COW-BOYS AND COLONELS

COW-BOYS AND COLONELS

Narrative of a Journey Across the Prairie
and Over the Black Hills of Dakota

---

by Edmond Baron de Mandat-Grancey
Translated by William Conn

The 1887 London Edition, Unabridged
Introduction by Howard R. Lamar

University of Nebraska Press
Lincoln and London

Manufactured in the United States of America

First Bison Book printing: 1984
Most recent printing indicated by the first digit below:
1 2 3 4 5 6 7 8 9 10

Library of Congress Cataloging in Publication Data

Mandat-Grancey, E. (Edmond), baron de, 1842–1911.
Cow-boys and colonels.

Translation of: Dans les Montagnes Rocheuses.
Reprint. Originally published: London : Griffith, Farran, Okeden & Welsh, 1887.
1. Black Hills (S.D. and Wyo.)—Description and travel. 2. Rocky Mountains—Descriptions and travel. 3. South Dakota—Description and travel. 4. Mandat-Grancey, E. (Edmond), baron de, 1842–1911. I. Title. II. Title: Cowboys and colonels.
F657.B6M3513 1984 917.83'9 83-23583
ISBN 0-8032-6562-X (pbk.)

INTRODUCTION

On the fourth of July, 1883, a drunken cowboy charged into a livery stable in Deadwood, Dakota Territory, and called out, thick-tongued: "They tell me there's a cursèd French baron here, and I want to see a cursèd French baron." As he shouted, a vigorous, square-built stranger seized him by his gunbelt and set him spinning into an empty stall. Sprawling there in the straw, the dazed, angry cowman pulled out his revolver, but he had the strength neither to rise nor to pull the trigger.

It is doubtful whether the cowboy realized that the big stranger who had thrown him down, and who now went back to saddling his horse, was Galiot François Edmond, Baron de Mandat-Grancey, as real and solid a French nobleman as the cowman would ever encounter. Nor could he know that the Baron was writing a book about the Black Hills which would excite readers all over France and acquaint a new public with this booming American mining and ranching frontier and its scores of uniquely western characters, anecdotes, and legends. Among the many incidents recorded was the meeting of the cowboy and the Baron.

The "cursèd French baron," Edmond de Mandat-Grancey, was a noted agriculturalist and a former naval officer who still lived on his family estate at the Château de Grancey near Dijon. Born in June 1842, de Mandat-Grancey had been schooled by Jesuit fathers in Paris and then sent off to the national naval school. After graduation he spent four years as an officer on the *Hermione*, a vessel attached to a French squadron operating along the coasts of Madagascar and Africa and in the Indian Ocean. De Mandat-Grancey then served an additional nine

Parts of the Introduction were previously published, in different form, as the Introduction to the reprint of Mandat-Grancey's *Coy-boys and Colonels* issued by J. B. Lippincott Company in 1962. Used by permission.

years as dashing aide-de-camp to Admiral Oyer, the French governor-general of Indo-China. This young officer, a devoted imperialist and a firm believer that France would continue to be a great world power, thoroughly enjoyed his stay in the Orient—a stay punctuated by visits to the main coast of Africa and by safaris into the Madagascar forests. Later in Indo-China he experienced local rebellions and participated in jungle warfare; but he also hunted tigers and looked forward to luxurious leaves of absence in Hong Kong.

De Mandat-Grancey's eventual return to France in 1870 was nearly as dramatic—and actually even more eventful—as his years in the Far East, for as a traditional royalist and an ardent Catholic, he found himself organizing volunteers that year to fight the Commune in Paris. The government honored these vigorous efforts by appointing him to a series of posts in the Ministry of the Marine, where he remained until 1877, when a new administration asked for his resignation.

The question remains, though: What was such a distinguished Frenchman doing in a livery stable in Deadwood? The answer lies partly in the fact that although de Mandat-Grancey was an excellent farmer and clearly loved his estate, he could not stay silent about public affairs, nor could he curb his interest in a broader world. Still in the prime of life and accustomed to command, he was furious at the way the new French Republic refused to employ thousands of gentlemen like himself. France, he maintained, was driving its most able men out to the colonies or to America. He was also convinced that newer lands in the United States, Australia, and South America would eventually ruin French agriculture, and he constantly sought a formula which would preserve both France's economy and use its wasted human talents. One of the answers, he felt, was for Frenchmen to invest abroad and to share in the wealth of new regions.

As the Baron pored over political newspapers, agricultural journals, and books about new frontiers, he became fascinated by the Black Hills gold rush of 1875–77, triggered when George Armstrong Custer led troops into the vast new Sioux reservation, created in 1874, which embraced the Black Hills. While there Custer and his men found traces of gold; indeed, Custer declared that there was "gold at the roots of the grass."

In the rush that followed, some ten thousand miners pushed past the army troops, sent to keep whites out of Sioux lands, and found both rich placers and quartz veins around present-day Deadwood and Lead, South Dakota. Given the sheer number of miners and the fact that many were veterans of other rushes, the gold deposits were exploited rapidly and professionally and news of their discoveries spread around the world.

Inevitably the miners' invasion led to conflict between those Teton Sioux under Sitting Bull and others who had never accepted the Treaty of 1874, and who therefore refused to settle on reservations. Instead, they began to gather by the thousands in the area to the west of the Black Hills in the Rosebud and Little Bighorn river valleys. In response, the government mounted a three-pronged full-scale campaign against the Teton Sioux. On June 25, 1876, General Custer and five troops of the Seventh Cavalry encountered the Sioux on the Little Bighorn, and in the ensuing battle Custer and his men were killed. By the close of the campaign, nevertheless, those Indians who had not fled to Canada with Sitting Bull were weakened enough to sign a treaty which ended hostilities and ceded the gold-bearing areas to the United States.

With peace restored, ranchers now joined miners in the Black Hills. All these events naturally kept Dakota well to the front of de Mandat-Grancey's thoughts. Meanwhile, other French gentlemen with francs to spare were soon speculating in mines in Dakota, and a few countrymen went into ranching there. Sometime in the late 1870s de Mandat-Grancey himself decided to follow suit.

De Mandat-Grancey's interest in America was whetted further by a dashing and somewhat mysterious ex-Confederate soldier named Gifford F. Parker. After Appomattox, Parker had left the South to fight for the French in Indo-China, where he had met de Mandat-Grancey. Later, the Baron found this freewheeling soldier of fortune living as a nabob merchant in Hong Kong; and yet again the two met in Paris. Always itching for a new adventure, Parker now appeared in the Black Hills as a promoter of mines, town sites, and ranches. Doubtless he acquainted de Mandat-Grancey with the fantastic prospects for wealth which Dakota now offered. In any event, by 1883 the

Baron could no longer resist a trip to see the new Eldorado for himself. Enlisting as a companion an old friend from Belguim, also a gentleman farmer, whom we know simply as Monsieur de Bouverie, De Mandat-Grancey boarded the French steamer *Provence* for New York in the late spring of 1883.

It would be a mistake to think that de Mandat-Grancey and Bouverie came to America merely to see mining properties. The Baron was already a frequent contributor to French newspapers and journals, and it is clear that he viewed this latest expedition as the possible subject of a book. Meanwhile, Bouverie, an amateur photographer, saw a chance to capture the wild West in pictures. Both men were also avid sportsmen, and they arrived in New York literally clanking with rifles, hunting gear, saddles, and camera equipment. Determined to appear truly "western," de Mandat-Grancey reports that he had even acquired a "bowie knife." After sightseeing in New York and Chicago, the two men boarded a train bound for the new railroad town of Pierre, Dakota, on the Missouri River. At this point Baron de Mandat-Grancey begins his informative and delightful narrative of a month's stay in the Dakotas.

At first de Mandat-Grancey's chatty style, humorous overstatements, and informal manner of writing suggest that he was just another tourist keeping a journal. But the Baron was also a trained reporter with a talent for catching the significant detail, so that under his pen the sound, sight, and smell of the booming American West comes to life. He had not been out of Chicago for a full day before he concluded that everyone about him was "in a hurry" and "on the make." Well-versed in English (Bouverie, on the other hand, knew not a word), de Mandat-Grancey listened skeptically to the persuasive land agents who clambered onto their coach at every stop and tried to sell the passengers tracts of land. He jotted down the details of the rough dress and manners of their fellow travelers. Dodging tobacco spittle, he stared fascinated at his first cowboys with their "bossy felt hats" trimmed in tarnished gold lace, their boots with Mexican spurs, their Colts, and the usual "big knife." Unlike so many Frenchmen who had been brought up on the novels of James Fenimore Cooper, de Mandat-Grancey was unsympathetic to the Sioux he saw hovering about the train stops. Imperialist that he was, he wrote that they "belong to an era anterior to ours and seem to be wanting in some inexplicable finishing touch."

All de Mandat-Grancey's acuteness and common sense, however, did not prepare the men for their Black Hills visit. The surprises began at Pierre, Dakota, on the Missouri. There spring rains had so inundated the area that the stage to Deadwood was delayed, and the team lumbered in such seas of mud that, once on the road, all passengers were ordered out to walk for most of the way! The situation took on some comic aspects when the stage driver, Stuart, fell in love with a young actress who happened to be a passenger and deliberately slowed down the trip in order to prolong the romance.

Furious at Stuart and impatient to explore the Hills, de Mandat-Grancey and his friend abandoned the stage at Rapid City. They joined Gifford Parker—now very much the frontiersman in a blue shirt and heavy boots—then bought horses and set out on a tour of the mines, settlements, and ranches of the Black Hills. Although they were frequently lost and short of food, the adventurers came through the experience without a scratch. For his part, de Mandat-Grancey attributed this largely to his superb horse, which he had bought from an unlucky gambler and named Jean-Leblanc.

De Mandat-Grancey's observations offer an excellent and varied view of the whole Black Hills region in a boom period. As he came into a new town he took time to describe the way it clung to a hillside or overlooked a gulch. He wrote of the loungers on hotel porches at Rapid City as "smoking and chewing tobacco with the gravity of an ecclesiastical council in moments of tranquility." He recorded, with an unusually good ear, the way Americans spoke, and how they used such phrases as "I guess" and "You bet," or ordered drinks with delightful names like "corpse revivers" and "gum ticklers." And he did not hesitate to satirize the curious American addiction for whittling.

Once in Deadwood, de Mandat-Grancey's impressions range from a physical tour of the town to lurid stories of vigilante groups hanging the wrong fellow because there was not moonlight enough to see who was the right one. Here the reader should be warned that de Mandat-Grancey was neither a scholar nor a historian, but a touring journalist who reported anecdotes about famous incidents just as he had heard them. His account of the shooting of Wild Bill Hickok by Jack McCall, for example, though a good story, is inaccurate. De Mandat-Grancey is at his best in describing events at which he was present. His mock-solemn account of the Fourth of July in Deadwood is unforgettable: narrow streets crowded with bearded cowmen and miners dressed in their best flannel shirts, their hair slicked down with sweet-smelling pomatum, all watching a motley parade of red-clad firemen and moccasined Indian hunters. The climax comes when a float passes containing forty little girls in white frocks (representing the forty states) gravely singing "Hail Columbia!"

Interspersed with these city vignettes are excellent physical descriptions of the rugged Hills country and patient, clear explanations of the mining process. It was de Mandat-Grancey's luck to be given a tour of the Homestake Mine at Lead, which had already become one of the most profitable mines in the West by 1883; he was also on hand when a large shipment of gold was sent off under the guard of a small army of men with Winchesters. Later, he toured lesser-known towns like Gayville, Tigerville, Central, and Galena.

He wound up his tour with visits to ranches and to a straggling mineral water resort called Cascade and with a trip south from the Hills to Sydney, Nebraska. There he and Bouverie, having parted with Parker, took the Union Pacific back to Chicago and the comforts of civilization. By late summer the two adventurers were again in Paris, regaling their friends with their exploits in *le Far West.* Indeed, de Mandat-Grancey was so full of excitement about his trip that in the winter of 1883–84 he gave a series of lectures in Paris and elsewhere which attracted great interest. The enthusiastic reception led him to publish his journal in June 1884 under the misleading title *Dans les Montagnes Rocheuses.* So favorable was the response to the book that the Académie Française awarded him the Prix Lambert et Montyon. The receipt of some nine hundred fan letters—no less than twenty-seven of which asked what had happened to the faithful Jean-Leblanc—persuaded de Mandat-Grancey to permit an English translation by William Conn.

That edition was published in London in 1887, under the more correct and certainly more lively title *Cow-boys and Colonels.* It is this version which is now being reprinted by the University of Nebraska Press, appropriately on the hundredth anniversary of de Mandat-Grancey's visit to Dakota Territory.

Why did a travel book about the American West—of which there were dozens circulating in Europe during the 1880s—enjoy such a success? Certainly one of the reasons is that the image of a last Wild West was being shaped in the 1880s, not only by mining rushes, Indian conflicts, and open-range ranching, but by dime novels, by the appearance of Buffalo Bill Cody's incredibly successful Wild West Show in London and elsewhere in Europe in 1887, and by the experiences of the Marquis de Morés and Theodore Roosevelt in the Badlands.

But there were other less obvious but perhaps more important reasons as well. Despite its casual style, The Baron's *Cow-boys and Colonels* was also a serious commentary on the American character and American democracy. De Mandat-Grancey sensed, for example, that on the Black Hills frontier he was witnessing the process which had made America great. As he watched miners and ranchers at work he found ample evidence of real equality, vigor, frenzied enterprise, and rugged individualism. The motto of these frontiersmen, he said almost enviously, was "self-reliance and a big revolver." It was a fresh, dynamic spirit which had moved, and was moving, mountains, a spirit he found absent in his own beloved France.

On the other hand, the Frenchman noted, some years before Frederick Jackson Turner, that this free and easy frontier phase was coming to a final end. Once law, order, and ordinary society were established in Dakota, he was sure the region would become merely a middle-class, security-minded, and often politically corrupt population such as he felt he had seen in New York and on the East Coast. Although de Mandat-Grancey was wrong about the impending future of North and South Dakota, he had been much impressed by the scandals of the Grant era and had followed closely news reports about the famous Star Route frauds in the Post Office Department, for this particular scandal was still making headlines in 1883. These events, plus his own royalist inclinations, led him to be pessimistic about the future as well as the desirability of democratic government in general. Thus his relatively innocent-seeming travel book was, in actuality, an argument against republican government in France! It was an argument which seems particularly ironic when we learn that de Mandat-Grancey claimed to be a relative of Alexis de Tocqueville, the very man who had familiarized the French with the virtues of republican government in his *Democracy in America.*

As for the American character, de Mandat-Grancey was annoyed at our bad food, prohibition, and the sloppy habits of frontier women, but his most basic criticisms were reserved for the two qualities which agitated him most: sham and violence. This French nobleman was fascinated by false-front stores in the West, and by a painter in Deadwood who was making a fortune by graining and painting ordinary wood to look like real mahogany or even marble. He was impressed and amused that nearly everyone he met was called Colonel, Major, Captain, or Judge. In another book about America, he drily noted that the last person to be a mere corporal in the United States died shortly after the War of 1812. From these related observations, de Mandat-Grancey generalized that pretense and sham were basic American traits. Hence the title *Cow-boys and Colonels* has a double and partly satirical meaning which must have delighted his French readers.

In a similar vein, de Mandat-Grancey criticized—as did many other observers during the 1880s—the cowboy as a kind of frontier delinquent, a living embodiment that the gun spoke in place of the law. To the orderly Baron, cowboys were "the plague of the West." As a military officer he admired their bravery, strength, and toughness, but he decried their lack of discipline and frequent resort to killing, as well as the vigilance mobs. These opinions were reinforced by the experience of another Frenchman in Dakota, the Marquis de Morés. Shortly before de Mandat-Grancey came to the United States, the Marquis had set up a huge ranch in the Badlands at a point where the Northern Pacific Railroad intersected the Little Missouri. There, in the town of Medora, he set up an elaborate packing and slaughterhouse and formed a refrigerator company with the intention of sending beef, already processed, from the West to eastern markets. But the very spring that Baron de Mandat-Grancey was in Deadwood, the Marquis was preyed upon by renegade cowboys, and in a showdown he shot one of them. Undoubtedly de Mandat-Grancey sided with de Morés in the affair, and although de Morés was exonerated, this incident as much as anything led de Mandat-Grancey to deplore violence on the American frontier.

But it would be wrong to say that de Mandat-Grancey was, at heart, a hostile critic. The book is full of enthusiasm about opportunity in America. In fact, one unexpected result of its publication was a new career for de Mandat-Grancey. His frequent observations that the Mississippi Valley needed strong, half-blood French Percherons for farming and for drawing trolley and brewery wagons persuaded a group of French families to send their sons to the United States under the guidance of the Baron himself to start a Percheron stud ranch. Located near Custer City, Dakota, in 1884, this unusual outfit bore the equally unusual name of the Fleur de Lis Ranch. De Mandat-Grancey took advantage of the enterprise to write a new and often humorous book called *La Brêche aus Buffles: Un Ranch français dans le Dakota* (Paris, 1889). In this second chronicle he included accounts of Billy the Kid and introduced audiences to the careers of Buffalo Bill, Calamity Jane, and many other familiar western figures.

De Mandat-Grancey's reading audience appears to have been so constant over the years that in 1885 and again in 1891 he published an account of the first part of his 1883 tour under the title *En Visite chez l'Oncle Sam,* which concentrated on the New York and Chicago portions of the trip. To the student of American social history, this volume is valuable in that a French visitor shrewdly and correctly figures out precisely those aspects of the American character which would intrigue and attract French audiences. His very pandering suggests an intimate understanding of the way Frenchmen—and perhaps other Europeans as well—perceived America. Having found a successful formula, de Mandat-Grancey also wrote books about brief tours of Ireland, Greece, the coast of Africa, and the Congo. In all of these he remained the royalist and the imperialist until his death in 1911.

Whatever his opinions and motivations, the fact remains that Edmond de Mandat-Grancey has given us an account of the Black Hills mining frontier which is valuable for its accurate on-site observations, its clinical frankness, its early reportage of stories and anecdotes which have become part of American folk culture, its appreciation of the American western idiom and its genuine humor. More than that, we know that he was instrumental in creating a specific image of the American West for thousands of French readers, just as James Fenimore Cooper had done for an earlier generation in France. Here, too, one sees an intelligent and shrewd foreigner seeking out the peculiar elements which made the American character and democratic institutions seem so different. Although Baron de Mandat-Grancey in his *Cow-boys and Colonels* does not demonstrate the rare genius of his more distinguised relative Alexis de Tocqueville, nor the insights of James, Lord Bryce, whose *American Commonwealth* (1888) appeared only a year after de Mandat-Grancey's English version of *Cow-boys and Colonels,* he deserves a return from obscurity and a chance to speak to and charm a new audience. Now, a century after his visit, his words bring to life again one of America's last and most colorful mining frontiers.

Howard R. Lamar

Yale University
August 16, 1983

Cow-boys and Colonels

NARRATIVE OF A JOURNEY ACROSS THE
PRAIRIE AND OVER THE BLACK
HILLS OF DAKOTA.

From "Dans les Montagnes Rocheuses" of Baron
E. de Mandat-Grancey

*WITH ADDITIONAL NOTES NOT CONTAINED IN
THE ORIGINAL EDITION*

BY

WILLIAM CONN

LONDON
GRIFFITH, FARRAN, OKEDEN & WELSH
(SUCCESSORS TO NEWBERY AND HARRIS)
WEST CORNER ST PAUL'S CHURCHYARD
1887.

INTRODUCTION.

THERE was a time when the primæval dwellers on the downs of St Germain, or of caves in the great hills of Montmartre and Chaumont—ground now occupied by Parisians in magnificent houses—came to hunt the bear and the beaver along the marshy banks of the Seine and over the spot where now proudly rises the Grand Opera of Paris. About the same epoch, and certainly also when Great Britain was a part of the mainland of Europe, and not yet an island, the great continent of North America bore no resemblance to the aspect it assumes at the present moment. An immense fresh-water inland sea, of a form almost triangular, occupied the centre, bordered on the north by the hills of Canada, on the west by the Rocky Mountains, and on the east by the Alleghany Range, this sheet of water of shallow depth flowed into the Atlantic by the Falls of Niagara, and into the Gulf of Mexico by the Mississippi.

The rocky bottom of the Niagara wearing away by the incessant friction of the rapid waters, and the barrier on the south having been probably broken down by some convulsion, this sea gradually subsided, and at last drained out, leaving an immense plain, in some parts sandy, marshy almost throughout, and barely undulated by the movements of the submarine currents that flowed over its bed for so many ages. Of this wide expanse of waters no more remains than the five great lakes that separate the United States from Canada, now discharged by the river St Lawrence. The work of degradation and subsidence is still going on, it appears, for their level is lowering very sensibly.

The first Europeans who inhabited these plains, already traversed by the trappers, were the French missionaries, and they gave to this vast extent of land of nearly two hundred thousand square leagues, the name of *Prairie*, which the Americans have retained. The topographical vocabulary, besides, is almost wholly French : a hill, for instance, is a *butte*, a cascade a *saut*, a tributary stream a *fourche*, &c.

At some epoch undetermined, following a subterraneous convulsion, an island, almost round, about a hundred miles across, rose all at once, not far from the Rocky Mountains, in this immense inland sea. An eruption, forcing its way through the various horizontal strata, lifted portions of them, fractured in the form of rings, around the crater that served as a vent. Each of these beds or strata, on coming laterally to the surface, naturally carried with it the minerals it contained, and from this singular displacement there resulted a series of concentric zones, each containing its special riches. On following a certain radius, the traveller traverses, in a few hours, beds of coal, deposits of petroleum, mines of gold, copper, and silver. If, on the contrary, he takes a circular course, keeping along any one of the several systems or beds that are met with at every step, he will come back to the point from which he started, and see an almost uninterrupted continuation of the same mineral.

This singular country remained a long time unknown; it was far removed from the settled abodes of man, and indeed, as if lost in the heart of the Prairie; but its approaches were guarded by numerous aud warlike tribes of Indians. It is now only about five or six years since the Americans took possession of it, at the end of a sanguinary war, in which they had not been always conquerors. At present the Black Hills of Dakota are becoming the centre of an agglomeration of mines, farms, and pastures, all growing daily in importance, and attracting around them a large population.

Having been drawn to this country through affairs,

in which we were interested, we thought that the narrative of the rapid journey there and back we have just accomplished would not be uninteresting to those who have not visited this remarkable spot of the North American continent.

CONTENTS.

CHAPTER I.

PAGE

Departure from Chicago—Pullman Cars and their Occupants—A Railway Refreshment Room—The Prairie and the *Cow-boys*—The *Colonels*—The Missouri—The Stage Coaches—The Sioux—Willow Creek—An Emigrant 1

CHAPTER II.

The Cheyenne—The Cattle Ranches—Passing a River—The International Hotel—Rapid City—Justice in America—American Manners—The First Bivouac—M'Donnell's Ranch—A Farmer of Dakota—Homestead, Pre-emption, and Free Claims—The Forest System—Hilly-Ranch 45

CHAPTER III.

Average Prices of Provisions in the Black Hills—The Percheron Horses in America—Uncle Sam's Mine—Galena—The Colonel's *Fighting Men*—The American Women—The Sirens of Deadwood—Wild Bill 105

CHAPTER IV.

The Great Mines of Deadwood—What the Absence of Policemen Costs—Caledonia—A *Soiree* at Deadwood—The Jesuits in America 143

Contents.

CHAPTER V.

PAGE

The Fourth of July at Deadwood—A Monarchist Discourse—The Monarchist Journalists of New York—The Jury and Lynch Law—The Minister's Prayer—The Cow-boy and the Baron—Introduction of the Spit into the Black Hills—Little Gimlet—The Art of becoming a Proprietor in Dakota . . . 171

CHAPTER VI.

Little Rapid Creek—The Beavers—The Pan-Bill—The Marquis de M—— and the Cow-boys—Tiger Hunting—Fair View—The Marmots 203

CHAPTER VII.

Departure from Little Rapid Creek—Castleton—King Solomon—French *Cuisine*—A Dead City—An Irish Ranch—Custer—The Whittlers—The Conquest of the Black Hills—Death of Colonels Custer and Crook—Sitting Bill and Manitoba—The Mica Mines—The Yellow Stone—The Misfortunes of a Sheriff—The Philosophy of a Cow-boy 235

CHAPTER VIII.

Departure from Custer—Mr and Mrs Kemish—"War-Horse" and "Red-Cloud"—A Sheep Ranch—Accidents—The Hot Springs—An Indian Princess—The Art of Scalping—Cascade—How a Village is Founded 280

Contents.

CHAPTER IX.

PAGE

The Return Journey—The Alkali Desert—The Indians—The Prairie Dogs—The Antelopes—A Sand Storm—Willow Creek—The River Platte—Jack Slade and Jules Burgh—Sydney—The Union Pacific—Omaha—Chicago . . . 302

CHAPTER X.

Something more of the Black Hills 343

COW-BOYS AND COLONELS

CHAPTER I.

DEPARTURE FROM CHICAGO — PULLMAN CARS AND THEIR OCCUPANTS — A RAILWAY REFRESHMENT ROOM — THE PRAIRIE AND THE *COW-BOYS*—THE *COLONELS*—THE MISSOURI—THE STAGE COACHES—THE SIOUX—WILLOW CREEK —AN EMIGRANT.

WHEN one has tramped two whole days over the miry roads to which the municipality of Chicago gives the name of streets, and has assisted at the transformation of a few hundreds of fat pigs into hams and bacon, which is, as everybody knows, the great business of the place, he feels impatient enough to get away from the unaccustomed proximity of so many styes. It is therefore with the most decided satisfaction that my friend and travelling companion, Monsieur Bouverie, and I prepare to quit the Grand Pacific Hotel, and say adieu for a few weeks to American civilisation. It seems, in fact, that we are going to plunge into sheer savagery: at least we have ground for anticipating as much from what we hear around us. At New York, for instance, when we spoke of our project of going to Deadwood, Dakota, our friends of the Union Club lifted their arms to Heaven in invocation for our safety. This morning we have been in the office of the hotel to settle our accounts, to give our address, and take our railway tickets. The clerk is a Canadian, and, since our arrival, has done all he can to manifest his attachment to "the French of the Old Country" we represent. On speaking to him about Deadwood, he reflected a moment, then questioning the other clerk, a Yankee with a long beard:

"Jim," said he, "here are two gentlemen going to Deadwood, Dakota. What is it that has occurred at Deadwood lately? Haven't the Indians scalped the whole population?"

"No," said Jim, throwing himself back in his chair and lifting his eyes to the ceiling with an air of deep meditation. "It is in Colorado where that took place, it was not in Dakota."

"Then the cow-boys have taken possession of the city, and burnt the whole of some quarter."

"No; that was in Montana."

"Well, at all events, I am sure something has happened at Deadwood."

"Ah yes, you are right. It is a flood: I remember now. The river has overflowed and carried away all the city. It was last month."

"Ah! after all, it is now some weeks since that. The post-office must be restored and reopened. Messieurs, you take your tickets to Deadwood, do you not? Forty-nine dollars each; thirty-six hours of railway and as much by coach across the Prairie. The omnibus will take you as far as the North-Western. Messieurs, allow me to shake hands and say good-bye. Always happy to see Frenchmen. Ah, here is the map of the railway."

We say good-bye to this good man, and we wriggle with some difficulty into an omnibus already three-quarters filled with our guns, travelling trunks, and saddles.

While it is taking us to the station, we glance over the map that has just been handed to us. In America, every railway company publishes, in the form of a guide, a map, a mere puff, in which the relative position of the chief cities is strangely modified in such a manner as to lead the uninformed traveller to suppose that the line in question is the only one that conducts him to the place where he desires to go. Upon the cover of this one is displayed, in large type, the following advice:—

"To the explorer!
To the pioneer!!
To the labourer!!!
To the hunter!!!!
To the tourist!!!!!
To the miner!!!!!
To everybody!!!!!!!
It is made known that:
If one wishes to succeed in cattle breeding,
If one wishes to have good harvests,
If one seeks for a delightful climate,
And wonderful situation!
He should never leave the country traversed by
The North-Western Railway.

Let him say this to himself!!!

for:

In Europe the mortality is	1 in 42.
In the Eastern States it is	1 in 88.
In the Far West it is	1 in 120."

I translate for Monsieur Bouverie this audacious puff.

"Ah, my friend!" he exclaimed, "what a consoling science statistics is. Since all the inhabitants of Deadwood have just been drowned, there is no one in the far West to die for the next ten years. Without this, the averages would be exceeded. And these good people of New York to tell us that our journey was dangerous, forsooth!"

Fortified by this reflection that unites so happily philosophy and arithmetic, we rush into a Pullman car, and this speedily carries us far away from the good city of Chicago.

The Pullman car is one of the rare public conveniences of which the Americans have an indisputable right to be proud. When one can find a place in one of them—and there are some in almost every train—he travels much more comfortably than on our most luxurious lines in Europe. They are carriages more than twenty-five yards long. In the centre of each side are a dozen little sofas, facing one another in couples; each of these sofas corresponds with a place, and two of them constitute what is called a "section." Joined together during the night, they form an excellent bed, furnished with sheets and pillows always perfectly clean. Another bed, hidden in the partition during the day, comes out from a sort of cupboard to spread itself at three feet horizontally over the first, and to receive the second traveller.

The front and back of the carriage are occupied by a smoking-room and dressing-rooms, always plenteously supplied with iced water, soap, and towels. In many trains there are, besides, a restaurant and a kitchen, but this supreme luxury is not often met with except in the East: beyond Chicago we have only *buffets*, and the American refreshment room deserves special mention.

Three times a day, at very odd hours, the train stops suddenly at a certain spot in some village. Then at the door of some house, more or less distant from the station, a *gentleman* shows himself, ringing vigorously a great bell. Here passengers hurry into a large room, where there are several tables covered with red cloths always very dirty.

Then a girl, generally very plain, comes up to you with a serious look, and rapidly utters the following words, which are always the same:

"Boiled beef, roast beef, salt beef, bacon, potatoes, cabbage, tea, coffee."

This is the bill of fare. It is quite useless to make a choice, for whatever you say, the result is the same. In about five minutes the same young lady returns with a dozen saucers, with which she forms a triple crown around your plate without saying a word. This initial ceremony having been performed, she disappears with a calm, dignified air, and you see nothing more of her.

But it is just at this moment when you must see, or rather not see, the Americans at work. Armed with their forks, they thrust these at random into five or six saucers, transferring their contents into their plate, then, having thoroughly mixed the whole, they swallow this hotch-potch with the aid of their knives in the twinkling of an eye. With a providential eye for accidents that might happen with the inexperienced, the said knives are always blunted by usage and so not so dangerous as they seem.

On the day of our departure we dined at Sparta. I was struggling painfully with some substance which might have been beef or the flesh of some other animal, when I heard Monsieur Bouverie suddenly utter an exclamation as if he had been stung by a wasp. Facing us was an old gentleman of respectable appearance, who had begun by first taking a slice of bacon, which he carefully cut into little bits, to this he then added a little cream, a few heads of asparagus, a poached egg, some raw tomatoes, the juice of a preserved peach, and pepper and salt in abundance; at last he saturated the mess with black treacle, and swallowed the whole with evident satisfaction, just as my friend's cry of distress made me turn my head. The spectacle was so repulsive that it made me shudder.

But the country where one eats so coarsely is decidedly charming. On leaving Chicago, the line, quitting the prairie, rises in the north on entering Wisconsin. Coming out of the marshy plains of Illinois, we see chains of little mountains covered with magnificent oak and fir woods, separated from each other by pretty verdant valleys of admirable fertility. This country, which only Indians inhabited fifty years ago, is now as densely populated as many provinces of France, at least along the line; for the absence of roads must, as a consequence, barely permit the existence even of a few villages in the interior. The water courses are mighty and magnificent. Standing upon the platform of the carriage we constantly see everywhere sheets of water and even lakes, on which numerous little boats are steaming away in every direction.

About nine, we cross the Mississippi at Winona, but unluckily the darkness hides almost everything from our view. We remain only a few minutes in a station brilliantly illuminated by the electric light, and then, the train going on its way, we take to our beds.

When we awake the next morning we find the aspect of the country quite changed. We have entered into the prairie; not the well-cultivated prairie around Chicago, but the prairie in all its immensity and naked wildness. Here the work of colonisation is only just beginning, and in the vicinity of the stations only may be seen, here and there, far away and apart, little wooden houses with clearings around them. Everywhere else the eye wanders without any object to arrest it over an immense plain, hardly varied with a mound or a hill, and covered with thick grass, reflecting singular blue tints as it undulates under the passing breeze.* Water is scarce: a few hollows filled with muddy pools trailing slowly their tortuous courses towards the Missouri; in other places the water, having no outlet, forms swamps, from which constantly rise long flocks of ducks.

The impression produced is gloomy in the extreme; for, evident as it is that incalculable riches are hidden in these monotonous plains, how many years more will our agriculturists of Europe, weighed down with burdens accumulated through many centuries of civilisation, be able to continue struggling against the invasion of products from this free land? An impulse has now been given to the movement, and to arrest it is out of the question. Good, however, will result from it, still not before fifty years hence, when the value of our lands will have been depreciated at least one half, and the half of our peasants have been forced to emigrate. And in this interval, what suffering!

We must not close our eyes to the inevitable consequences; unless a total change takes place in the system of our customs duties the struggle will be fruitless, and every year that passes away will see the ruin of one branch or another of our agricultural

* Blue grass (*Andropogon furcatus*). It is the best summer fodder known in America. The hay is always superior. This grass is conspicuous on the rich limestone land of Kentucky and Tennessee.

industry. First the corn and next the wine, for California is beginning to send its wines to Bordeaux, after having sent us the phylloxera, and then it will be the rearing of live stock. Every line of railway that opens in the Far West, opens at the same time a new wound.

It is interesting to examine the manner in which the American government favours this movement. Sometimes, as in the case of the *Union Pacific*, the great artery that first traversed the Continent, it gives directly a subsidy to the company, though lately it has not proceeded in this manner.

As soon as the course of the line is settled, the zone to be run over is divided into little squares, having their base along the line a mile in length, each being called "a section." The company, by the terms of the concession, becomes the proprietor of the half of these lands, the other half remaining with the government.

During the first years especially, the only benefits the shareholders can hope to realize, arise from the sale and rise in value of these lands; the company therefore uses every means to attract immigration thither.

The settler, as he is called, generally comes to choose his land in autumn. Upon a simple declaration, they give him a run, almost gratuitous, over the line. As soon as he has made his choice he goes in quest of the company's agent. If he has no money, as it unluckily happens in most cases, they give him a credit of five or six years. The land is sold to him at the rate of from one to five dollars the acre. He must still have a house, agricultural implements, and live stock; all these are furnished to him by special establishments. These expenses, however, are relatively considerable: a house costs from 350 to 500 dollars; a milch cow, 25 to 30 dollars; a good pair of horses, 100 or 150 dollars. But in the spring, about the 15th of April, he has only to turn the turf of the prairie and throw down a few handfuls of oats, to garner, about the end of July, 25 to 40 bushels per acre. After the first year, they sow wheat, that returns from 20 to 40 bushels the acre, and this with a simple turn of the soil, without even a spadeful of manure. They showed us lands that had given as much as twenty-five successive harvests of corn by this simple treatment, without any appreciable depreciation of the soil—a black alluvial earth, in which not a stone can be seen.

To feed his cattle in winter, the new farmer may cut as much grass for hay as he thinks proper; and if he has need of a little ready-money for his current expenses, he has only to go to his neighbours to work a while, and he will earn two dollars a day. At the end of the first year something comes in, and if his visits to the bar at the station have not been immoderate, the farm and stock should, at the end of four or five years, be entirely his own, freed from all debt.

At Tracy, where we arrived at nine in the morning, we were obliged to leave our Pullman car, which proceeded no further. The compartment in which we are now installed contains a class quite special, entirely different from that we had been accustomed to see in the East. Four or five women of very mysterious bearing occupy one corner; they seem to be under the surveillance of a stern-looking couple. The other places are occupied by men bespattered with mud up to their ears, habited in well-worn flannel shirts, and with their breeches tucked in great long boots. They are all inveterate tobacco-chewers. There are a few women and some groups of children. At every station men with their hands full of prospectuses rush into the carriages: they are land agents, and come up to us offering farms. One of these pushing men of business is pestering me to buy a whole quarter of a town with some sounding name, Athens or Paris, I forget which. He spreads out before me the plan. I see there grand avenues intersected by innumerable streets, and the whole well sprinkled with squares, two public gardens, seven or eight railway stations, churches and chapels by the dozen, and ten or twelve banks. When he is quite convinced I am not going to buy anything of him, he admits, pleasantly enough, that there are only one hundred and fifty inhabitants in this city, who are dwelling in about fifty wooden sheds; but he asserts that in two years there will be more than twenty thousand, and this is not at all impossible. The children begin frolicking at once, and make their *début* by shooting adroitly a ball into the eye of the gentleman, the vendor of the city, who smiles graciously, for it is well understood that in America all the children are charming. After this comes my turn, and I immediately open the window behind me, hoping that the ball will consequently roll into the prairie. The wickedness of my proceeding is instantly detected, and the young gentleman, a terrible seven-year-old urchin, springs forward to close it without my permission. I oppose, and away he goes, rapping out an oath with a *resonance* that seemed to gratify his vengeance.

Every moment some one in passing along the passage reserved through the middle of the carriage, stumbles and jostles against us: they tread on our toes also, and without a word of apology. But for all that they are in one respect superior to the ill-bred class among us, inasmuch as they consider it quite natural that others should treat them in the same mode. One of my friends was travelling lately in a saloon car; all at once he was startled at seeing two great feet stretched out on each side of his face! But his neighbour behind him was merely putting himself at his ease. To have shown any indignation, of course, would not have been *comme il faut* from a Yankee point of view, and besides useless. Fortunately he finds an easy chair unoccupied behind this amiable Yankee, takes possession of it, and returns the compliment precisely in the same way. The other kept as still as a mouse with the most perfect composure.

Here is another incident of the same kind that was related to me. Two travellers, the one French and the other American, were sitting face to face in a tramway. The American, who was chewing tobacco as usual, began spitting, with remarkable dexterity too, through the open window beside the Frenchman. The latter, feeling annoyed and getting irritated, would have his revenge, but sets about it so unskilfully that he hits his antagonist plain in the face. Naturally, he was overwhelmed with confusion and apologies, which were received by the Yankee with very good grace, who calmly took his handkerchief and applied it as if he were wiping away a drop of rain, remarking at the same time with a somewhat patronising tone, "All right, stranger! I guess you are a beginner!"

These people are very coarse, because they have never been taught to be otherwise; but for all that, they are in many respects superior in behaviour to people of the same class in France. Their attitude towards women is admirable. Not an obscene word in their presence ever escapes their lips. Moreover, equality with them is so thoroughly ingrafted in their minds, that one never sees, as in France, that sullen hostility so often manifested by the man in blouse towards the man in frock coat. This observation, however, though quite true with respect to the West, would at least be subject to some reservation regarding the states of the East, which are becoming rapidly Europeanised.

Around the stations are already grouped a few houses and each of these sends forth its contingent of sickly-looking ragamuffins who come, dabbling through the mud with their naked feet, to look at the train. The population of these villages is throughout of the same character. Two or three grocers, a few dry-goods stores, shoeing smiths, saddlers, one or two little chapels which do not look as if they were frequented, and hardly ever any butchers or bakers. In America they eat nothing but bacon. As for bread, everyone makes at home for each meal balls of a sort of unfermented paste, baked in a stove, as a substitute! Accordingly, especially in the West, nine Americans out of ten who have reached the age of twenty are afflicted with chronic gastritis.*

But there are some things never wanting—an hotel for instance, and then a collection of "saloons." It is under this fine name that the public houses and taverns are known, and it is here where the best part of the profits of the farms around changes hands. Before the doors endless files of agricultural machines, thrashers, harvesters, mowers, all painted in bright colours, are displayed. Their employment, which with us in France is only yet exceptional, is quite the rule here. The well-levelled soil of the prairie, besides, seems specially adapted to their use.

As we proceed on our way the number of our travelling companions diminishes in the same ratio. At one of the last stations two *cow-boys* get into the train.

* The Author's ideas are here a little too strong for the facts of the case.

With their bossy felt hats set off with tarnished gold lace, their great boots bristling with Mexican spurs, and their girdles furnished with a brace of Colts' revolvers, cartridges, and a murderous, big knife, these "boys" have the look of actual bandits. These in our company behave very well, but it is not always so with these gentry. A few weeks ago a drunken cow-boy, intent on indulging, it seems, in one of their favourite pastimes, shot away the cigar from an inoffensive neighbour with a ball from his revolver. Thereupon the guard blew out his brains with his pistol on the spot; the body was cast out on the line, and everything thus promptly settled without bier, bell, or burial.

These cow-boys are the plague of the West. Recruited generally from among men too idle to work in the mines or on the farms, passing their life on the prairie, day and night in the saddle, watching their herds, constantly at war with the Indians, they make their appearance in the towns only on pay days, when they invariably get drunk and become a terror to the inhabitants, who, on the other hand, get as much profit out of them as they can, regarding them as very proper subjects for *exploitation*. The newspapers, romances, and tales are full of their exploits. Now and then one hears that a troop of cow-boys have taken possession of a little town on the frontier and pillaged the inhabitants, or that, solely from mere wantonness and wild spirits, they had driven all the population to a certain spot, and there forced them to dance for hours together before them for their diversion, sending bullets into the calves of their legs if the performance did not proceed with sufficient animation. Then some fine day a Vigilance Committee is formed, who take three or four unlucky individuals by mere chance, and hang them at the first tree they come to, the others continuing their exploits a little further off. After all, they are the best boys in the world in the estimation of the saloon keepers, whose fortunes they make.

Our neighbours draw near and begin talking with us. The brakeman also comes up, and salutes us with the well-worn phrase, "Well, stranger, how do you like the country?" The conversation then becomes general. They tell us all about the five women who are ensconced in the end of the carriage. They are gay women, as they call them, under the protection of an old gentleman, who has the sanctified look of a methodist preacher. They travel all through the country, remaining a fortnight in each town, where in certain hotels they are received gratuitously.

The brakeman brings us some bad news; he is not quite sure whether we shall arrive or not at Pierre this evening. Yesterday a bridge broke down by the passage of a train, and they don't know whether it is yet restored. Accidents of this kind are too common here to produce much impression on the people. If one only understood the way in which the line is made he would be surprised that accidents did not occur more frequently. This morning, on passing, we saw some work of this kind going on, where they were busy in laying down a short line across the prairie to join some coal mines recently discovered.

A steam scooping-machine was placed on a truck, and the scoop, cutting into the rich soil, ploughed out a trench through every intervening rise it encountered on its course. In proportion as its work of levelling had been supplemented and accomplished by the aid of seven or eight men, for a length of a few yards, they laid down the sleepers and rails that were brought up by three or four other waggons in the rear. The locomotive placed behind made then a few steps in advance, and the same operation was resumed for another stretch. On certain lines they have laid down and completed by such means ten miles in a day, but, to use a vulgar expression, they had to "sweat hard" to reach this limit.

When they meet with a small water-course they span it with an open timber-work bridge. They rarely put down any ballast; I have seen it merely on the lines of the Eastern States, and then the Companies do not fail to make it well known to the public, that they may profit accordingly. The rail is simply built up, and when the jolts are rather too rough they fill in a little, and gradually everything settles down. The main point is that the line be opened as soon as possible.

If the permanent way is rather loose, the rolling stock, on the other hand, is admirable for its solidity and even elegance. The *personnel* also appear to me to be very good. I am surprised to learn, however, that notwithstanding the hard work exacted from their *employés*, their remuneration is not at all liberal. If we take into account the difference of the value of money, and of the fact that the companies provide neither pensions nor a fund in case of sickness, it must be admitted that they are not so well paid as in France. An engineman earns from sixteen to twenty pounds a month. It is true that this pay corresponds with a daily course of a hundred miles, and that every additional course of the same length carries the right to receive another day's pay. A few of them get forty pounds a month sometimes, but these lucky individuals are not numerous.

It is getting dark as we arrive at the place of the accident. We are close by the Missouri, which a few days previously had overflowed its banks. A little bridge had not only been carried away, but the waters have so undermined the permanent way, that, over a length of forty or fifty yards, it has fallen five or six feet below its original level. The immense locomotive lying on its side, like a horse fallen in the shafts, has almost disappeared in the soft mud of the rivulet. A little further on, half-a-dozen waggons, loaded with wood, are piled up over each other, with their wheels in the air. A score of men are at work, and the way in which they repair the mischief done is characteristic. Every sleeper is brought up to the required level by means of wooden posts piled up under its extremities which rest on the still soft mud. The contents of the waggons have furnished this material. The work is not yet finished; we have, therefore, plenty of time to visit the scene of the accident.

It is here where we see the Indians for the first time. There are two clad in their great red blankets, with their arms crossed, and they look on the busy people around them without moving.

One of our travelling companions remarked to me; "See those long lazy louts! They have only to stoop to earn honestly two or three dollars, but they like better lying, and picking, and stealing!"

It appears to me that this reflection explains the instinctive antipathy between the two races. These men, tall and strong as they are, will not work; they are repulsively ugly, and have a sinister look. Certain animals, the rhinoceros and hippopotamus, for instance, seem to belong to an era anterior to ours; and these men with their large features, stern and immovable, seem to be wanting in some inexplicable finishing touch, which suggests the same idea of imperfection. We fancy we see conjured up before us specimens of prehistoric man.

Besides, there is nothing attractive in their costume. They have breeches of buff leather; their long, black, stiff hair is half hidden under pointed felt hats, for they no longer wear the famous scalp lock, ornamented with eagle's plumes, which the imaginative Fennimore Cooper has so much overdone in his romances. They have not, however, abandoned the custom of scalping "the pale faces," and when a young warrior can find an emigrant dead drunk in some ditch, and not too bald, he feels it very gratifying, and considers it a duty, moreover, to carry off his scalp, an exploit that procures him the esteem of his chiefs and the love of all the young squaws of his tribe. He will also have encountered the risk of being hanged like a dog by the friends of the scalped, if he should take it into his head, as it sometimes happens, to boast of his prowess in their hearing when it is his turn to be groggy.

It is dark when the brakeman calls out the familiar "all aboard," and we rush into our carriages; for in this country they never wait an instant for loiterers. But we could very easily have overtaken the train on its way, for as far as Pierre the permanent way is so uncertain that we proceed very leisurely. On the left, we see in the darkness the stars reflected on a great sheet of water stretching far away out of sight. The Missouri has not yet drawn back within its normal geographical limits, for when we arrived at the station about ten o'clock, the locomotive was immersed up to the springs. Before us the lights of a town were everywhere glittering, and yet not a single house stood on the spot three years ago. It is inhabited by the labourers and mechanics, who came here for the construction of the railway, and these have raised it. At present it contains 2500 inhabitants, and among these five or six newspapers are edited and published.

An imitator of M. Boltin has even just published a Pierre directory, containing the names, *titles*, and professions of his fellow citizens. I deliberately use the word *title*, because a pestering urchin having absolutely compelled me to buy this interesting work, I notice therein with pleasure that the taste for these distinctions is far from dying out among the people of the West. Among 1500 names there are 800 colonels, and 200 or 300 majors or judges. The others appear to be satisfied with the title of captain ; they are, no doubt, people of a modest and retiring disposition, for whom I have the warmest regard, as if through instinctive sympathy.

Of course among all these good folks, there is probably not one who has even a remote claim to such a title. Nothing is more amusing than to ask an American, travelling in Europe and calling himself Colonel or Major, in what regiment he has served. However recently he may have "hailed from the other side," the question generally makes him feel very uncomfortable. I remember one who used to call himself Colonel F——. I put to him my usual question. He replied with commendable candour :

"I have never served. I had an elder brother who never served any more than I have. But as he had a very military look, they used to call him the *General.* Being younger, I naturally took the rank of *Colonel.*"

A considerable portion of this brilliant staff encumbered the platform of the depôt (station). Some of them, no doubt, belonged to the corps of bridge toll-gatherers, for a footway had been thrown over six inches of water that interrupted the road to the grand hotel of Pierre. It is a great wooden booth that looks as if it were the rendezvous of another series of colonels, judging from the collection of faces, not very reassuring, that encumber the grand room when we enter therein with our portmanteaus on our backs, for the most ragged of these valiant warriors would not condescend to earn twenty cents at this work.

The hotel proprietor, a kind of colossus embellished with formidable moustaches, is reposing behind his bar from the fatigues of the day, with both feet stuck up on the said bar, above the level of his head. He is also a Colonel, for a traveller passing before us addresses him with this title. He makes us sign our names on the register, which he pushes before us without disturbing his comfortable posture; then he deigns to summon a captain, whom the fortunes of war have reduced to the grade of waiter, and who leads us rather sulkily into a little room fitted up with a big bed, where he leaves us with the intimation that the bed is quite big enough for two. These surprises are some of the delights reserved for travellers' in America. However little cramped they may be for space, even in the best hotels, they propose to you in a perfectly unconcerned manner to sleep two in a bed. Sometimes, however, on complaining persistently, a more congenial arrangement is possible. But at

Pierre it was just as impossible to obtain a second bed as to get a dinner, and accordingly with empty stomachs we had to try to sleep, side by side, as well as we could, to the roaring of a raging storm as it brought down another flood on the already inundated roads.

"Take an Englishman, and take away all his good qualities, and you will have a Yankee."

This definition, not very flattering, comes from an English traveller, one too prone perhaps to grumble at everything. Entirely false so far as it concerns men, it becomes a striking truth when applied to institutions—to the cooking and to the stage-coaches, for instance. What admirable descriptions Dickens and Thackeray have given us of these journeys on the top of a coach by the side of a jolly stout driver, whose instructive conversation left no one ignorant of the interesting details of the private life of every dweller along the roadside! The four high-mettled horses, well harnessed, flew on the wings of the wind between the hawthorn hedges. At the entrance of the villages, on the sound of the horn, the fowls scampered away scared, and the women caught up hurriedly their children straying in the way: and then, at the changing, the fat ostler was seen lolling against the kitchen door, through which one caught a glimpse of a spit turning a substantial sirloin before a cheerful bright fire.

This was the mail-coach of the past in England or the *malle-poste* in France, and on passing the Atlantic we find the institution singularly decayed. The Americans, however, not very exacting in what pertains to comfort themselves, declare that a journey in a mail-coach in the Far West is one of the most painful trials to which the members of poor humanity can be made to undergo. It was, therefore, with a resignation, not deprived of anxiety, that, on the day after our arrival at Pierre, we made our way towards the ticket-office of the mail-coach that was to take us from Pierre to Deadwood, across the two hundred miles of prairie that separated the two towns.

At first sight, the equipage standing in the middle of the inundated road looked anything but attractive. It was a kind of tumbril, summarily suspended and perched on two pairs of very high wheels; the whole being covered with a double fold of canvas. Two or three porters were occupied in heaping up a lot of cases and other baggage in the interior, reserving for us but a very small space in the middle. As soon as we took our places there, a cow-boy doing duty as driver mounted the box; another, enjoying the name of "conductor," sat beside him, and four horses of good appearance, standing up to their knees in water, set the heavy machine in motion without much pulling. In about ten minutes they stopped on the banks of the Missouri, which the rise, rather steep, had hindered our seeing till then.

This very muddy and rapid river is not less than 800 yards across. The clear, bright day enables us to see distinctly a range of green hills bordering the opposite side, broken in certain places by abrupt and rather high precipices, known here by the name of *bluffs*. In winter, during four or five months, the passage is made over the ice, which in this latitude acquires a considerable thickness. During summer the company makes use of a little steam ferry-boat of a very primitive kind, and this is now quite ready to receive us. Our horses, well broken to this manœuvre, trot on board without the least hesitation, and in twenty minutes we reach a little creek on the right shore, protected against the current by the hulk of a steamboat, which the last break-up of the ice had thrown on the bank—a wreck that no one seemed to consider worth appropriating.

Hardly had we got aboard than a serious discussion arose. One of our four horses was lame in the foot, and the question was whether we should continue, or return and take another. Then four or five loungers come up and give their advice. But the conference, that threatened to become interminable, is cut short by a man on horseback, who gallops off to the nearest bluff, and soon returns with news that gives unanimous satisfaction.

He arrives from Willow-Creek, the first stage, sixteen miles from here. The storm of last night was accompanied with such a flood that a bridge has been carried away, and he had much trouble to get across by swimming. And then again, there has been no coach from

Deadwood for two days, and probably similar accidents have taken place elsewhere. It is decided, in this dilemma, that we repass the river to take orders from the superintendent.

There, two hours pass away in *pourparlers.* The superintendent, who at the same time is a large shareholder of the company, is in a rage with everybody, and swears like a pilot in a storm, in which he is exactly imitated by his subordinates—a fact that proves to us again how poor the English language is in good round oaths. It is really extraordinary, since the Americans have been working at it, that people so inventive have not been able to perfect it in this respect, and that they should remain so far behind other nations, such as the Mexicans or the Germans. If we remember how the Tudors used to swear, the English have certainly not advanced in this accomplishment.

At last they come to an important decision: they leave behind half of the load, and then we shall be accompanied by a waggon carrying a boat to take us across the creeks. The notion seems to us rather original, and we welcome the arrangement all the more, inasmuch as we have more room to stretch our legs.

Our third passage across the river is accomplished as happily as the two preceding. This time we have a companion. He is an old Indian, lame, and covered with ignoble rags, who seems idiotic, but who, nevertheless, is a personage of some importance, for he is attended on the river bank by a dozen of his tribe, well armed.

All these Indians are Sioux. It seems that this name, by which they are known to the whites, is a corruption of the French word *saoul*, which the old trappers gave them on account of their decided taste for the divine bottle. This explanation, at least, is given by the Père de Smet. They call themselves "Dacotahs," which, in their language, means "cut-throats;" they have, therefore, not much to lose in changing their name. All the territory we are going to cross, between the Missouri and the Cheyenne, forms part of the reserve, conceded to them by the treaty of 1877, which was concluded at the end of a long war—one in which the American Government was really not in the right, and their troops not invariably successful; for "Sitting Bull," their great chief, after having beaten two or three detachments of the Federal army, was able to retire into Canada, where he remained two years, and did not return to his own country till at the conclusion of negotiations with the American Government, carried on on the footing of recognised belligerents.

According to the terms of the treaty, which guaranteed to the Indians absolutely the property of this country, the whites have no right to raise therein any permanent establishment: they cannot cultivate there any land, nor introduce into the country, even for personal use, any fermented liquor. Special functionaries, named Indian agents, who have at their command a certain number of Indians duly armed and organised, are empowered to execute these regulations which are to some extent observed. But the unfortunate Indians will not long enjoy the tranquillity that this treaty should ensure them, for the Government is already exercising a pressure on them to force them to give up this territory to enable the North-Western to carry its line from Pierre to Deadwood. It is said that negotiations have already terminated, and that Congress will be asked to sanction a new treaty. The Sioux feel themselves at present too much hemmed in by the rising wave of civilisation to think of recommencing the struggle, and they will be obliged probably to go in search of a fresh refuge in the plains further north.

The policy of the Americans with regard to the Indians is, in general, abominable, its object being their extermination. The representatives at Congress, far from disavowing it, excuse themselves by saying that it is the only way of dealing effectually with the Indian question. Now this is absolutely false. When the French established themselves in Canada, they found tribes there of the same race as these. Our Colonial Government showed itself a faithful observer of treaties and did not hesitate to punish publicly and rigorously any whites guilty of any injustice towards the "savages," as they were and are still called even in official language though the term was not used in a derogatory sense. This policy was not slow in being duly recompensed. During all the wars we had to sustain against the English, the savages were always our faithful allies, in spite of the efforts that were made to detach them from our cause; and later, after our defeat, when the English conquest had become definitive, seeing that their new masters observed towards them the old traditions, they maintained with them the most friendly relations. Not only not a single Indian war has burst forth, but the old tribes, while preserving nominally their organisation, are so thoroughly obliterated in the white population, that it is now difficult, it seems, to find Indians of a race absolutely pure.

Many have definitely abandoned a nomadic life to become farmers. At the last census their number rose to 1,100,000, and they owned 6000 head of horned cattle and 15,000 horses. At present the grand hereditary chief of the tribe of the Tortoises, the descendant of the famous Chingachgoock, whose exploits have been sung by Fennimore Cooper, exercises the profession of notary in the city of Quebec.

Nothing of this kind has taken place in the United States, but the fault proceeds from the institutions much more than from the sentiments of the people. Instability, the inevitable condition of a Democratic Government, is not a quality that gives security for the obligations of a treaty. Those who have signed it are soon replaced by others who, having nothing to gain, see in it merely its burdens. This is what constantly happens. The administration that concluded treaties with the Indians acted, no doubt, in good faith; but, at the end of short intervals, often a few months only, new difficulties arose. As is frequently the case, the reserved territory, which was thought to be of no value, was found to contain some mine. Emigrants flocked there, and the Indians naturally resisted the invasion; shots were exchanged on each side; the Federal troops intervened, and, after a few months' skirmishing, a new treaty was imposed on the Indians, who often found themselves forced to go very far away to occupy a new reserve, which was soon destined to become the object of fresh contestations.

There were other difficulties besides, that presented themselves. The nomadic Indians lived almost exclusively on the flesh of buffaloes; now, on the one hand, the buffalo, chased incessantly everywhere by the white trappers, who every year kill some thousands solely for their skin, is beginning to disappear; and, on the other, the reserves, smaller and smaller as they are, into which the Indians are thrown back, are carefully selected among territories the poorest in pasturage, and into these the buffaloes naturally never come. It has, therefore, been necessary in the later treaties to stipulate for the regular distribution of food and clothing. It is the Indian agents who have this duty to perform. But this administration, like all others in the United States, is recruited from political favourites, who obtain these places as a recompense for their services, and who know they will only keep them so long as their party is in the ascendant. They, therefore, only think of making their fortune as quickly as possible. It is estimated that they will succeed in appropriating more than half of the credits open for the Indians. But a moment invariably comes when these, dying of hunger, procure food at the expense of the farmers of the frontier. All the Indian wars have begun in this way. At the time we were in America, the Government was obliged to send an important expedition, commanded by a general, against the Apaches, a great tribe on the Mexican frontier, who, exasperated by the depredations of the agents, rose in a mass and devastated a whole district of Texas with fire and sword.

These wars are much more serious than is imagined. The Indians always find money to buy arms, and whites also ready to sell them to them. They all have repeating Winchester rifles; they have besides a great number of horses of a special breed, which they well know how to turn to the best account. I have heard American officers maintain that they constitute the most formidable irregular cavalry in the world, and this, indeed, may well be true. In their engagements with the regular troops they have often had the advantage. It has been often said that their number is diminishing rapidly, but this is much contested. The census returns prove that among many tribes the population is stationary, and that it has a tendency even to increase. That of the Sioux is estimated at about forty thousand souls; there is nothing to prove that they have ever much surpassed this total. The Père de Smet, who lived among them for about forty years, estimates their number at about sixty thousand, but other reports do not bear out his statement.

In spite of their numerous faults, among which must be reckoned cruelty and inaptitude for work, these people certainly do not deserve all the evil that has been said of them by the Americans, and the example of Canada shows what could have been done with them under a more humane policy. On some points, however, the work of their transformation has been undertaken not without success; at the beginning of this century particularly when some Jesuits, having insinuated themselves among them, lived a long while under their tents. One of them, the Père de Smet, who died a few years ago at Yankton, had been able to acquire an extraordinary influence over them. It may be affirmed that he educated the greater number of their chiefs, and notably the famous Sitting Bull. The Americans themselves admit that many imminent massacres have been prevented by him. The souvenirs of this man who did so much good are still fresh and vivid. They have given his name to one of the last depôts of the railroad before arriving at Pierre, as well as to one of the richest mines of the Black Hills.

After his death, the examination of his papers revealed that this missionary, so well informed, had long known the existence of their valuable deposits of minerals and precious metals, the discovery of which was to be the cause of so many misfortunes to his dear

Indians, and having a presentiment of these evils, he had accordingly resolved never to speak of his great treasure-trove. Since his death, the hostilities that have taken place, and the forced emigrations that have followed as a consequence, have obliterated nearly every trace of his work. Many Indians, however, are still nominally Catholic.

And what will be the future of this race ?—a race in which the French feel it a duty to interest themselves especially, for they have been, during more than a century, their faithful allies, when fortune has smiled on them, and equally so when she has frowned on them. There is at the present moment a portentous transformation working itself out in the West. The plains, till now reserved for the buffaloes and the Indians, are invaded by herds led there by the American cow-boys. It is the pastoral life succeeding the savage life of the hunter, there, as formerly in many other lands of the old continent. To make use of an expression much affected by the Americans, and which is very *à propos*, the Far West is destined to become the manufactory of meat, where a great part of the civilized world will come for their supplies. It seems to me that the Indians should easily find a place in this new social state.

The wild warrior who resists absolutely any attempt at culture, would easily form himself, I think, to a pastoral life, and would very advantageously replace the cow-boy. This idea of mine is not at all utopian. Besides the Creeks and the Cherokees, tribes of the south-east, which have entirely entered on the road to civilization, they are beginning to speak of several tribes or portions of tribes who are proprietors of many herds of cattle. Others, desirous of following their example, are soliciting the government to supply them with reproducers instead of rations.

If the missionaries could only resume their work, I believe it would be in their power to favour most signally this transformation; especially, if the Federal government employed them as intermediate agents, for its direct influence for good is very feeble at present, so great is the corruption of the official agents now standing in the way.

The company enjoying the concession of the service of the mail coach between Pierre and Deadwood—a service for which they receive a grant of ten thousand dollars—pretends that the journey is made in thirty-six hours. Its friends affirm that this has happened once in four years. On the other hand, many people have told me that they have never been less than four days on the road, and often eight or ten: the distance, besides, is no more than two hundred miles, and the returns should be sufficiently remunerative, for the fare is twenty dollars each, and the baggage paid for at the rate of ten cents per pound; but, then, we must admit that the absence of any trace of a road inevitably gives rise to much uncertainty.

And hardly are we on our way when difficulties begin to spring up. On the west of the Missouri, the general level of the prairie rises a little, and attains an average height of about a thousand feet above the sea-level. In order to reach this elevation we are obliged to ascend hills covered with black mud—called *gumbo* in the country—into which the wheels sink almost to the axles. It is so tenacious that it fills up the intervening spaces between the spokes, and has to be constantly cleared away with a shovel. Our horses, of course, can only get on at walking pace, but they draw the coach with remarkable spirit, and this, too, without a touch of the whip, for I noticed a fact which has often struck me since, and this is the admirable tenderness of the Americans for their teams. I make another remark flattering to our national *amour propre.* I was admiring our leaders for the beauty of their form and their vigour, which were much superior to the shaft pair, and asked the "conductor" if they were not of French origin, and he informed me that they were half-blood Percherons. The Americans justly appreciate this admirable breed, and they are beginning to import every spring some hundreds of these Norman stallions.

We again fall in with a few little troops of Indians: one of them is on march for a change of encampment; the men are on horse-back leading, wrapped in their red blanket, which covers even a part of their face. They all have a Winchester slung across the pommel of their saddle. Behind them come the women, also mounted; on each side of their horses are attached bundles of long poles, their ends trailing on the ground, bearing the leathern tent folded up and the domestic utensils. These ponies are thin, but they seem good; they are rather less than the Algerian horses, which they resemble a little.

Further off a warrior has halted on the side of a hill, and five or six horses are feeding on the buffalo grass around. The man stretched out, flat on his chest on a skin, is following us with his eye while smoking a pipe without moving. His two squaws are squatting beside him. One quite young, fifteen at most, is holding an infant totally naked, to whom we give a small coin. The husband continues impassable: he is a fine young fellow of about twenty-five, and has quite the look of a gipsy.

About two o'clock we come up to an encampment of cow-boys: they are employed by the mail-coach company, for they have also a waggon service that conveys an enormous quantity of goods from Pierre to Deadwood in fifteen or sixteen days. Last year this traffic exceeded 23,000 tons. Their day's work is already finished, and the oxen are pasturing around. Every team consists of eight or nine pair. There are always two, and often three waggons, hooked on one after the other. By these means the weight is distributed over many wheels, and in the passage over difficult spots they may be easily separated. The men united under a tent are having their dinner. They invite us at once to share their repast, composed of bacon, haricot beans, and coffee. We accept it with eagerness, for we are dying of hunger, and, at the rate we are progressing, no one could form any idea when our turn would come to dine. I wish to give two dollars to the head man—*boss* as he is called—but he positively refuses, and looks even offended at it. This is one of the good points of the Far West and of America in general: gratuities and *pourboires* are quite unknown here.

At last, about four, we arrived at Willow Creek. The creek—the generic name of water courses—is, for the moment, really a river, twenty-five or thirty yards across, running between two muddy banks which are rather steep. There is hardly more depth than four or five feet of water, though the current is still very rapid; but the flood must have been tremendous. Beside us is a coach, unloaded and abandoned. When we reach the other bank its conductor comes up to us, loudly lamenting that there were no means whatever of taking it across last evening. The travellers, however, had managed to cross on a sort of raft, since carried away. They are now waiting at the station for a coach to arrive from Deadwood, and then they will change. We begin by unloading the boat that has brought us over the stream, and, after a long discussion, it is decided that the coach be drawn across where fordable. I can hardly believe what I hear, for the banks are inclined at least fifty degrees without any gradual rise on approach, and yet these men consider the operation in question quite simple.

They send us four horses from the station, which are

put in before ours, then, without a cry, without a lash of the whip, our postillion leads, with wonderful precision, his eight horses, guided with long reins, quite regularly to the bank. With a mere word of encouragement the noble animals proceed steadily, gliding on all fours, one after the other, the coach, firmly dragged, descending at their heels.

The coach and team once launched into water, there is a moment of intense confusion. The leaders and second pair, overthrown and carried on by the current, fall one on the other, with their legs caught in the traces. The men leap also into the water, and lift their heads to prevent their drowning, the wheels of the vehicle meanwhile gradually submerging, and the coach beginning to disappear. In this dilemma a man comes forward, and, with the end of a long chain in hand, he plunges down and fastens it to the pole. The horses are then attached to the other extremity, and the carriage, rising again from beneath the stream, climbs in its turn the other bank.

It was a success, but for all that the horses had run too great a risk to encourage a repetition of the exploit; they therefore decided on leaving the second carriage on the other side, which would serve the travellers coming from Deadwood. Our baggage was brought over in a boat and reloaded on a waggon, and we then made our way a-foot to the station, having only a few hundred yards to march.

There we found the unfortunate travellers awaiting

us, who, having started twenty-four hours before us, were in great distress for want of conveyance. There were six or seven, and among them two women. One of these was immediately recognised by our travelling companion, Mr Morgan, who hastened to introduce us to her in due form. She was, it seems, the chief artist of the lyric troop of Deadwood, Miss Sally Rodgers, and appeared not to have suffered much from a sleepless night. The stations, however, are not particularly inviting for a sojourn, and to look at them one would not suppose that they formed an important item in the capital of the company. All those we have seen are nothing but long sheds of rough planks, serving as stables for fifteen or twenty horses, forming the relay. One of the extremities, separated from the rest by a partition, serves as a lodging for the postillions, and travellers too, who have the ill-luck to be detained there.

Just as we are setting out, a rather warm discussion keeps them well occupied. This having ended, the two *conductors* coolly informed us that we have to follow on foot the waggon conveying our luggage. In the end we yield, on the promise that they will find place for us in the first carriage coming from Deadwood. High words have already been exchanged. At all events, there being no alternative than to remain at Willow Creek for some time longer, we start in a tolerably good humour. The ground at once becomes a little firmer, and we are again in the open prairie.

We have plenty of companions on our way at present, for all the travellers by the other coach have joined us. I ask them to explain to me why trees have not found their way into soil so rich. Opinions are divided as to the reason. Some attribute it to the fires the Indians light there periodically, and remark, in support of their opinion, that the shores of the creeks are often covered with a certain vegetation, the trees, willows, or Canada poplars becoming there protected by the swampy lands around them; but the general opinion is that the upper layer of the soil, the *gumbo,* is impregnated with alkaline salts, which hinder all arborescent vegetation. When they desire to plant trees, they find it necessary to plough the soil, and give it some months' exposure to the rain, that it may be well washed; after this preparation the young trees thrive wonderfully well.

These people are all rich farmers or ranchmen. Their conversation is interesting, and they discuss with much animation an event that has recently taken place. It was a debateable point lately to choose between the cities that piqued themselves on the honour of becoming the capital of the State of Dakota. Each county has nominated its delegates, who have met within the last few days. Since the first meeting it was admitted that their choice could hardly fall on any others than Pierre or Bismarck—the latter a town recently founded on the North-Western line. The advantage conferred by the preferences consists in this: the tribunals and the seat of the government about to become united there, the men of the long tongue, barristers, and politicians of every class, would flock to the chosen capital immediately, thereby augmenting the population, and this would produce a corresponding rise in the price of land. A syndicate of proprietors was immediately formed in each town, and it was with the help of good, ringing, solid dollars that they were enabled to come to a prompt decision.

Proceedings of this kind, unfortunately, are not rare in Europe ; but those who take an active part in them hide them at least from the world, and those who talk about them blame their authors. But here everybody considers operations of this nature quite regular. The discussion turns on a question of figures. They are all agreed in opinion that the people of Pierre, who have not had the upper hand in these biddings, have only got what they deserved ; they should have offered more. As to the delegates, they have only done their business.

We meet with a convoy of five or six carts drawn by horses, with a score of cows and a few fillies following at liberty browsing along the way. It is an emigrant travelling with his family. The mother drives the first cart, from which we see peeping out the fair heads of three or four bairns too young to walk : three lads and two tall lasses, with flaxen hair uncombed, their legs and feet quite bare, follow the file. The father, a little aged, with a gun on his shoulder, and his cheek puffed out with an enormous quid, brings up the rear.

I begin talking with him by praising his teams.

"Yes, indeed! stranger," said he, "they are really fine animals. I take care of them, for they have still 500 miles to go to take us into the Yellowstone."

"And where do you come from?"

"From Arkansas; and it is two months we have been on the march."

"But why do you go so far? Is not the land good here?"

"There are some, perhaps, who think it good: that depends on what you are going in for. For wheat, it is too dry. See how it cracks."

"And are all these children your own?"

"I guess they are, all of them; we have already ten. We reckon on making up two dozen."

"The deuce, you do! I can only congratulate you. And your wife? Is she not afraid to travel like this, quite alone, in plain Indian country, with all her little ones?"

"Oh! she is well used to that. We have had a farm for fourteen years in Arkansas, but that State is getting too populous. The newspapers say there are good lands in the Yellowstone. We have sold out, and that is the long and short of it."

I take it into my head to make him talk politics. The result of their educational system is that they have all the same instruction—one, moreover, very superficial, for at fourteen they all pass from theory to the exercise of some trade or profession; but they all read an enormous quantity of matter in the newspapers, and they well remember the style and the phrases, therefore the pettiest farmer never hesitates to discuss the most complicated questions of political economy.

My man explains to me that he belongs to a party who finds that the creditors of the State, having already received, in the form of interest coupons, more than they have lent, all that they take up now is stolen money.

" Precisely," I replied ; " there is among ourselves a certain Monsieur Proudhon, who has already found out that."

He has never heard of Proudhon, but he develops at some length his demonstration. " The country is in the hands of a party of aristocrats, who oppress the people, and crush them systematically with taxes, in order to keep them in misery."

As I had already heard this at Belleville,[1] I left my good man with the hope that he might find in the Yellowstone less oppressive aristocrats than those of Arkansas, and I went on to rejoin Monsieur Bouverie, who was walking in advance.

As it was getting dark, my travelling companion called my attention to the strange appearance of the country. One often sees in summer dried-up ponds in farmyards—the black mud there forming the bottom is traversed by a lot of little streams, which hollow out

* Belleville is a suburb of Paris, where the disciples of Socialism principally reside, and Gambetta, who was deputy for this arondissement, found it no easy matter to pacify these restless spirits.—W. C.

gutters in it, and by these the soil passes away; at the end of a few days it cracks and becomes covered with vegetation. Now, this is precisely the prairie, since the time when the waters of the great inland sea ran off and left millions of acres dry, which for ages they had covered with fertile mud, that now furnishes so much riches.

At midnight we at last arrive at Lance Creek, having come fifteen miles afoot. Everyone apparently was sound asleep. At length, however, by dint of shouting and outrageous taunting, we succeeded in rousing an Irishman, the sole guardian of the station, who deigned to consent to give us some potatoes, accompanied with rancid bacon, the only nourishment known in the country. Just as we are preparing to do honour to this frugal repast, the door opens, and a dozen individuals, as famished as we are, come to share it. They were the travellers coming from Deadwood, and they had been six days on the road. We set out again, each party on our way, at one in the morning.

CHAPTER II.

THE CHEYENNE—THE CATTLE RANCHES—PASSING A RIVER—THE INTERNATIONAL HOTEL—RAPID CITY—JUSTICE IN AMERICA—AMERICAN MANNERS—THE FIRST BIVOUAC—M'DONNELL'S RANCH—A FARMER OF DAKOTA—HOMESTEAD, PRE-EMPTION, AND FREE CLAIMS—THE FOREST SYSTEM—HILLY-RANCH.

THE second day passed almost as badly as the first. The two coaches kept company, so that they might be enabled to lend one another their teams in moments of difficulty. At frequent intervals we fell in with creeks just as deep as the first one. Sometimes the carriage overturned in the mud, and then it took two or three hours work to pull it out again. We began to dread the endless prairie, and, to make things worse, we were daggers drawn with the conductor, Stuart, who, absolutely captivated with the charms of Miss Sally Rodgers, seemed bent on prolonging the journey as much as possible. We passed the second night on a heap of half-rotten hay. The third evening, while they were taking the horses out of the coach at a station, we wandered away a little in the interval to have a shot at some wolves that showed themselves on the horizon, and, on returning, we found the horses of the relay unharnessed, and every preparation made for resting the night. Stuart, who was sauntering about the neighbourhood, told us very coolly that we should wait till to-morrow to cross the Cheyenne, from which we were only a dozen miles. On this we lost all patience, and we made such a row that he at last decided on putting in the horses, swearing all the time that he should hold us responsible for anything that might happen. As the Cheyenne is very wide and rapid, it is decidedly rash to attempt the passage by night.

But the other coach having started, and his fine project having accordingly been frustrated, he could hardly refuse to set off likewise, though, in reality, he was quite right. The old French trappers were the people who named this river the Chienne, which the Americans have since transformed into Chayenne or Cheyenne. It is formed of two tributaries, the Belle-Fourche, or North Fourche, and South Fourche, which, taking their source near one another in the west of the Black Hills, run around the base of the mountain mass, unite on the east on the same parallel, and, keeping an easterly course, pour their waters into the Missouri. Collecting on the way all the streams from the mountains, it is subject to sudden floods which swell out the ordinary course by several yards in a few hours. The fords, therefore, are always dangerous.

We arrive at the shore about midnight. A brilliant moonlight fortunately lights up the great stream, three or four hundred yards wide, as clear as day. In the discussion the postillion had sided with us, and now does not flinch at the moment of trial. But here he seems less confident of his task, and goes down to reconnoitre the ford. Generally the men of the station on the other bank mark out with signal lights the line to be taken on crossing, because the banks of sand and gravel, constituting the ford, are often shifting. But this evening, in spite of our shouting and shots from our revolvers, no one appears. At last the postillion discovers a place where a pebble bottom seems to indicate shallow water. The water, in fact, has fallen so much as to hardly reach out seats, but the current is so strong that the carriage, taken athwart, is carried with the stream. Fortunately our brave horses hold on well, and, in the end, we arrive without accident on the other side.

And here we are at last out of Indian territory. We hoped that the refreshment rooms would be better supplied, but in this we are deceived. There is nothing but the omnipresent bacon on the table, followed, as usual, by potatoes. It is impossible to obtain even a bottle of beer. They tell us very gravely that fermented drinks are prohibited by the company. The Americans recognise the frailty of human nature in general and of their own in particular; accordingly, so soon as two among them find themselves invested with any kind of authority, their first care is to enact Draconian laws in order to hinder the poor devils who have the ill-luck to be thirsty from drinking at their discretion. Thus all travellers are made to suffer for the misconduct of a few, instead of putting these into the stocks as our ancestors would have done. A few years ago the State of Illinois was just on the point of passing a law, wanting but eight or ten votes, that was to declare the act of having taken in public any fermented beverage whatever, a felony subject to a heavy fine. It was the Catholics who succeeded in rejecting it, for if it had passed, a priest would have been liable to a fine of one hundred dollars every time he celebrated the mass.

The Americans start from the principle that every man enjoying the liberty to drink gets drunk. It must perhaps be granted that it is true among them. In New York they even go a little further in quite another order of ideas. If you ask for a private room in a restaurant, the waiter will tell you with a frown that it is forbidden to give one to fewer than five persons. Can these Americans be so dissolute, and feel their sense of propriety so feeble, that they are driven to take such precautions! And yet, how they moralise when they come to Europe. At Paris it often happened for me to dine at a restaurant, in a *cabinet particulier*, with Americans of both sexes, and I am happy to say that my sense of decorum never had cause to feel embarrassed.

June the 27th.—About one in the morning we quit the inhospitable banks of the Cheyenne. In order to reach

Deadwood we have still a hundred miles to travel. During the last four days we have been on the road we have accomplished only one hundred and four. The prospect of remaining perhaps three more days cooped up in this abominable vehicle, or of being forced to follow it afoot, seems to us so distasteful, that we decide on abandoning it at Rapid City, the first city of the Black Hills, from which we are only forty-five miles distant, and where we can communicate by telephone with Mr Gifford F. Parker, the person we are come to see.

Besides, since our animadversions last evening, our intercourse with the conductor has become so acrimonious, that if we would avoid entering into the country with an open quarrel, which, considering the habits of the people here, might be rather serious, we should do well to mind what we are about.

We interchange our reflections on this matter in the thick of a very dark night. The jolts are so sensible that every moment we are putting the solidity of the carriage roof to the test at the expense of our heads. Then to add to our discomfort, we are assailed by a swarm of mosquitoes, consequently, on reading again our notes, I find this written portion of our journey bristling with sharp strokes and constellated with dots, placing thereby our mental irritation on record.

At Shoon's, where we arrive at day-break, they inform us that there is nothing to eat, but console us by intimating that a little later they should find a ranch where we can breakfast. The country is a little more attractive, a few poplars lifting their heads now along the creeks. At the end of another hour of a fresh series of jolts, they pull up in the middle of a bare plain. At the door of a hovel, standing isolate thereon, an elderly man appears, smoking his pipe; we then enter into a room poorly indeed furnished, though clean, where a woman is boiling potatoes and frying bacon, the sickening odour of which has been pursuing us for the last three days. While we are eating, turning our morsels with a recoiling tongue, I ask Mr Morgan if he knows who these people are, whose distinguished air, in spite of their evident wretchedness, puzzles and interests me singularly. He tells me that the husband is an old major in the Household Guards of Her Majesty Queen Victoria, who, at the end of a course of numerous adventures, is come to hide his head in this hole with his wife and daughter—a young lady who, perhaps, has assisted at the splendour of Her Majesty's drawing-rooms. He lives by trafficking in furs with the Indians. I have, in my wandering life, already fallen in with a large number of these men, waifs and strays of society, who, after having fallen always lower and lower, though not often from their own fault, close in obscurity and misery, in a foreign land, an existence brilliantly commenced. None of these has inspired me with more compassion than the poor hermit of Shoon's Ranch.

A fresh passenger comes to join us just as we are starting. It is a man of about fifty, with a countenance lighted up with energy and two honest blue eyes, that look at us straight in the face, and which prepossess us in his favour at once. He wears the costume of rich ranchmen, set off with a pair of revolvers and a silver-mounted bowie-knife. He comes up to us mounted on a rather fine horse, which half disappears under an enormous Mexican saddle. On setting his foot on the ground, he fastens the bridle to the pommel, and giving the animal a touch with his whip, it gallops off at once to rejoin the troop to which it belongs.

Our new acquaintance, whom they call Colonel W——, is evidently a man of importance, to judge from the manner in which he is received. Morgan informs us that he has gained in different speculations a large fortune, and that he is the proprietor of more than ten thousand bullocks. He passes his life in riding from herd to herd, overlooking his cow-boys.

The heat is now becoming quite suffocating—one of our horses, consequently, can hardly draw himself along; he has been touched, I suspect, with sunstroke. The postillion jumps down from his seat and sticks his bowie-knife nearly an inch deep into the animal's palate. I was quite ignorant of this method of bleeding, but it seems to me quite efficacious. After discharging a moderate quantity of blood, mingled with foam, the animal is so far relieved that it is able to recommence its course. Naturally, we can only move forward at walking pace, and we are soon invited even to get down and walk. We avail ourselves of the opportunity of having a shot at some of those birds that the Americans call *woodcocks*, and which are served up under this name in the restaurants of New York. But, in fact, they have neither the woodcock beak—theirs being curved—nor, certainly not, the flavour, for it is a very poor sort of game. The unlucky birds run in couples along the side of the road and await their fate with indifference.

After having peppered away with the prospect of something better than bacon for dinner, I begin talking with the Colonel, who, by-the-bye, from the first has called me Captain, a rank not at all calculated to give me a high opinion of my appearance. He speaks about that production of cattle which, for the last few years, is taking such a development, that it at once raises grave questions of political economy; for if it is such an incalculable source of profit for America, it constitutes henceforth for us as great a loss, and threatens the sole remaining branch of our agricultural industry, that has so far kept its ground.

Since the end of the American war, the vast prairies of Texas have become the pasture lands of immense numbers of horned cattle; but it is only since the opening of the Union-Pacific that they have thought of turning the plains, to which it gives access, into a breeding-ground for cattle, and which, until then, had only fed herds of buffaloes and troops of wild horses.*

* A few figures will give an idea of the importance and rapidity of the movement produced:—

In 1868 there were not, on the lands conceded to the Union-Pacific

When two or three partners, having at their command about 20,000 dollars, desire to embark in a speculation of this kind, one of them goes into Texas to buy there a thousand two-year-old animals, taking care to have a bull to every fifty cows. The price is generally 16 dollars a head—the seller undertaking to conduct the herds by stages into the North.*

During this time the other partners go in search of a vacant ranch.† The plain should be covered with an abundance of grass of good quality. It is very important that a considerable portion contain buffalo-grass, which has the property of drying standing, without rotting, and constitutes for winter an excellent forage, which the animals eat through the snow. The ranch should also be indented with some little valleys, to afford a refuge from the inclemency of snowstorms.

Company, 20,000 head of cattle. In 1883 the official returns reported the presence of 700,000 bullocks, 30,000 horses, and 45,000 sheep.

In 1876 the whole space comprised between the two forks of the Cheyenne and the Black Hills was entirely inhabited by the Indians, whose only domestic animals were a few horses.

In 1878 there were 100,000 bullocks in the mountains, and especially in the prairies at their base.

In 1882 there were 500,000.

In the spring of 1883 this figure was carried to 800,000.

I speak only of Dakota. In Nebraska, and the States or territories around,—Colorado, Montana, and Wyoming,—the proportion is, perhaps, still more considerable.

* These figures would now be no longer exact. It would be necessary to reckon on 25 dollars a head. (July 1884.)

† The word "ranch" is of Mexican origin, and generally signifies the plain whereon the cattle pasture, but it is applied also to the little dwelling built thereon.

It is for this reason that the ranches situated at the base of mountains are so much appreciated. Finally, as a matter of course, water is needed, and in abundance.

With regard to the extent, it is calculated that 20,000 acres of average prairie are required to feed 1000 animals. This is about eight times as much as would be necessary in France, with good grass; but it must not be overlooked that in this country, where the work of man has done nothing for the shortcomings of Nature, there are many spots where grass does not grow. In fact, I have often seen some portions of prairie equal to the best lands of Normandy.

When the ranch is once chosen, it may be acquired on making the demand to the government, which claims payment for it at the rate of 1 dollar 25 cents per acre. It is asserted, even, that a few gratuities, judiciously distributed, procure a great reduction in price; but hardly anyone resorts to this medium, because it is found to be too costly.

It often happens that the run of the springs and water-courses admits of another plan of procedure, which consists in simply becoming the owner of a strip of land on each side of the rivulets in such a way as to become owner also of all the approaches thereto. One is thus proprietor, in fact, of the whole plain, because if herds were brought there by any other breeder, they could not be maintained without water.

But the Americans, who are, in general, very practical

and much opposed to round-about ways, find this means still very complicated. The most common practice hitherto is to occupy the land by right of first occupant, advertising in the newspapers, which are full of these announcements, that such a party has established itself at such a place, and has taken such a brand for his cattle. Naturally, also, rights so elementary occasion many disputes, and the difficulties are settled by the revolver—the *ultima ratio* of the interested, and sometimes this assumes the proportion of a little war. Lately, two ranchmen in Montana quarrelled about a stream: their cow-boys entered the lists, and took sides for their respective patrons. There were cavalry charges, six or seven men thrown on the ground killed or wounded, and the vanquished thereupon disappeared with their herds. Excepting the revolvers, not then invented, matters passed much in the same way in the time of Abraham, proving once more that there is nothing new under the sun.

When the herd is once established on the ranch, there is nothing to do but to let it increase and multiply, and this they hasten to arrive at with the most laudable zeal: for all that, they must be kept. It is here, in this pursuit, where the favourite hero of the modern romancers of America appears—the inevitable cow-boy. A disciple of M. Le Play, should he wander in the Far West, will one day, perhaps, be tempted to give a monograph of the cow-boy. It would, doubtlessly, be interesting to the world, though presenting to him some difficulties, because the cow-boy, for reasons best known to him, moves generally in the world under a purely fanciful name. Many are natives of Texas, and a few others come from Europe. I have heard of one who was even a clerical member of the Anglican Church! In general, their origin is rather mysterious, and they by no means like questions on the subject.

If these ill-starred mortals, however, have any peccadilloes on their conscience, they are always well expiated by the kind of life they lead. It is calculated that five of them are required for a herd of 1000 to 1500 head. Each of them is furnished with six horses for their use. Constantly in the saddle from morning till night or from night till morning, they have only three nights out of five they can call their own, for two of them watch all night; and often, when the proximity of another herd or a storm renders the animals restless, all are obliged to be on the alert. They seldom come together except in the morning, and then near a waggon that brings their provisions. Every day they move from place to place to economise the pasturage, constantly riding around the flanks of their herd, bringing up with a stinging lash of their stock-whip any straying beast, and stopping only in their rounds to change horses; no sooner are they re-mounted than they are off again in a constant gallop. When one thinks well of the life these men lead, and this too for a petty pay of forty dollars a month, he cannot much wonder at the orgies with which they celebrate their pay-days.

Every year, generally about autumn, they bring the whole herd together in a narrow valley. The calves of the year are then marked with a red-hot iron with the brand of the owner: then they put aside any bullocks bearing a strange brand, and all those that have become three-year-olds in the spring. The former are conducted to a central depôt, fixed by the syndicate, where every ranchman comes to claim his own cattle; the latter are driven to the nearest railway station, and then conveyed to the great markets of the East, Saint Louis and Chicago.

Hitherto the profits have been enormous, though during the first three years nothing is returned, for they sell only beasts that are becoming four-year-olds. But when this term of three years is once passed, the return for the capital is about 40 per cent. from the beginning, and the capital goes on always augmenting, because the herd doubles in number nearly every three years. The losses arising from cold or accidents do not rise to the rate of 8 per cent. In short, a bullock of four years, which weighs living from 1100 to 1600 pounds, has cost no more than five dollars, and sells for fifty on the average.

But these brilliant results will not be slow in shrinking to more modest proportions, in consequence of the occupation of the ranches which are becoming scarce in some districts, and these must be paid for in earnest, if the ranchmen are bent on having them. Certain large companies are already entering on this road. They are especially English who go into these speculations. Many landlords of England have lately become owners of immense domains, which they let out in due course to ranchmen. They speak particularly of the Duke of W——, who bought at a single bid six hundred thousand acres.

All this flesh-food serves for the consumption of the East, but it is employed chiefly in the preparation of those canned meats that now flood the whole world. During the last few years, the exportation of live bullocks and beef to England and France has been carried on on a very large scale. On taking into account the losses, it is estimated that on selling the meat at sixty centimes or sixpence per pound very large profits are made.* The Governments, however, that feel the danger, especially in England, have thrown so many impediments in the way of this trade, that it is not quite so active at present; but it is certain that it will be resumed before long, and in such proportions that it will be expedient to take a decisive course, which will either encourage or impede it. Perhaps, however, it will be advisable for France to take a middle course, to consist in permitting the introduction only of lean beasts that would be fattened subsequently at home. The graziers buying their beasts at a much lower price, might then well be content with a proportionately lower price for meat without thereby incurring any loss.

* In 1883, the Port of Glasgow alone received 49,000 carcasses of American bullocks, brought over in ice, the whole of which was consumed in the neighbourhood.

Thanks to our incredible ignorance of what is going on in foreign countries, these questions, serious as they are, seem to occupy the attention of no one among us. We have no adequate idea of the figures that represent the extent of the business on this side of the Atlantic. A single butcher of Chicago, Mr Armour, whose establishment we visited last June, had already killed and prepared since the beginning of the year 450,000 pigs, and they kill there also 300 bullocks a day.

In the early days of the enterprise, cattle stealing was common enough, but owing to precautions taken, it is now almost unknown. Every thief caught in the act is immediately hanged without any form of trial. The syndicates, moreover, keep agents at all the principal stations, who, advised by telegraph of the consignments, verify on passage every mark, and immediately seize any animal bearing a suspicious brand. The expenses of prosecution are covered by an annual subscription of 10 dollars per 10,000 dollars of capital. Finally, the ranchmen take a last protection—one very effective, though accompanied with disagreeable consequences for the public. They refuse absolutely to supply the local butchers, for fear that the regular sale of one of their beasts would afford facilities for the theft of many others; for if their brand were once in the open market, it would be very difficult to recognise which were stolen and which sold, and, consequently, to detect the thief. And this it is that explains why butcher's meat is so scarce in the country, and why they live on bacon and canned meats ; and again how policies, affecting a whole community, may bring about changes in the habits of a people.

Monsieur Bouverie having, in his turn, got tired of the sport of bagging pseudo-woodcocks, came up to join me, and since in such heat trudging along under a fierce sun is neither invigorating nor pleasant, we lag behind our companions and then slyly slip into the carriage, with the innocent design of indulging there in a gentle nap. But, unluckily, Conductor Stuart, having spied us out, takes it into his head to remonstrate insidiously, by beginning to complain of the fatigue of his horses. This gives rise to a fresh scene, in which we insist so vigorously on our rights, that he goes off grumbling to rejoin the Colonel, who heroically continues his way a-foot.

But all our attempts to sleep are in vain, and this we quickly find out, for no sooner do we begin to nod than a tremendous jolt sends us up in the air, and we come down on the floor of the carriage. With our poor heads leaning against the canvas covering, we gaze bewilderingly on the endless green plain and dusty track.

" Just look there," exclaims Monsieur Bouverie all at once. " See how the Colonel and Stuart are laughing together, as they eye us so mischievously. One would say that they are putting their heads together to play us some trick."

At this moment the carriage stops abruptly, and we find ourselves on the banks of a rather broad creek.

"Now then, Captain!" the Colonel cries out to me, "you must get out. Come down here to us; we have a boat, and I will get you across."

We are so thoroughly uncomfortable in the carriage, and being glad of a pretext to quit it without seeming to yield, we hasten to get out of it. Stuart and the Colonel lead us on a few hundred yards, and show us a canoe hidden in the rushes. It is the trunk of a pine hollowed out, about two yards long.

"Is it in that we are going across?" I ask.

"Certainly," replied the Colonel; "and it is I who am going to pilot you over."

"Much obliged; give me the paddle and I will go alone. I have no wish to be with another in that *galère*."

"Nonsense!" cried the Colonel, laughing, "you will see."

I am fool enough to yield, and I take my seat aft, the Colonel kneeling down in the fore part: in eight or ten strokes with the paddle we are on the other side. On landing, he jumps up briskly and springs ashore, giving the canoe such an impetus that it capsizes. Happily I suspected a trick, for I had seen him give Stuart a wink, with a triumphant smile. With one hand I seize the branch of a willow, and with the other his leg, sending him rolling into the middle of the stream. With this *coup de grâce*, I leap ashore scarcely splashed.

I almost danced in triumph. On the opposite bank I saw Monsieur Bouverie shaking his sides with outrageous laughter, and the temptation, little generous as it was, to chaff my vanquished antagonist was irresistible.

"Now then, Colonel," I said, sitting calmly on the bank, "you see what it is to indulge in little jokes of this sort on people. Take a good, hearty draught of that cool water, Colonel; it will do you a world of good."

But he swallowed too much of it, I fear, the unhappy man; for, encumbered with his boots, and his spurs, and his pistols, he was turned over two or three times by the current, and seemed to be buffeted about so badly that I had already thrown off my coat and prepared myself to leap into the water; but at this moment he was enabled to seize a jutting branch of a tree, and to swing himself on land. He ran directly up to me, holding out his hand.

"By Jove! 'tis well done, Major," he cried, shaking my hand so heartily that it was nearly disjointed. "You are a good 'un! I have only got just what I deserved. We will have a milk-punch together when we get to Rapid City."

"Do you hear him now?" called out Monsieur Bouverie from the other side. "He calls you Major, at present: your exploit has raised you in his estimation."

"Don't trust yourself with Stuart, he is going to throw you into the water also."

"Pooh-pooh! Let him try, and we'll see who will have the last laugh."

Just as we expected; he was hardly in the middle of

the stream when Stuart capsized the canoe, and then threw himself into the water to swim ashore; but at this moment, Monsieur Bouverie, putting both hands on his shoulders from behind, gave him so vigorous a push that it sent him to the bottom. At ten yards lower down his face, red and convulsed, reappeared above water, but the unsparing Monsieur Bouverie, who was waiting for him, recommenced the operation without giving him time to collect himself. Having been satisfied, my friend gave a few bold strokes and joined me, leaving our conductor to have a chase after his immense hat, already carried some distance down the stream.

The Colonel was wringing his clothes while Stuart rejoined us in a very bad humour.

"We must be off," he said, shaking himself like a Newfoundland dog. "We are late."

"Whether we are late or not, it is all the same to me. But this I know, we don't stir an inch till I have changed everything from head to foot. Tell them then to open my portmanteau."

It was a rare sight. It is related of Goethe that he made one of his friends one day walk about in a meadow quite naked that he might realize more fully in his imagination the aspect of the terrestrial paradise. Stuart, the driver, the Colonel, and I were just in the same picturesque condition on the prairie. But it was one not at all to the taste of Stuart, who swore like a trooper, declaring he would start and leave Monsieur Bouverie behind to his fate.

"Oh! oh!" exclaimed my friend when I told him what was said. "We will see to that. Tell him if he stirs an inch I will send a bullet through the first horse that moves."

He looked so droll, brandishing his revolver, with as little costume as Ajax, the son of Telamon, that the Colonel and I laughed till tears started in our eyes. The Colonel now sided entirely with us. In about half-an-hour, Monsieur Bouverie, decked out daintily in white linen, with his moustaches curled like a masher's, declared himself ready to start, and the mail-coach resumed its way.

We soon catch a glimpse of a range of mountains covered with pine, with others faintly rising behind, depicting their outlines on the pale greyish blue of the horizon. Altogether it is precisely like an island we sight in the middle of the ocean, and this is the first view we get of the Black Hills. About seven o'clock, after having crossed a pretty river, which is Rapid Creek, we make our entry into Rapid City, and the carriage at last stops at the door of the International Hotel.

The first aspect is characteristic. The dinner, apparently, is just over. All the frequenters, great strapping fellows, with long uncombed beards, are sitting in little groups of six or seven around the pillars that support the upper floor, smoking and chewing tobacco with the gravity of an ecclesiastical council in moments of tranquillity. All their feet are elevated in the air, resting against the wooden pillars at an altitude that leads the spectator to apprehend a serious fall head over heels. These people are by no means talkative. Now and then, however, escapes from a nose—for here they speak only through this organ—some phrase invariably beginning with, *I guess*, and others reply, *You bet*, in a confident tone, and this is followed by a silence. All these *nature's noblemen*, as they call themselves, smile a little at the sight of the Colonel, who is evidently "one of our prominent citizens," and give him a warm greeting.

Feeling we are rather in the way among these intimate acquaintances, we begin by informing Stuart of our decision, and invite him to unload our luggage, and then we go to look for the hotel proprietor. He is a tall Irishman called M'Carthy, and, verily, one of the best fellows to be found anywhere. He scans me from head to foot for a moment without a word, then all at once he asks:

"Colonel, aren't you the French baron Parker is expecting?"

"How quickly one is promoted in this country!" whispered Monsieur Bouverie. "Here you are colonel already."

"Is Parker here?"

"No; but he was here this morning, and will return this evening. Colonel, you are welcome; come and take something."

These so far are our beginnings of the life in the Far

West. I am writing my notes in a room, tolerably clean, beside a bed, rather inviting, and whereon I am going to repose with delight from the jolts of that execrable mail-coach. I rise in due course, refreshed for the dinner of which I cannot say much in praise. The milk punch, however, offered to us by our worthy host was delicious.

June the 28th.—This morning I was awakened by two knocks at my door, and presently entered a fine young fellow in a blue shirt and high boots up to his knees, whom I did not directly recognise. It was that good fellow Parker, of whom I shall have much to say.

I introduced him immediately to Monsieur Bouverie, to whom he could not make himself well understood, for, four or five years sojourn at Saigon, and another as long at Paris, have still left him his rather fantastic French; though this does not prevent them from becoming excellent friends.

After I had finished dressing, we went into business matters. Parker finds himself at the head of two groups of properties; one, the Little Rapid Creek, thus named from a tributary of the river that we crossed last evening, is an undertaking of mines and forests; the other, quite to the south of the Black Hills, is of a more miscellaneous character. It involves cattle that are increasing, a city that is rising, and a railway that is extending; and we will say something of these when we get there.

In the interval we draw up our plans. In the first place, it will be necessary to buy horses, and then we shall go to Deadwood, the centre of all business of the country. We shall remain there long enough to visit the principal works and manufactories; then traversing the country in its whole length from north to south, we shall go and stay awhile, first at Little Rapid Creek and next at Cascade, to reach again, through the desert of Alcali, the line of the Union Pacific Railway, this time at the town of Sydney. Parker entreats us not to take with us either guide or servant, because it is the law of the country that the first comer who discovers a mineral lode in any property whatever, becomes the proprietor on a simple claim to it. One is therefore very cautious in taking a stranger in his journey through the country.

Having now settled our plans, we begin putting them into execution, and under Parker's guidance we beat up the town to provide ourselves with horses. In about five minutes some are brought to us from all quarters. Nearly all of them are ponies which, they say, come from Oregon; they are nice little animals, about 13¾ hands high, admirably built; and among them it is only rather difficult to choose. Out of twenty-five or thirty shown to us, not one is unsound. In France they are quite right in saying that it is the hard roads that ruin the horses' legs. Here, God knows what the cow-boys make theirs go through, and yet I have never seen a windgall nor a vessicon. They assert also, though it seems to me an exaggeration, that there is not a broken-winded horse in the country, and that all those having arrived here in this state have been cured. Many are restive: at a moment, when the least expected, they will put their head between their fore-legs, bring their feet together, raise their back into a hump, which no girth is strong enough to resist, and then leap on all fours till the cavalier comes to the ground, which he infallibly does in due course. This amiable trick of *buck-jumping*, as it is called, is also practised by the Australian horses, but I have not seen it elsewhere.

Monsieur Bouverie has, at first sight, taken a fancy to a little dun-coloured mare, which in fact is one of the prettiest little things to be seen anywhere, in spite of the frightful tatooing that disfigures her, for here they brand horses as well as cattle with the red hot iron. We pay fifty dollars for her to the seller, an old farmer, who says good-bye to his pet so touchingly, that I begin to suspect its genuineness, remembering similar demonstrations of the Norman horse-dealers when they part with an animal which they had never hoped to get rid of.

As I do not find among them one sufficiently high to carry easily the 85 kilogrammes of bone and flesh constituting my portly personage, without reckoning

* "Buck jumpers" are not so very rare in England, and are probably well known to most of our principal horse dealers.—W. C.

the supplementary kilogrammes represented by my saddle, my courier's bag, and my gun, I decide on going in the afternoon to see a troop of horses which they tell me is in the neighbourhood. We return to our hotel, loitering on the way.

The town of Rapid City, which counts 400 inhabitants, is beginning to enter into its second period, that is to say, there are already two houses of brick. The others are mere wooden sheds, the oldest, the log-houses, being trunks of pine unplaned and put together, and the more recent dwellings of plank. Among the latter are a few belonging to occupiers, who pique themselves on their taste for architecture. They have on the frontage a false story, that is merely a simple *façade*, in which are pierced mock windows. What would Mr Ruskin say about this? It appears that this adds a great deal to the importance of the proprietor.* There is always a wooden footway along the street.

The hotel is crowded. Besides those in the Far

* This simple fact singularly reveals the character of the inhabitants. It shows that they estimate the value of things by what other people think of them, and not by their intrinsic worth. On the other hand, from an æsthetic point of view they are now probably too familiar with the deceptive imitation for it to produce disgust, just as we tolerate wall papers and grained doors, we are most accustomed to, that look wonderfully like oak and marble. It seems that close imitations of real things can only become beautiful when we are perfectly habituated to them. This perhaps may explain the hostile criticism at first provoked by the tinted Venus. Imitations intentionally deceptive, however, must lose all their effect on being detected. The moral element would be wanting. "Rien de beau que le vrai."—W. C.

West who do no cooking at home—and these are the immense majority, coming here to dine—there are others, it seems, brought here by the Courts, now being held. We dine with the presiding judge, and a score of lawyers who follow him. In France, it would appear to us somewhat extraordinary to see a *président d'assises* dining at a *table d'hôte* with the bar and the judges. But here, these free and easy habits shock no one. All these people address one another with the title of "Colonel" with the most perfect ease and affability.

After dinner we take a carriage, which conducts a Mr H——, one of the "prominent citizens" of the city, who most courteously offers to pilot us in our search of horses. We traverse one or two charming little valleys, where we admire the beautiful rivulets and pines, and then a very rudimentary sort of brewery; but wherever we look for horses, not one is to be seen.

At last we learn that the troop has been led away to the North. This information is given us by a cow-boy we meet on our way, a very characteristic specimen. His costume consists of a grey felt hat, holed through and turned up *à la Don César de Bazan*, with a golden end well tarnished and rubbed, a red shirt and an Indian buff-leather breeches with long fringe hanging from the seams. These breeches have the peculiarity of being destitute of a seat, and held on to the girdle merely by the front piece and a kind of scarf that passes between the legs. The Indians ride like this on bare skin, probably not very tender, but I must not forget to mention that this individual had on a pair of drawers, though this too is likely enough spared the friction on the ranch.

While he is talking with us I examine the horse. It is a fine grey animal about 14½ or 15 hands high, with splendid limbs, and looks as if it could carry with perfect ease the weight of an enormous Mexican saddle, a lasso of plaited thong, and of the rider decked out with his revolvers and cartridges. He has already done seventy-five miles a-day without appearing the least fatigued. Unfortunately, the owner positively refuses to part with him.

We return to dine at the hotel; then, in spite of Parker's remonstrances, who maintains that it is not prudent, we go into the *saloon* of the hotel. The bar-keeper, in his shirt sleeves, stands behind the counter. A great trough filled with ice is at hand, and with the help of this he makes all the drinks, bearing extravagant names, that the customers come up and ask for—*gum ticklers*, *corpse-revivers*, and so forth. But the majority of these tipplers ask only for whisky, which they swallow glass after glass, standing at the bar, without winking or uttering a word. All these gentry have a gallows look, but for all that they are quite polite. Many draw near us: some of these, Canadians, speak of the "vieux pays;" others want to sell us some mines,—for every one of these has a sample of some mineral in his pocket. The old man who has sold us the dun mare treats us as old acquaintances. He tells me he has come here on a law suit: a pig worth two or three dollars had got into his fields, and wounded itself there, by accident, he affirms. The owner commenced legal proceedings against him, and these have been going on for three months. At last he has found a lawyer who undertakes to conduct his case for fifty dollars, and it is in order to pay him that he has sold me his mare. Another, who has apparently taken a drop too much, tells us that he is an Englishman. He deeply regrets the good ale and gin of Old England, but he has emigrated because he was obliged to bow down so much to the nobles! In the interval he has turned his hand to every trade, and has gained just enough to live; but at last he is going to make his fortune, for he has found a mine. Then, having groped in his pockets, he pulls forth the specimens of his treasure.

These people, in short, manifest no unfriendliness towards us, and those who speak to us are polite and even cordial. We do not see many revolvers, yet for all that assassinations are frequent; but I believe they are almost all the result of pot-house brawls between armed men. The judge tells us that Rapid City is kept in admirable order. The police regulations are so severe that the simple act of firing in the town any firearm whatever is punishable with a fine of ten dollars. But when I ask him whose duty it is to arrest the culprit, he admits that the only personage duly authorised for this purpose is the Sheriff, who lives at about sixty miles hence—that is, at Deadwood. Thereupon, I am edified.

June 29th, Friday.—I have often heard related of a shipowner, a free-thinker, who, determined to protest against the superstition about Friday, had a ship laid down on the stocks on a Friday, waited for a Friday to launch her, named her "The Friday," had a crew of thirteen; sailed on a Friday for her first voyage and never returned; and this greatly troubled the ship-owner in the first place as owner, unless he had over-assured her, but at all events as a free-thinker.

I think of this well-authenticated story in recognising that it was on a Friday that we definitely quitted our well-beaten path, and that, so far, we have not marched from one success to another.

Last night, *poker*—the favourite game of the Americans—probably was not favourable to the cow-boy we met yesterday, for this morning at day-break he came to Parker to offer him his grey horse for seventy-five dollars, which he at once accepted for me. I am going to see my new acquisition at the livery stable, where it is standing. It is probably the first time this hardy animal has ever entered a stable. He stands perfectly still at the end of his tether, but in a state of consternation that is quite amusing. They give him some oats. This also is quite unknown to him ; but after a while, making up his mind to taste it, he seems to take to it like a Highland crofter.

Then we go from store to store to make our last acquisitions. Fortunately, we have brought our saddles from France, but then we want spurs. We look at these—wonderful works of art that come from Mexico, and ornamented with rowels quite an inch in diameter. Our friends, the Canadians, continue loading us with civilities, and they come from all quarters to wish us good-bye. One of them went to his farm last evening to fetch his younger brother in order to present him to me.

Every moment the French words taken in an English sense mingle with his Norman *patois:* one would fancy he was an English actor playing the *rôle* of a peasant of Molière.

"When my mother heard he had come from some French noblemen of the old country, she pressed us very much to tell you to come to our house."

"Thank you very much: if we can do so, we will not fail. Where do you live? Is it far from here?"

"Oh! no. I have taken a farm on the creek not far off. It is excellent land."

"And everything goes on well? Are you married?"

"Married! Ah! ah! *Ben sûr non* that I am not married. With whom do you think one can get married in this country. In the first place, it is much shorter to get unmarried than to get married. When I want to get married I shall go to look for a wife in our parish near Montreal, and then I shall bring her into the States. Here there are no Catholics but the Irish, and I do not much like the Irish."

On re-entering our hotel, I ask M'Carthy to show me a place where I can write a few letters while waiting for the luncheon. He leads me very obligingly into a sort of drawing-room, on the door of which is written, *Ladies' Room.* Then follows a fresh adventure. In another minute I become conscious that someone is reading over my shoulder. I turn round briskly and see a tall fair girl, one of the two or three *ladies* who sometimes condescend to wait at table.

"Well! My dear, does it amuse you what I am writing here?"

"But I can't read very well," she replies, with an air of vexation. "You write so small!"

"Ah! Had I known it, I should certainly not have neglected to write larger. But perhaps you do not know French?"

"No, I don't know French. Is it French you are writing there?"

"Yes."

"Ah! but I know only Swedish and English." And then she disappears with the conviction probably that I am rather disobliging in making use of a language she does not understand.

At luncheon we find one of our Canadian friends. He is a painter and grainer, and is so proud of his work, an imitation of mahogany on the panels of the doors of the Court-house, that he cannot rest till we have inspected his work of art. We therefore hurry over a poor meal to gratify him.

In America the first outlay incurred in a rising town is for a school and a court-house, and the first forms the lawyers and politicians that encumber the second. The "Rapid Citizens" have not yet a school, but they have a court-house that cost 15,000 dollars, not yet paid for, and, quite possibly, never will be in the opinion of our friend the painter, who is waiting for six or seven hundred for his work. It is a great building in brick, with a French roof or mansard-roof—the perfection of architectural art in the estimation of the Far West. We arrive here just as the Court is sitting. The judge, our acquaintance of yesterday, is seated in a rocking-chair behind a green table. On his right are the men of the jury in their shirt sleeves, because it happens to be rather warm. On the left a lawyer is standing up pleading his cause, hemming and hawing over it most painfully. The judge, the jury, and the bar have each a large jug of iced water at hand, and they quench their thirst with large draughts every five minutes.

I ask to be enlightened on the case. It is a scene of national manners and customs, and one rather curious. In a tavern quarrel one man has beaten another almost into a pulp. The next day, the aggressor, becoming a little sober, gets himself prosecuted by an obliging friend before a local judge. The friend complains of having been hustled a little; the judge condemns the delinquent in a fine of two dollars, and each party goes his way.

Two days afterwards, the actual victim of the assault comes before another judge and states his case. The defendant, duly summoned, arrives, admits candidly the facts, but produces an office copy of the judgment that has already condemned him, and goes his way, confident of his sound demur, for no one can be tried twice for the same offence—*non bis in idem.* This is all the Latin they learn in America, but they know well how to apply it.

It appears, however, that this Norman of Dakota has not the merit of having originated this artful manœuvre. The same proceeding had been resorted to lately, with complete success, in New York. It was even in this case more piquant, inasmuch as the pot-valiant aggressor was himself a judge. In the great metropolis of the East, the complainant did not press his case and did well. The Dakotian, a pig-headed passionate fellow, was determined to appeal, but he will certainly have to pay the costs.

All this seems very natural to the Americans. In the old States, the judges are nominated on their election for a period varying from two years to life. They have a very low salary, and, besides, they are obliged to relinquish, at least ostensibly, the practice of their profession during their term of office. Then again, their election always costs them dear, and they undertake, like all other functionaries, to hand over to the fund of their party their first year's salary. They must therefore make their fortune in four years, and the suitors well recognise this exigency.*

In the territories like Dakota, the judges are appointed directly by the President of the United States for a period of four years. The choice therefore is not so bad; at most they are reproached with having gained their position for electoral services.

Our friend, the painter, has not made us a present of one of his artistic panels, but he has made us dance through the court-house from top to bottom, introduciug us here and there with the most perfect freedom, and we cannot refrain from testifying to the imperturbable good humour of all those functionaries of the law. We enter into the chamber of the Recorder without even warning. He shakes our hands with a heartiness that almost dislocates the wrist, and asks us *how we like the country*—a phrase that inevitably proceeds from every mouth. A little further on we meet the Sheriff—another elected functionary. He is a kind of magistrate invested with various functions, from that of the bum-bailiff to the hangman. In fact he is the undertaker of the police of a county, and is paid in proportion to the services he renders; so much for the arrest of a murderer, so much for his hanging, so much for summoning, on subpœna, a witness. If it is a question of having bought police, or hired hangmen, he pays for them out of his own pocket, but this proceeding is so little to his taste

* This is absolutely untrue—if elected for ten years, why make their fortune in four?—W. R. B.

that he invariably does the work himself, without feeling ashamed of it. The office too is no sinecure. In this territory, though the fees and charges are not very high, the Sheriff of Deadwood last year netted 75,000 dollars.*

I was told this by a judge to whom I have just been introduced—judge, at least, according to the unknown individual who, in presenting me, addressed him as judge; but then another comer called him colonel, and a third professor. This is the way these titles are bandied about. "You must be somebody," says their countryman, Emerson; "then you may do this or that, as you will." But the wonder is when they are known, as in the majority of cases, to be supposititious, that they do not lose their dignity and become ridiculous, and consequently distasteful. This morning I was on the point of stirring up a quarrel with the boots of the hotel. As he appeared to me to occupy the last grade of the social scale, I took it into my head to call him *corporal*, but he indignantly protested, and declared that he was a *captain.*

At last, about noon, we had our horses out of the livery stable, in order to try our hands at loading a pack-saddle. When one has been all his life a gentleman farmer or a naval officer, like Monsieur Bouverie and me, this art is not perfectly understood, especially when the equilibrium of such unaccommodating objects as a

* The sum of 375,000 francs is given by the Author, which would be about 75,000 dollars, and it seems almost incredible. [This is untrue.—W. R. B.]

photographic apparatus and two Winchester rifles have to be well maintained on the backs of two half-wild animals. We get there without unduly exciting the idle curiosity of all the *bakers* around us. In America, they call the habitual man-about-town the lounger—*baker.* I leave to a more learned etymologist than myself the care of discovering whether there is not in this term an ironical allusion to the way in which they make the execrable bread we are forced to eat everywhere in the country.* Parker, who travels in the fashion of the country, that is, without luggage, is already perched upon his Mexican saddle, while we are contending with unmanageable buckles. At last he gives the signal to start, which we do in an imposing canter, opening our way through a crowd of admiring colonels.

To-night we are to sleep at Fort Meade, having a letter of introduction to the commander from General Sherman.

We press our horses into a gallop along one of the three or four valleys leading out of Rapid City. The country around is charming. The end of the valley is occupied by a tributary of the Rapid, which runs through magnificent natural meadows, where some fine cows, much like our Norman breed, are up to their knees in sainfoin. Then there are fine woods of birch, oak, and willow, grouped here and there in such masses of verdure, that one would suppose the ground was laid out for an English park. Over all this rise hills covered

* If *loafer* be derived from loaf, may not *baker* have been suggested and adopted as a synonym?—W. C.

with a magnificent forest of Scotch fir. What is called the road is nothing but the wheel-track left on the elastic turf by a few passing vehicles. We see here two or three farms. In a snug nook, a log-house, low and well-smoked, used now as a barn and stable, recalls the humble commencement of the squatter. It was about four years ago that he built this hovel to shelter his family, that had then just traversed the prairie in a great, covered waggon. And then, when he had established himself, he passed many a long night, with his hand on the Winchester, listening to the howling of the wolves around his dwelling; and when this ceased, he remained in painful doubt as to whether they had not fled at the approach of the red-skins. They point out to us, half-way up the hill, a white stone, marking the spot where five men were scalped by the Sioux in 1879.

And then at the end of two years they had done well. The farmer has abandoned the already half-decayed log-house, and has constructed, facing it, a pretty little house of plank, painted white, with a verandah and a bow window. Through the open windows we can distinguish the carpet covering the floor, and a piano—the inevitable piano. We French are often reproached with not being colonists; but if our colonies often showed spectacles of this kind, I think we should soon become colonists.*

* It has often been said that the English make colonies with colonists, the French colonies without colonists, and the German colonists without colonies.

I have decidedly made a good acquisition in purchasing Jean-Leblanc—the name we have given to my grey horse. He keeps well ahead of all the others in spite of the weight he carries. His pace is neither a trot nor a gallop, but much nearer to a gallop, and some moments he ambles along; at all events, he goes five or six miles an hour, and this is the important point.

We have hardly passed the last farm when Monsieur Bouverie's dun mare overtakes me, fleeing, like an antelope, without a rider, with a Mackintosh and the leg of a photographic apparatus flapping between her legs. I start immediately in chase. She plunges into the thick of the firs, and here we are in a mad pursuit over the great slabs of slate that strew the ground. Jean-Leblanc seems to understand the business so well, and takes to it with so much spirit, that I let him have his head, wondering every moment if he will select a comfortable spot to go head over heels. At last, I lose sight of the fugitive, which, according to the amiable trick of runaway horses, has allowed me to approach twice or thrice, just near enough to touch her. I return now with some difficulty to the skirt of the wood, where I find Mr Parker, and this gentleman goes off in pursuit of the mare. It appears that she started while the unlucky rider was in the act of adjusting his pack. He has just come up, gathering on his way, with a most melancholy air, all his nick-nacks scattered along the track. But this does not hinder him from putting the best face on the affair, and declaring that it was a lucky thing the accident did not happen after we had left far behind every inhabited spot.

At the end of another hour Parker returns. His insinuating ways, with the beau-sexe in general, seem to have had some influence over the dun mare, who allowed herself to be caught. But this animal is really a little too wild, and, I fear, will give us further trouble.

At last we resume our way. Parker leads us through the forest, assuring us that, in spite of our misfortunes, we shall arrive at some inhabited spot by night-fall. I will not undertake to say how many fearfully steep hills we have scaled, nor how many brooks we have forded. Whatever the difficulties may be, the scenery is everywhere lovely, especially in crossing a number of little valleys and ravines, ensconced between hills covered with pines.

This country has by no means the wild and grandiose character that one expects—I know not why—to find here. It has the smiling and congenial aspect of the little valleys of Switzerland and Savoy. A painter here would put in the foreground a little shepherd with a pointed hat, playing the *Ranz des vaches*, and not a Sioux in war paint, with a ring in his nose.

About seven o'clock, our good leader, Parker, candidly confesses that he is lost. We find ourselves on the bank of a river, which, judging from its importance, should be the Rapid Creek, or, at all events, one of its main tributaries. The waters rush forth, foaming, from a narrow gorge, which they have scooped out at the foot of a rock, and this, on our side, completely bars the valley. The rays of the sun at present light up no more than the tops of the pines. We fancy, however, we can distinguish on the other side something like a passage leading up the valley, and it would be only necessary it seems to get across the stream, but herein lies all the difficulty. It is at least fifteen yards from bank to bank, but we can form no opinion of its depth, and the rapidity of the current by no means tempts us to feel our way to the other shore. The horses, good judges generally in such cases, appear to remonstrate strongly against the attempt ; but Jean-Leblanc, an animal apparently ready for any emergency, consents to advance one or two paces. In an instant the water rises above the girths, and, being almost carried along by the current, he turns back briskly from the treacherous stream, quite determined, it seems, not to venture in the enterprise. But since we have to find some means of continuing our way, I decide on putting into practice a manœuvre I had often seen successful in our expedition to Cambodia. I wind around my body one end of Parker's long lasso, and then my two companions, standing over the jutting point of a projecting rock, and holding the other as I enter the current, sustain me with all their might. Being thus suspended at the extremity of this long line against the force of the stream, I oscillate on its surface from side to side, like the movement of a pendulum, till I at length succeed in reaching a branch from the other shore, and this I immediately grasp. Then, fastening thereto the end of the lasso, I return by hauling myself over the river. Having everything now arranged, I take the horses by the bridles in one hand, holding on to the stretched lasso by the other, and, urged forward by a few smart lashes of the whip, the unwilling animals, partly by swimming, partly by scrambling over the submerged rocks, triumphantly accomplish the perilous adventure.

Parker and Monsieur Bouverie, who can hardly swim, were not very confident of success, but they have managed to pass over on the backs of their horses without having been deeply immersed.

At last on the other side, I dress myself again as quickly as possible, for the water was icy, and the air now feels quite cold. We start again across a little marshy plain, but no sooner have we proceeded a few hundred yards than we are obliged to pull up once more. We discover that we are merely in a ring of the water-course, and completely closed, this time on our left, by a wall of rocks precisely similar to the other, that had already forced us to traverse the river. We are therefore compelled to re-cross; but since it is now quite dark, it would be madness to think of repeating to-night with our tired horses the exploit we have just achieved. There is no alternative from pitching our camp.

Over our heads, at the foot of great rocks, extends a little plateau or shelf, where a scanty grass barely grows under the shadow of gigantic pines. Some prospectors even must have sojourned on this plot, for we find here the remains of a log-house fallen in ruin. If we had only something to eat we should not, after all, be so badly off. I have passed many nights in Madagascar and in Cochin China under worse conditions. We begin by abusing Parker, a proceeding that affords us some relief without unduly disturbing his equanimity. Then I fumble in my pockets for some matches, but it is impossible to find any, remembering then I had left them at the hotel. Happily Monsieur Bouverie is a man of resource, and I call to him to supply me.

"Where am I to find matches?" he replies, groping all the time in his pockets. "Ah! here are some; but as I had them in my pocket when I fell into the water the other day, I fear they will not light. Happily, they are not French matches,* and there is still some hope."

I had already brought together a great heap of dead wood, and then, as we lie flat on the ground, face downwards, to intercept the least breath of air, we strike one match, and the little spark, passing from blue to pale yellow, soon lights up one branch of fir, then another,

* The "allumettes de la régie," as the French matches are frequently termed ironically, are the product of a monopoly, favoured by the Government for the benefit of the revenue; and the privileged company, having no competitors to fear, give themselves little trouble about the quality of their manufacture: these matches, therefore, form the subject of constant jokes among Frenchmen.—W. C.

till the whole pile gets well ablaze, casting its lurid glare over the dark boles of the lofty pines, the ruined log-house behind, and the horses tethered beyond, as they are cropping, with mournful look, the sparse, dry grass that forces its way with difficulty between the scattered stones.

Squatting around the burning faggots, it amuses me to listen to the animated polemics between Parker and Monsieur Bouverie. The former has passed four years at Saigon and four at Paris, yet speaks the strangest sort of mongrel French ; and the other does not know a word of English. But this does not hinder them from launching into discussions on theology and all sorts of subjects. It sometimes happens, however, that while each is following out his idea, without clearly comprehending the replies of the other, their arguments are taking divergent courses, and this leads them on insensibly to observations which, as responses, are ridiculously irrelevant. Then they call to me to come and unravel their difficulty.

But this evening I am very far from their conversation. Here once more I am squatting at the foot of a tree, near a bivouac fire. I recall to mind many a night passed long ago in this adventurous way ; the encampments under the great *ravenals* in the woods of Madagascar, near to some lagune, the carriers crouching a little way off, eating their rice, or dancing with the great brown girls that have come up from the neighbouring villages ; and then, a little later, the scene changes ; I am pursuing some rebel bands in the jungles of Cochin-China. The *matas* have arranged for me a straw mat to protect me from the dew; the fire-flies are sparkling in the bushes; the arecas depict the outline of their groups of leaves against the sombre blue of the sky; and on the edge of the swampy arroyo I see my sentinels, with their muskets, gliding along like shadows, not a sound arising from their footsteps; afar off resounds the low growling of a tiger chasing its prey, or the sonorous trumpeting of an elephant passing on to its feeding-ground amid the rice fields.

Countries resemble their inhabitants; rather, the inhabitants are formed by the nature of their country. In yonder lands, all those indolent populations are contented to live without a thought for the morrow, sure, as they are, of finding each day sufficient for the day, without troubling themselves overmuch about the mortal maladies lying in wait for them from the depths of the lagunes. Here, nature offers a climate remarkably healthy, but this is all she provides gratuitously; labour she recompenses a hundred-fold, but without incessant work one dies of hunger, for spontaneous productions nowhere exist. The red-skins, whom the Americans consider indolent, can live only at the cost of incessant work. What can be more arduous than those long-sustained hunts over the deep snows of winter, or under the burning sun of July? And if they are not successful, or if the warrior disappears in some sanguinary adventure, the children die inevitably of hunger in the wigwam. Stories full of such like incidents are constantly related by the trappers.

June 30*th.*—This morning, notwithstanding Parker's care and activity, who has passed all night in heaping up wood on our fire, we were awakened by the cold and perhaps also by the teasing of our stomachs. Our poor horses, which we did not venture to let loose on account of the inopportune fancy for freedom manifested so recently, do not appear to have passed any better night than ourselves. Except in point of picturesqueness, our encampment is far from being desirable. We are within a little curve of the river, which has been abruptly turned from its course by the two walls of rocks to which we owe our misadventure. Some gold seekers have tarried here before us, and as traces of their passage, they have left a log-house, now fallen, near which we have passed the night, a dozen of fine firs thrown down from the need of a clear space, but which have furnished us with an abundance of fuel, and then some remains of washed gravel that were apparently not very productive. The sun lights up, a hundred yards above our heads, the great trunks of the pines springing from the fissures, formed in the vertical beds of slate rock, thrown on end by the marvellous subterraneous force that raised these masses of strata into a mountain island, from the depths of an inland sea. Before us, the valley relieves the severity of the wild landscape by its smiling green meadows saturated with dew. About five hundred yards beyond, we spy a spotted doe followed by her fawn. She comes out lazily from the thickets of willows and birch bordering the forest, on her way to drink at a little pond formed by the beaver-dam.

While I am busy in taking a photograph of all this, I try to render myself worthy of the confidence of my companions and of the office of ferryman of the expedition to which they have appointed me. I begin, however, to find out that these duties are more glorious than agreeable, for my night's bivouac and empty stomach already make me shudder at the prospect of another immersion in the frigid waters of the river. Besides, it is here much wider than at the spot we crossed over yesterday, and quite as deep; the current therefore will carry me much further, exposing me at the same time to the unpleasant contact with a greater number of large rocks scattered over its bed. To add to our troubles, Monsieur Bouverie's mare breaks her bridle, has a fresh spree, and is not caught again till after an hour's chase. At last, about nine o'clock we are all landed with our animals on the other side, without any accident worth mentioning; but while I am dressing, my teeth are chattering in my head like the click of a telegraphic indicator.

The landscape, at all events, is enchanting, though wanting perhaps in a little more diversity. Still, I could not do full justice to any description in my famishing state, for the stomach very sensibly modifies our perceptions. While jogging along behind me, on his runaway mare, that tiresome Monsieur Bouverie, who lays claim to decided talent in all matters of *cuisine*, is enumerating to me the good things he is going to prepare for our breakfast. He is talking so eloquently about an omelette with bacon, that I already taste it in anticipation, and this is only aggravating when it is not accessible. Parker tells us there is a farm or ranch somewhere about here, called MacDonnell's ranch, where we shall find many good things, but we were so much disappointed by his promises yesterday, that we do not receive them with the same confidence to-day.

About eleven, however, Jean-Leblanc, trotting as usual at the head of the column, takes it into his head to scale a little rise of ground dividing the valley. His performances during our difficulties of yesterday have given me so high an opinion of his sagacity that I refrain from opposing this caprice, and I am fully rewarded, for, from the summit, I see lying at my feet a little log-house, surrounded by a *corral*, in which a dozen fine cows are pasturing. I scamper away at once from my observatory at full gallop, trusting my neck to the acrobatic aptitudes of my wonderful roadster, and arrive almost breathless before a little hut, in the interior of which we see a tall Yankee busy filling his churn. Without a word I seize the bucket and take a long gulp of the best milk I ever tasted in my life—at all events the milk I have most highly relished. Fortunately he turned out to be a good sort of a fellow, and my voracity afforded him endless amusement. During this interval Monsieur Bouverie lays violent hands on the other bucket, but Parker, invariably gallant, is engaged in tattling with the farmer's wife, a bouncing young woman with a face as round, though not so ruddy, as a Dutch cheese, who, in leaving the care of the dairy to her husband, seems to be taken up with one of her cows, whose tumefied udder is causing her a world of anxiety. Monsieur Bouverie having declared that there was nothing in it but a splendid case of cow-pox, and that she might avail herself of the opportunity of vaccinating all her friends and acquaintances with sound lymph, she appears quite consoled, and goes immediately to resume her seat in the rocking-chair, one well worn from having to do, no doubt, the duty of two; and this with a filthy pallet, the sight of which makes one shudder, and an old cast-iron stove, constitute their entire stock of household furniture.

A few pints of milk having put us in better humour, we accordingly receive proposals from Parker in a better spirit, who tells us that MacDonnell's ranch, the land flowing with milk and honey, is no more than seven or eight miles from here, and that the best thing we can do is to get there as soon as possible. Consequently, we say adieu to this hospitable couple, paying them, on their demand, two dollars for our milk, about ten times as much as at the Pré Catalan in the Bois de Boulogne, and we turn our horses' heads towards the mountain before us, for we have to get into the valley on the other side, and this leads us to infer that Parker was mistaken in the road he took yesterday, though he still firmly maintains he was right.

This country must be very humid, for even the little plateaux that we traverse are covered with fine thick grass throughout, where firs do not grow. Besides, we are constantly falling in with streams of water, all as clear as crystal and excellent, and as it is very hot, nearly 90° Fahrenheit, we drink an enormous quantity. The spring is now nearly over, and the wild strawberry and the wild raspberry, that abound here, are already in bloom. We pass thicket after thicket of little wild red and white roses, and the soil besides is quite spangled with charming flowers. Conspicuous among these is a multitude of superb orange lilies with very short stems.

At last we descend by a pathway, which European slaters would consider dangerous, into a large valley, in the centre of which rises the long hoped-for ranch. Mr MacDonnell, evidently, is not so insensible as his neighbours to the attractions of architectural art, for he has erected a house in plank with an upper storey. He has, at starting, left far behind the age of the log-house.

We begin by unsaddling our horses, and turning them loose into the corral to crop there a little grass, for in this country they fancy—though I don't know why—that there is nothing so bad for a horse as to eat oats after a long journey; then we enter into the house. Parker's eloquence is quickly accounted for. The famous omelette with bacon is still uncertain, but the farmer's wife is decidedly pretty. Monsieur Bouverie, quite a practical man, is dismayed at the poor prospect of a breakfast. The fact is, appearances are not at all cheering. Who is it that has not retained the souvenir of a *dejéuner* at a French farm-house: the welcome of the house-wife, the joyous rattle in collecting the plates and dishes from the cupboards, the eggs pattering in the saucepan, the shrill cry of the chicken having its neck twisted, while its companions scamper away scared across the dung-heap? But here, there is nothing of all this. The farmer's wife is clad in a yellow cotton *peignoir*, or rather what was once yellow, for it is now stained, worn, and torn so much that the original colour can only be conjectured. She is stretched out in a rocking-chair, whilst her husband, a hideous little man, who does not reach to her shoulder, is comfortably smoking his pipe in the only other chair in the house. The house-wife, however, deigns to rise to light the fire in her stove, and to give Monsieur Bouverie six eggs. There is some bacon, too, it seems, that comes forth from a Chicago cooked meat-can, but it is so rancid and strong-smelling, even at arm's length, that we object to a more intimate acquaintance with it. After this effort, she reseats herself, and resumes her title-tattle with Parker.

This fine tall woman, slatternly withal, is so little

like a farmer's wife, that I amuse myself in my turn in making her talk. She tells me that she has been married a year, and since then has been living here. Her father, a "captain" of some kind or other, with eight children, is also come to this country, and is established in the neighbourhood. But he occupies himself less in agriculture than in hunting buffaloes, wolves, and bears for their skins; last year he killed two hundred buffaloes.

Her husband, of Scotch origin, but born in America, came from the Eastern States with some money. He has at present a hundred acres of wheat, which I saw from the window; the harvest is a little later than it is with us, though it takes place in July. It has not a very wonderful look, but in a country where flour sells for 25 cents per lb. sometimes, and never less than 15, they always get on. He has also a score of milch cows. It is the husband that milks and makes the butter, which is sold at three shillings per pound in winter, and at a little less in summer. But they do not make much, because it is too fatiguing, forsooth, notwithstanding the sale is certain, the miners buying all they can get. The cows are splendid; they give as much as seven gallons of milk.

I rally her a little on her laziness.

"Is it your husband who does the cooking?"

"Oh! The Scotch are so hard to please. He *will* eat soup, and he may, for my part, with all my heart. The Americans are satisfied with boiled potatoes and slices of fried bacon; the thing is done in a moment."

"They told us at Rapid City that he had just arrived from the country of the Mormon missionaries. Now, are you not afraid that your husband will be converted, and will take a second wife, to do the cooking for him? You see the house is large enough to cover more heads, and he is making money."

"Ah! I should just like to see that: they have only to come, that's all. There is no house too big for me. When my husband has made plenty of money, he will take me to Paris, and then I shall have one still bigger."

"By-the-bye, what church do you belong to?"

"Me! I ain't of no church."

And, talking all the time, my amiable companion gets up, takes off the hook behind the door a plait of false hair, and fastens it on with the most amusing indifference to any spectator of this occult department of female *coiffure*.

We have disposed of our six eggs, and, having nothing more to hope for, we saddle our horses, which in their turn have eaten at least a little oats, and we prepare to start after settling our account, amounting to six dollars! Scotch hospitality is decidedly different from good claret, for it does not improve after a voyage.

As a faithful historiographer I am bound to recognise that, from this moment, a slight melancholy pervades the members of the expedition. Our stomachs, deplorably unsatisfied, are hard to pacify, and as we are ascending the course of a little river we find the road execrable. It describes in the valley very graceful meandering, no doubt, but this kind of beauty has the inconvenience of intercepting the road every hundred yards. Our horses, for the last twenty-four hours, have had as little to eat as their good masters; they therefore lose courage, and will only move forward on being urged at the point of the spur. Our passage of every ford is accompanied by some fresh occurrence or mishap; and Monsieur Bouverie is himself on the point of becoming demoralised. He looks at his thermometer, sees the mercury at 90°, and indulges himself in remarking that this temperature is well adapted to drying our persons quickly after every successive bath, and this we fully admit.

Parker has lost much of his authority as a guide. We reproach him bitterly, on the one hand, with his blunder of yesterday, which we had to pay for by a long night without shelter; and, on the other hand, with certain tendencies, by far too gallant, towards the fair sex, which have led to the long roundabout way this morning, and the miserable breakfast that followed. A rigorous course of questioning, however, having elicited that we are still twenty-five miles from Fort Meade, it is unanimously decided, seeing that our horses are incapable of carrying us there, that we change our course, if we would not expose ourselves to a disaster like the fate of those left on the raft from the *Medusa*. There is, it seems, in a neighbouring valley a farm only about twelve miles distant, where we are sure of finding something to eat. Monsieur Bouverie makes rigid inquiries respecting the farmer's wife, and having reason to infer that she is not a beauty, we are reassured, and make our way to Hilly Ranch.

Four or five wearisome hours pass away. Every now and then the river becomes a swamp, and the unfortunate horses, belly-deep in black muddy peat, advance only by convulsive leaps, and then have to climb hills fearfully precipitous in traversing a forest of burnt fir trees. Great trunks, half carbonised, are lying across our way, others, almost entirely burnt at the foot, are ready to fall at the least touch: I push two or three with my hand, and they topple down with a crash.

An interesting fact in forestry may be noticed here. Generally, when a forest of resinous timber is burnt, it either does not grow again, or it is replaced by other species; but it is a general rule that the same species does not succeed immediately. In tropical countries this rule is absolute. Whenever the soil of a virgin forest is laid bare by a conflagration, it is followed by a grove of bamboos, and there is nothing but bamboos growing in its place. But here the new growth is of the same species as the old wood; this is Scotch fir, and it grows vigorously. To judge from the age of these trees, the conflagration, the result of some Indian war or of some accident, occurred probably about fifteen years ago.

I get Parker to explain to me the forest laws of Dakota. They are wonderful for their simplicity, and will attain their object in a future not very remote, and this seems to be the destruction of all the forests. The State is proprietor of all wooded lands, and never alienates them; but it authorises every comer to take what he thinks necessary as timber for building, for fencing, for mines, or for fuel. It is communism put into practice, and the result is not backward in showing itself. An insatiable emulation is brought to bear on this policy, and every one considers it a clever stroke of business to cut more timber than his neighbour. The heedless waste is enormous. I was looking this morning at the fences of our friend MacDonnell. They form an actual wall, composed of these great firs, 20 to 24 inches in diameter, separated by logs of wood of the same dimension, which serve for filling up. These fences do not last very long, and unless they take the trouble to bark the timber, which they very seldom do, it is quite decayed at the end of three or four years, and sometimes sooner if cut at a wrong season.

The Federal Government, recognising its impotence in guarding against the destruction of the forests, going on with accelerating speed from year to year, has resorted to an expedient to a certain extent efficacious.

Every American citizen, who has not yet enjoyed this right, may take from among the vacant lands belonging to the Government 160 acres for the purpose of a homestead, and he may also take another lot of 160 acres by way of pre-emption. In order to exercise this double right it is necessary:

1. To be an American, or to declare an intention to become naturalised.

2. To construct a house in the homestead, and to reside there actually during five years, or at least to produce, whenever required, a certificate from the neighbours, attesting to the fact that the person in question is living there; but this is not exactly the same thing.

The definitive title, giving the right to sell, is delivered only at the end of five years. If the emigrant wishes to dispose of it before this time he must previously buy it from the Government at the regulation price of one shilling per acre. Besides, in this, as in many other things, there are always ways and means, and thousands of homesteads change hands without Uncle Sam ever seeing a cent of the money he is entitled to demand.

To the 160 acres which the emigrant has acquired in this way he may still add 160 more, on condition of entering into an engagement to plant ten of them during the course of the first two years in trees of forest timber. This applies, of course, only to the prairie, and is called *Tree Claim.* This measure has produced unquestionable results. When the traveller takes the railway west from Chicago, he passes over hundreds of miles of prairie that were quite bare of timber thirty years ago. But at present they are covered with farms, for all the land has been long occupied, and one sees distinctly that every house is the centre of a plantation of eight or ten acres, and this modifies not only the aspect of the country, but also its climatic condition. They are generally Canada poplars and alders, and sometimes even oaks, that have been thus planted; they thrive admirably, but their culture requires some precautions.

While Parker is giving us these explanations we are wending our endless way across the forest. Jean-Leblanc is suffering from an atrophy. So soon as he sees a tuft of grass he devours it with insatiable voracity. At last we enter into a valley, much wider than the others, on the other side of which we discern a group of five or six wooden hovels. This, it seems, is Hilly Ranch, but the aspect is anything but attractive. Besides, in order to get there, we are obliged to cross a meadow so swampy that we fear every instant to end our days under the mud there; but our appetite gives us desperate energy, and we resort to a procedure so persuasive to our poor animals that we end by reaching the other side.

Having, at all events, compassion on our poor beasts, we go straight to the stable, and find there a few handfuls of hay, which they seize with avidity; then we enter into the house, where Parker, according to the custom of the country, presents us ceremoniously to all the members of the family. We cast our eyes at first on an old man, with light, long, grey hair, falling over his back, of the most beggarly aspect; he has on his head an old felt full of holes, and as to his trousers and flannel shirt, they are such rags as to lead one to doubt their utility, to the wearer at least, in the way of clothing.

"Captain," says Parker gravely, "this is the Baron de Grancey."

I salute him courteously, but the man, with both hands in his pockets, stirs not an inch. At last he draws a short pipe from the hideous black aperture that represents his mouth, spits, blows his nose, without the luxury of a pocket-handkerchief, and then without moving a muscle of his face:

"Ah!" he exclaims, "what do ye say he's called? I haven't well heard his name."

"Grancey, the Baron Edmund de Grancey."

"Oh! Baron de Grancey; delighted to see you."

"And so am I to see you; but could we have something to eat?"

"Ask the women; I don't do the cooking!"

This gracious reply fills me with hope. We then go into another room, and are honoured with another presentation, this time to two very slatternly women, sitting in rocking chairs, like Mrs MacDonnell. The first of these opens her mouth and seems to say something, though I hear nothing but a faint vague sound.

"She has a very sweet voice, has she not?" Parker remarks to me in French, apparently enraptured.

The unfortunate woman is afflicted with obmutescence; at last I manage to understand that the old man, to whom I spoke at first, and who, it seems, is her brother-in-law, killed a buck this morning, and that they are going to give us a bit. Monsieur Bouverie, to whom I announce this cheering prospect, brightens up immediately.

Alas! In the course of ten minutes they bring us something smoking in a tin porringer, the strong putrescent odour of which has already reached our olfactory nerves. On inspection we find the contents to consist of rough pieces of venison, chopped with a hatchet and fried with rancid lard. Monsieur Bouverie immediately demands the receipt for this dish; he intends publishing a book that will form a supplement to the great work of M. Gouffé, *ancien chef de cuisine* of the Jockey Club, and will complete it. It will be entitled: "A Collection of Receipts to be avoided." He affirms that every meal he has taken in America furnishes him with matter for a whole chapter of this work, which will be for the *cuisine* of the future what in theology is the collection of the cases of conscience.

After dinner, and also during this execrable meal, a musical entertainment was provided for us by the mosquitoes of the country, the old man living among them like a salamander in the fire. It seems he has served in the Confederate army. Parker wears also the grey uniform, and while these two old soldiers are entertaining one another with their exploits, I am sitting at a corner of the fire writing my notes in a cloud of smoke that makes my eyes run with water, while relieving me, however, in some measure from the persecution of the mosquitoes.

At eight o'clock the master of the house makes his appearance on horseback. He takes a newspaper from his pocket and comes to read it at the table where I am writing, without saying a word to anybody.

What a charming country ! and what charming people too !

CHAPTER III.

AVERAGE PRICES OF PROVISIONS IN THE BLACK HILLS—THE PERCHERON HORSES IN AMERICA—UNCLE SAM'S MINE—GALENA—THE COLONEL'S *FIGHTING MEN*—THE AMERICAN WOMEN—THE SIRENS OF DEADWOOD—WILD BILL.

SUNDAY, *July the 1st.*—Last evening, about half-past nine, the old relic of the Confederate armies pulled out of a corner a bundle of rags, which formerly might have been blankets, wrapped himself up in them without taking off his boots, and then lay down across the doorway, after having hung on two nails, within convenient reach of his hands, a Winchester rifle and an enormous Colt revolver. This homage having been duly rendered to the security of the country, he resigned himself to a sleep of innocence. We began to consider whether we should not do as much and in the same condition, when Parker, who had disappeared since dinner to carry on a bit of flirtation with the lady with the *sweet voice*, came back to tell us that we were to have two beds. When he added that there would also be sheets, our countenances lighted up with a grin of incredulity. The promise, however, was carried out, and in five minutes we were in a sound and sonorous sleep.

This morning I am roused rather early by an obtrusive sunbeam. The weather is brilliant. About fifty milch cows are distributed over the prairie under my window, eating *à pleine goulée*, as they say in Normandy, the fine grass growing on the banks of the little river. The sight of the river suggests at once to me the idea of a good plunge, and I dress quietly, so as not to wake Monsieur Bouverie, whose snoring makes the air tremble like the great organ of Haarlem. Happily my way is not barred by the old Confederate, who is already up. His long, lanky body has the look of a rusty machine in want of grease, wherein the joints do not work easily. He is, moreover, crippled with rheumatism, like all people of this country. I told him yesterday I had seen at Cherbourg, twenty years ago, the fight between the *Kearsage* and the *Alabama*, and that I had shaken the hand of Captain Semmes. This seems to have raised me in his estimation. He did not say good-bye to me, but addressed me with a little grunt, evidently kindly, and this would answer the same purpose.

I go down the valley. There are ten or twelve hundred acres of land there within a fence of fir timber. These people must make enormous profits. They are not more than fifteen miles from Deadwood, a population of six or seven thousand miners, who pay for what they consume without looking at the money. The figures I have heard quoted are almost incredible. Wheat sells for 8s. the bushel of eight gallons; oats, 4s.; potatoes, 4s.; onions, 10s.; flour, 20s. per 100 lbs.; eggs, 2s. per dozen.

On the other hand, notwithstanding the little labour bestowed on the land, it returns largely. An acre yields 50 bushels of wheat, 60 of barley, 110 of oats, 400 of potatoes! Their hay, that costs them only the trouble of cutting and carrying to Deadwood, sells for from 1½d. to 2d. per lb.! They have been established here four years, and they have sold hay even at 6d. per lb.! It is true that the Indian war had officially just ended, but bands were still scouring the mountains in search of scalps. The man who had laid out the farm a few months previously was afraid to remain, and sold it to them for a pair of ponies.

I am obliged to give up my project of a bath, the banks of the river being too swampy. In order to cross it, they have laid down what they call a *corduroy road*—a contrivance that seems well adapted to breaking horses' legs. It consists of timber poles as big as a man's arm laid close together over a marsh. They settle down in the mud, and present to the feet a stable surface. It answers its purpose thoroughly for pedestrians, but for horses it is nothing but a treacherous break-leg trap.

I go back to the farm, and see rising from the roof a bluish smoke that recalls my dainty dish of yesterday. Our horses are no longer in the stable, but are turned into the *corral:* it is a little enclosure close by all the houses of the country.* Jean-Leblanc greets me well,

* The term *corral* came from Mexico probably; there are corrals also in the Philippine Islands, but these are enclosures in the sea made with rattans for capturing fish.—W. C.

notwithstanding my having made him pass the night bridled, and does not seem to have a bad opinion of me, for he lets me get hold of him without the least hesitation, whilst his two companions mistrust my good intentions and scamper away at full speed. As I stand here, a dozen mares, accompanied with their foals, that have their freedom around the house, come up to see what is going on. They are rather fine animals of half-blood, having good limbs, but are too long in the reins, like all the American horses: in short, of a conformation much too light for farm work, and especially for waggons. I make this remark to their master, who seems more disposed to talk to-day. He takes his pipe from his mouth, and, having scrutinized me attentively from head to foot:

"You are French," he says.

"Yes, I am."

"You ain't a Britisher?"

"So it seems."

"I will just show you a horse of your country."

He then leads me into a separate paddock, from which he brings forth with pride a very indifferent stallion, but a genuine half-blood Percheron. In Paris, the *compagnie des omnibus** would not look at it, and, in a fair of La Perche, if any young countryman paid more than eight hundred francs for such an animal, he would be well rallied. Here, last year, for his services

* The fine horses in the Paris omnibuses are all Percherons.

at the price of fifty dollars, he has earned something like five hundred pounds!

In America they have now a great fancy for the horses of La Perche. The first importations date from 1831, but for a long time they arrived only in small numbers. The light American horses were well suited for the stony roads of the eastern states, but when colonization removed further west, and the culture of the prairie took a great expansion, it was soon discovered that they were not equal to the work. America may be said to be almost without roads. In fact, no one being charged with their maintenance, it is easy to imagine what sort of communications they are in winter without any metal, traced as they are by accident or caprice across the soft mud of the prairies. A farmer in the neighbourhood of Chicago, living about five miles from a station, told me that, to bring home a little barrel of whisky, he had often been obliged to take a waggon and pair. The carriage must have rendered this precious liquor as dear as Tokay or Johannisberg.

The Americans have therefore been obliged to turn to Europe for a supply of strong draught horses. For a long time the Clydesdale breed was in favour of the public; but gradually they discovered that these heavy, lymphatic animals, loaded with fat, without being stronger than the Percheron, were very much slower in their pace. Accordingly, since 1870 the importation of stallions from La Perche has acquired an importance that increases from year to year, and has not yet arrived at its maximum. In 1881 the farmers of the arrondisements of Mortagne, Alençon, Condé, and the country around there, have sold Percherons to the value of three millions of francs; in 1882, to that of nearly seven millions; and this year, I should not be surprised if it arrived at ten millions. A single house in Chicago imported last year one hundred, which, bought in France at an average of 4000 francs, cost them at least 6000 francs landed in America, where they sell generally for 3000 or 4000 dollars.

While I am looking at the pseudo-Percheron of my host, I hear myself called by Monsieur Bouverie, who has overlooked the preparation—summary and simple enough—of our breakfast. We eat up the remains of the venison of yesterday evening, then high enough, take a cup of what the Americans call coffee, and, having caught our horses after much trouble, we settle our account, which does not exceed the modest sum of ten dollars, and take our departure from Hilly Ranch.

The programme for the day is well charged. We are expected at Galena, to visit there two silver mines, which we have heard spoken of; and then, from there, we go to sleep at Deadwood. To accomplish this, our poor horses will have to carry us thirty miles before night.

The night's rest and the oats seem to have done them some good, for they take us across the wood that surrounds the valley of Hilly Ranch at a gallop. We continue at a good pace for two hours, through a country really lovely. There are little *combes*, with rivulets running along the bottom, hardly to be seen, half hidden as they are in thick brakes of roses in full bloom; then these are followed by open turfy spaces, with a few trees grouped together, like an English park. Now and then, we make a short halt on the top of a hill that rises above the others, and from this point we contemplate the chains of mountains, extending above and beyond one another in the distance. Far away, we see isolated peaks, marking their outline against the slatey blue firmament. Near at hand vast forests of pines cover the line of the horizon with their luxuriant sombre verdure. The soil, formed from the accumulation of shreds of long slender foliage from the resinous trees, deadens every footstep passing over the elastic surface, and along here our horses, insinuating themselves between the enormous trunks of the pines, pick their way in silence. Then, on leaving the forest and entering a valley, rather marshy, we see the flank of a mountain rising on our left, covered with magnificent *Épicéas*.

In a few minutes more the scene changes; we perceive at our feet a few houses. It is Brownsville, the head of a line of railway which the mining adventurers of Deadwood have laid down to bring up the timber necessary for their mining operations; for, within a radius of ten miles, they have already hewn down every tree. In fact, from the high ground where we are standing, we see distinctly before us the poor mountains scalped of their coiffure of fir—all quite bald and disfigured. They will be avenged in their own way. With the first rains the water will run down in torrents, carrying away the soil into the valleys, and the houses into the Cheyenne. This is what took place a few weeks ago at Deadwood.

Just as we cross the narrow line of this railway, we see a train starting in the direction of the north. In spite of its ill-omened work, one cannot help admiring the desperate efforts it has cost, and the almost incredible tenacity it represents. All this material, from the little locomotive to the rail, has been brought more than four hundred miles over prairie and mountain in waggons drawn by oxen.

Three valleys open before our eyes : the first on the left leads to Deadwood, from which place we are not more than a dozen miles ; the next leads us to Galena ; but before going there, we shall ascend the third for about a mile, taking our course towards a pretty cascade, which we see glittering in the sunbeams on the right. It is here we shall find Uncle Sam's mine, one of the mines we are about to visit. Its history is very curious.

A young American named Weber came three years ago from the Eastern States, attracted, like many others, by the stories that were everywhere told of the riches of the mineral lands of the Black Hills; and like everybody else, he arrived without any other baggage than a pick, a shovel, and a little mortar for pounding the quartz. He wandered about from one spot to another for two or three months, finding throughout a few spangles of gold, but nowhere anything of importance. At the end of this time, almost exhausted from hunger, hardship, and misery, he decided to enter into the mines of Homestake. Here he gained at least three or four dollars a day, which enabled him to live; but the passion for *prospecting* had seized him and overruled every other thought. He saved all he could from day to day, and, at the end of five or six weeks, so soon as he had the means of buying a side of bacon and a sack of flour, he set off again. In this way he recommenced four or five times, returning to Homestake when he had nothing more to eat.

One evening, on coming back this way to the fold after an expedition as fruitless as the preceding, thinking he was too far from Deadwood, he took it into his head to sleep under a pine at the foot of a rock, intending to set out again early the next morning. When day broke, he picked up his tools to start, and taking a glance at the rock that had sheltered him, he fancied he could distinguish a vein of quartz cropping out between two walls of slate. A stroke or two of the pick soon proved that he was not mistaken, and, at the end of an hour's work, cutting away the slate right and left, he laid bare a great block of quartz, partly translucent and as hard and compact as iron. His experience as a miner told him at once that he had at last found a valuable mine. Returning to Deadwood, he prevailed on his brother and two comrades to come with him. They set out at once and commenced in earnest on the quartz.

It was then about the middle of the summer of 1880. The four men, straining every muscle at their work, broke away the quartz, crushed it with a hammer, and then washed the matter in the brook. In this way they gained seventy or eighty dollars a day. When winter came, however, they were obliged to suspend the work of washing, for the water was frozen, but they continued heaping up the blocks of quartz. The vein took a downward course, and, in following it, they found themselves at the bottom of a shaft, now a few yards in depth. Then one day in the spring, after they had just blasted away a rock, the two Webers went down again into the shaft, and soon sent up some stones covered with mud and black with powder, when one of the men, who remained above at the mouth, called down to them through the ascending smoke:

"But it isn't quartz you're sending up; 'tis slate!"

The two brothers, understanding at once the significance of such a change and quite agitated, light a candle. The flame, instead of showing them the white, porcelain-like fracture of the quartz, reveals only the lamellar surface of a grey slate. Nothing but barren slate is to be seen anywhere; the vein of auriferous quartz is interrupted.

During a whole season these men continue hard at work, driving levels and cross-cutting right and left, eating up even to the last sou of what they had gained, drawing in their waist-belt when they were suffering from hunger, but never for a moment losing courage.

One day in the month of October 1880, the younger brother's pick gave out a metallic ring. For some weeks they had been driving a gallery descending obliquely. The lucky vein was now found again, and the first specimens brought to light proved it to be richer than ever. For many days it yielded gold at the rate of fifty, sixty, and even seventy dollars per ton of quartz!

From this moment the capitalists began to open their eyes. One of them, Mr Miller of Deadwood, came one day to offer them one hundred thousand dollars, with a share in it. But the four co-adventurers had faith in the riches of their mine, hesitated a moment, and then refused. They at length succeeded, with their own resources, in setting up a water-wheel, making use of the waterfall that had hitherto furnished them with water for washing. This wheel set going only one stamp-head for crushing the quartz. This was the extent of the machinery they were able to provide, and on the day even it began to work the four miners were in debt to the amount of fourteen hundred dollars. Fortunately, good luck did not abandon them. The average of the first month's work was one hundred and thirty dollars a day, and a little later they were gaining even so much as four hundred dollars a day. At present they are economising their earnings in order to buy a stamp of fifty heads, and, particularly, a steam engine as motive power, for their waterfall, dry in summer and frozen in winter, permits only four months of effective work in the year.

This interesting story was related to us by the elder Weber. He is a fine young fellow of about thirty or thirty-two, with a calm but energetic looking face. This man is already gaining twenty or twenty-five dollars a day, and he is quite sure of acquiring in a year or two a handsome fortune, one that he can discount immediately. We have found him in his shirt sleeves shovelling the stones of quartz into the iron trough in which the stamps are working. A wretched hovel built of trunks of fir, now rotten, serves them for a house; bed they have none, and they live entirely on rancid bacon, which they cook themselves.

The American, it seems, is a wonderful machine for making money, but he has no idea whatever how to enjoy it.

We go down into the mine, where the three other partners are at work. The communication below is simple and summary. In a corner of the shaft they have erected a fir pole, in which are inserted a series of short sticks, reaching from top to bottom, many of which are rotten. The bear, Martin, the old friend of my childhood in the Jardin des Plantes, would certainly complain of the administration of the Garden, and even "strike," if his ladder were so rickety. We descend perpendicularly fifty feet, and then as much again by an inclined gallery. They have just been blasting, so that the air is hardly respirable; the smoke, however, soon clears away, and then we see at our feet the blocks of quartz that have just been detached.

Whenever a gold mine is offered to a European, the first thing he invariably says is, "Give me a specimen to get analysed." It is only now that we fully understand the embarrassment this demand causes a conscientious miner.

When the gold, vaporised or simply melted by the internal heat of the depths of the globe, has been ejected near the surface by some internal convulsion, analogous to the explosion of a steam boiler, the metal has encountered a solid layer of quartz that arrests it. It has penetrated into the irregular crevices of this vein, and lodged there, becoming here a mere spangle of an extreme tenuity, when it has permeated a minute fissure, and there a nugget, if, by chance, a larger flaw existed in the vein of quartz. Then later, in certain places, fresh convulsions have broken in their turn these veins of quartz, and projected them occasionally to the surface of the earth. These are the *débris* that constitute the gold mines we work.*

* The author, in describing the quartz veins terms them *couches*, *i.e.*, strata or beds; they are not *couches* but *filons*, *i.e.*, veins or lodes. Quartz is not a sedimentary deposit, but an eruptive mass, filling dykes, veins, and fissures. Gold, no doubt, has been melted by the internal heat, but there is no evidence, I believe, that it has been vaporised as suggested.—W. C.

Admitting this theory, it will be easily understood that the metal would be very unequally distributed throughout the crystalline mass that imprisons it, which it is in fact. It is therefore only with large quantities that an average produce can be determined. Then one says, such a mine contains two, three, ten, thirty dollars to the ton ; but an isolated specimen signifies absolutely nothing. On submitting to analysis a block of quartz, in which may be seen a little nugget, and then estimating from the quantity found, the yield of the mine, the inexperienced calculator would arrive at an extravagant figure and be woefully deceived if he paid for it at this rate.

The mode of treating the mineral is most simple; the blocks of quartz, previously reduced to stones of an average size, are thrown by hand or mechanically into an iron trough in which is rising and falling a stamp, also of iron, and weighing seven or eight hundred pounds. Five of these stamps are generally set up in a trough constituting a crushing machine.

A constant stream of water arriving there in a regulated quantity, transforms the quartz into a liquid mud, which runs through a metallic gauze, covering grooves in the bottom of the trough, and issues in a very thin sheet of liquid over a copper table, slightly inclined, the surface of which is rendered slimy by the presence of mercury, poured into the trough in the proportion of three or four spoonfuls a day. The gold coming into contact with the mercury is transformed into an amalgam that adheres to the copper table, and this, swept morning and evening with a leathern brush, yields a yellowish slimy product, which is an amalgam of gold. It only now remains to submit this residue to a high temperature in order to separate the gold from the mercury, and find again the two metals rendered perfectly pure by the volatilization of the second.

It is already ten o'clock when we come up covered with mud from the only gallery that is to make the fortune of the Weber family. We shake hands with the proprietors, who, through their economy and industry, seem to us to distinguish themselves signally from their neighbours, and we go to remount our horses which we have left on the other side of the river. We are expected at Galena, and we are still six miles from there. The country is everywhere lovely. The mountains luckily are so precipitous on this side, that the woodcutters of Deadwood have hitherto left the trees alone. We pass by some pines which, measured at a yard from the ground, show a circumference of from 6½ feet to 8 feet. At every step there are traces of prospectors: a shaft sunk on the summit of a rock with its abandoned windlass half decayed; a tunnel fallen in, opening its dark mouth on the side of a mountain, and beside it the remains of a miserable hovel, where some unfortunate miner came every night to sleep, on emerging half drenched from the hole where he had hoped to find a fortune, and where, nine times out of ten, or more likely ninety-nine times in a hundred, he has reaped nothing but bitter disappointment and ruin.

The success of a fortunate miner, like Weber, induces thousands of men to abandon their farms or their lucrative occupations to lead the life of prospectors, and when they have once launched into it they never draw back.

At last about noon, we find ourselves at the head of a little valley, so narrow, that one might almost throw a stone across from one mountain to the other. In this spot is Galena. We follow a rivulet that takes its course, first in one cascade, then further on in another. The music of its silvery ripple is so alluring, the sight of its pellucid water, sparkling in the sunbeams, in the little basins hollowed out of the yellow rock, is so very inviting to draw near, that we dismount, leaving our horses to frisk on a patch of luxuriant grass that falls most opportunely in our way, and quickly divesting ourselves of our costumes, we plunge into one of the most delicious baths it is possible to conceive. After this, coming out delightfully refreshed, we make our triumphal entry into Galena, a town composed of thirty plank houses, among which are a livery-stable, three or four *saloons,* and two hotels.

On our way Parker has been giving me a lesson, for it will be necessary to resort to a diplomacy whose depth quite bewilders me. We have to visit two silver mines in course of working here. Now, this is the aspect of the matter, and it is typic if not epic.

A certain *colonel*—who, by-the-bye, is no more a

colonel than I am—has discovered, on the summit of a mountain that rises on our right, a silver mine of extraordinary richness. He has fulfilled the formalities necessary for its appropriation, has built very important works for treating his minerals, and has found the means, for the last eighteen months, of making them turn out the modest sum of two thousand dollars a day, reaching in certain months even an average of three thousand dollars a day.

Then a *brilliant* idea, but one I should call decidedly knavish, at once flashed in the brain of certain New York capitalists. Having ascertained that the levels of the *gallant colonel*—such is the usual appellation—were extending around a central shaft, sunk in the middle of his concession, they schemed between themselves to acquire, as quietly as possible, a zone of land around the flanks of the mountain, encircling completely the said concession. Having accomplished this, they set men to work, and in a few months have driven a circular level, with the object of closing in the gallant colonel on all sides by *coming around him*—a circumvention at once in both senses of the word. It was nothing but an operation of deliberate extortion on a large scale, and the New Yorkers demanded only one thing, which was an arrangement that would have diverted into their own reservoir a copious stream of that pretty argentiferous cascade that falls into the colonel's day after day. But the latter was equal to the emergency. He did not yield a jot. A point of law, rather obscure, gives to the proprietor of an *in-clined* lode the right of following it throughout,* when he is already possessor of the ground where it comes to surface. This, it seems, is the colonel's case, and he has declared loudly in all the saloons of the place that he well knows how to maintain his rights. Thereupon, he recruited five arrant scamps, each having at his private account half a dozen assassinations. In this country, this should not have presented to him much difficulty. These desperados, fed like game-cocks for the pit, have been three months in the mine, day and night, armed with Winchester rifles and Colt revolvers. In proportion as the level advances, they establish traverses, epaulments, and other works of temporary fortification, familiar to the corps of sappers and miners, but generally unknown in mining engineering. It is quite understood that so soon as the levels cross one another, the miners will unmask the body of reserve, and the *fighting men* will open fire immediately.

The New Yorkers on their side are not abashed. They have addressed a cheering allocution to their men, and these, inflamed by the martial eloquence of their patrons, liberal rations of whisky, and promises of high pay which accompanied the whole, have declared with bluster that they will leave to no stranger the honour of fighting the colonel's myrmidons. Consequently, since this critical stage of the affair, they

* That is, within a line drawn perpendicularly downwards from any point on the bounds of his concession.—W. C.

work only with revolvers in their belts and rifles at hand in a corner, and the *fighting men* are duly warned that they will find their match.

I call to mind a reflection that was suggested one evening, a few years ago, on seeing the first representation of the *Amants de Vérone*, the fine opera of my friend the Marquis d'Ivry. After a night brawl, which must have nicely hindered the good citizens of Verona from sleeping, these appear on the spot abandoned by the combatants, and impart their complaints to one another, accompanied with a very pretty air, in words like these: "Good God! what a plague are these Capulets and Montagues! What happiness will it be for us when they are all spitted, and we hear nothing more of them!" It struck me that this was one side of the subject that history has too much neglected, and that in a town as unfortunately divided against itself, the situation of an honest man indifferent to the quarrel might be very disagreeable. In consequence of the speculation of the New York Montagues and the resistance of Colonel Capulet, the peaceful townsmen of Galena—if there are any—find themselves precisely in the situation of the citizens of Verona. The saloons have been obliged to take sides, and the taverns also. The livery stable, being the only one there, could remain neuter, though only with difficulty. For a long time the Colonel and his son only went out accompanied by a *fighting-man*—not one of those attached to the mine, for these never stir, but another specially engaged as a body guard. It happened even one day that Capulet, junior, having made a prolonged visit to the tavern, and having treated there his fighting-man beyond moderation, the latter took for a Montague a man having a friendly discussion with his good master, and, full of party zeal, lodged in his back two balls from his revolver. This affair made some noise, and the person who related the story to us gravely affirmed that "the indignation of the public was such that it has cost the Colonel no less than 10,000 dollars to bribe the jury, who have acquitted the man!"

On entering into the town we are received by Mr R——, a pleasant young fellow of about eight-and-twenty, who fulfils the duties of chief engineer—superintendent, as he is called here—of the works of the New Yorkers. He takes us immediately to his tavern, where he gives us a *déjeuner*—execrable, as usual.

I mention an incident very characteristic of the people of this country. Mr R——, after having scrupulously scrutinised the seven or eight saucers that were laid out before him, and tasted the nameless hotch-potch they contained, declared that he was as hungry as before he began. We then timidly suggested whether we could not have a chicken cooked for us—I did not say roasted, the spit being an implement that is used in this country only by the Sioux when they have a "pale face," a prisoner, and the opportunity as well of submitting him to slow torture. We had not long to wait: they brought in a can of cooked chicken from Chicago, a delicacy we by no means appreciated.

The further we go the more are we surprised at the total absence among the American women of a taste for the cares of the household, especially of that sentiment, so predominant with French women, which consists in a fondness to prepare with their own hands all the little dainties destined to be consumed in the family.

The execrable education they receive is, no doubt, the cause. We see constantly, in Europe, American ladies, whose origin, we well know, is of a humble character, and who, having had their fortunes made for them, make a good figure in the world—one much better than that of French ladies in the same situation. We duly esteem the instruction they have received in their village school, and we are right in doing so. But we do not see among us all those women whose husbands have not had the good luck to make a fortune, and whom this same education has rendered totally unfit for the cares of the household or of the poultry-yard. They would rather go to their grocer's and order a can of cooked chicken, which is at once unwholesome and tasteless, than give themselves the trouble to procure or keep fowls; they would rather serve up the rancid bacon of Chicago than exert themselves ever so little to provide for the table sweet and wholesome meat from a pig of their own feeding. I have already visited seven or eight farms, and not one of them had a garden! Yesterday, while Parker was dandling and dallying with the women of Hilly Ranch, I was looking about the house. In the kitchen there was linen thrown into a corner all in rags, and besides the disorder, it was a hole of abominable filth. The women themselves were dressed in linen *peignoirs* that had never been washed, and full of rents unmended, and the husbands' clothes were no better. Having made this interesting inspection, I returned to the "salon." Here, in a corner, were five or six books, Tennyson, Longfellow's "Evangeline," and a few others of the same kind. These ladies told me that they decidedly preferred *Marmion* to the *Song of Hiawatha.* While replying that I was of their opinion, I thought of the lamentable solutions of continuity presented by the husbands' breeches. When he becomes a millionaire, and has an *hôtel* in the Champs-Élysées, his wife, perhaps, will well maintain his salon, but in the interval she is not of much use to him.

Immediately after our meal we took our way, under the guidance of Mr R——, along the goat path leading to the works. On proceeding along the flank of the mountain we pass directly above the Colonel's house. We have evidently been noticed, for six or seven individuals of both sexes are assembled under the verandah, and two telescopes, passed from hand to hand, are brought to bear on us. As it is a part of Parker's plan to conduct us by-and-by into the fierce Colonel's retreat, we defile under the fire of these glasses, assuming a modest attitude, equally removed from bravado on the one hand and timidity on the other, imploring God and our patron saint that they will be pleased to dispel from the mind of this vindictive warrior any idea of opening hostilities at this moment, for our persons, clearly depicted against the light grey rock, would present to his satellites a most tempting target. Our prayer, no doubt, is granted, for we reach the orifice of the shaft without a Winchester ball having whistled in our ears, and we descend, with grateful hearts, by a ladder less primitive than that of *Uncle Sam's Mine.*

The New Yorkers have well managed their enterprise, sparing by no means their money. Fifty-five thousand dollars have already been expended without the return of a sou, of course, for they have not yet found an ounce of metallic ore. And so far, there seems to be little chance of cutting the Colonel's lode outside the vertical passing by the limits of his concession, though they are already one hundred feet in depth. Still, we hear very distinctly the blows of the pick from his miners, and yet the stratum of gneiss in which we are is so compact, so favourable for the transmission of sound, that the distance between is possibly still considerable. In any case we shall not be witnesses of the Epic combat announced for the day of meeting, for which the three miners now at work seem prepared with very good grace. They are young fellows with truculent looks, and I foresee that the Colonel's fighters would encounter fierce and desperate foes. According to custom we are presented to them. They shake our hands vigorously, and then we go to take a glance at the tortuous level that winds around the silver mine—alas! without touching it,—and we scale the four enormous ladders that reconduct us from the darkness visible and the subterranean coolness into the bright sunshine and ninety-five degrees of heat which it maintains at the surface.

Before going downhill we rest a few moments to draw breath. The fine firs around us move to and fro gently in the breeze; the air is embalmed with the perfume of roses; a multitude of little brown squirrels, called *wood-chucks* in the country, are gambolling around us; a little cascade is running at our feet, taking its course into the river along the valley, almost before the Colonel's white house, which stands out dazzling from the shade of the great trees. How lovely all this is, and what a dismal, dark, doleful life is that of those poor devils of miners, the dull blows of whose picks still reach our ears amid the joyous sounds of animated nature!

We say good-bye to Mr R——, or at least for a while, for it is decided that we pay a visit to the Colonel, whither, of course, he will not accompany us. In order to reach his house, we have only a march of twenty minutes by a path quite precipitous, along which we proceed by scrambling and rolling, preceded by showers of stones we have set in movement, and with this *facilis descensus* we save much time. The ladies disappear, and when we arrive before the plank verandah of the house, we find ourselves in the presence of the formidable Colonel and his inevitable *fighting-man*, who, sitting in deal easy chairs with their feet—two feet at least—above their heads, are chewing their quids with that grave and embarrassed air of people desirous of concealing their displeasure at an unwelcome visit.

The Colonel is a little man of about fifty, whose sociability is not the most conspicuous trait in his character. The sparse hair that still remains on his head, and the few red bristles, tipped with white, constituting his moustache, seem individually to be affected with the same amiable disposition, for they all stand well apart from one another and like quills on the fretful porcupine. As for the *fighting-man*, whom I regard with special curiosity, he has an enormous moustache, such as is necessary to his calling, but still the look of an honest man.

Parker with his insinuating ways begins to speak. He at once presents us in the most approved form, and this is received by a kind of growl of bad omen. Seeing that I was not offered a chair, I take one uninvited, and the little eye of the Colonel remains fixed on me from this moment. Without feeling discouraged, Parker returns to the charge.

"These gentlemen, visiting the country, desire to see all the principal mines. Mr R——"

"Mr R—— is ——," roars the Colonel, with a delicate expression which cannot be printed. This is followed by a prolonged silence.

"And he won't stop long in the country," again breaks forth the irascible warrior.

At this stage I consider it time to interpose.

"Nor we either, Colonel," I said, courteously; "but we should have been deeply disappointed if we had been obliged to leave without doing ourselves the honour of visiting a man whom every one speaks of as the pioneer of civilisation in these mountains."

You must always tell an American that he is the *pioneer* of something, or the *prominent citizen* of some place. The effect is infallible. In about five minutes the Colonel and I were chatting together like old chums. He then shows us his receipt for the week, represented by a respectable number of ingots of silver just turned out of the furnace. Unfortunately he cannot take us down *Spotted Tail Mine*, as he calls his property, for the work is suspended in order to repair the shaft; but he shows us all his specimens, which are very curious. The silver occurs as a sulphuret of silver in enormous veins that have only to be *stoped* away. Some blocks are so rich that they present a crystalline appearance. The average yield is 1070 ounces to the ton of ore, but certain specimens have given as much as 8170 ounces per ton.

He takes us afterwards to see his works where he treats his mineral, and these are very well appointed. We see the crushers and the roasting furnaces; but time presses, and we are obliged to take leave of the excellent Colonel, who at last is become the best friend in the world.

It is still very hot; therefore, before allowing us to depart, he obliges us to come once more to his house for an instant, and there cordially offers each of us a glass of clear, cool water, and insists that we come again. This is the extent of hospitality in this land of teetotalism. One of these fine days, I must try this sort of reception on a Norman farmer.

We soon return to our inn, where we again find Mr R——. The company is increased by a journalist of Deadwood, who is having a ride on horseback in company with the school-mistress, and they take their departure after a light lunch. I do not know whether horsemanship forms part of the programme of instruction of the young ladies of this country or not, but if they are to be taught to leap a five-bar gate, they would grievously need a more efficient professor.

Three quarters of an hour later we take the same road, after having emptied, on principle but without pleasure, six or seven of the little saucers placed before us, which are in every respect worthy of furnishing Monsieur Bouverie with the subject of a fresh chapter.

It is after six when we set out, accompanied part of the way by Mr R——, to whom we say adieu, thanking him for the cordial manner in which he has received us at Galena. He has cautioned us that the road, torn up by the late rains, is particularly bad, and this is by no means comforting, for we have ten miles to travel. We accordingly hasten our steps.

In about two hours it becomes dark. We find ourselves at the end of a valley, from which we emerge by climbing a fearfully steep mountain, and, having surmounted this difficulty, we come into another valley, where it is so pitchy dark, that we cannot see where our horses put their feet. The brave animals, however, with their noses to the ground, pick their way with admirable precision, passing through water sometimes up to their girths. At last, about eleven, we arrive on a little plateau, from which spot Parker points out a number of lights glittering below us: we are at Deadwood, or, rather, are very near there, but the entry into it is by no means easy.

In the first place, we must reach the valley. The hill is so precipitous, that I deem it prudent to dismount, and let my horse go first, I following, firmly grasping his tail, and in this way we proceed some distance. At length, all at once, I hear the sound of planks under his hoofs, and he springs back at a bound, throwing me aside. I stoop down, and, feeling with my hands, try to make out the meaning of this plank in such a spot.

"Look out!" cries Parker, beside me; "you are on a roof!"

And there was no mistake about it. I had passed

on to the roof of a kind of store built against the wall of the rock. We turn around, and soon come up to the bank of a river. Parker, being uneasy, is looking out for a bridge, and hails a man passing on the other side.

"The bridge?" replies this one; "why, it was carried away the day before yesterday."

Fortunately they have put down a foot-way for pedestrians. It is composed of a thick plank resting on two trestles. We are so fatigued, and the idea of fording the river attended with a cold bath is so little enticing, that one of us proposes to pass the horses over the foot-way. Jean-Leblanc, whose acrobatic accomplishments are the subject of general admiration, understands what he is expected to do, but hesitates a little. He puts down a foot, snuffles at the wet wood, and snorts loudly; but at last he decides, leads the way, and the others, thus encouraged, follow.

Reaching the other side, we come abruptly into a wide street brilliantly lighted up. At first I fancy I have alighted on a Chinese village. At every house sign-boards are hanging out recommending to the public Ah-Chin as linen-washer, or Wan-Loo-Ting, as tailor, and at every door, notwithstanding the late hour, the "Celestials" are bawling and gesticulating, or simply airing themselves, squatting on their heels, with their pigtails wound round their yellow skulls. A slight odour of opium pervades the air. A little further on the scene changes. We quit the Chinese quarters and enter the American city. Out of every three houses bordering the street two at least are *bars*, and the footway is encumbered with miners and cow-boys in top-boots, sitting with their feet in the air. Through the windows we see others standing before the bar, gulping silently the glasses of whisky handed to them by the *bar-keeper*, who is decked in a clean shirt, with his hair artistically arranged, and rings glittering on his fingers. Here and there are women, who are also taking a drop. At the windows of the upper storey there are a crowd of others, who address the passers-by, recalling to mind at this time some virtuous declamations of the *New York Herald* on the scandals of the Paris boulevards. At last we arrive at Wentworth House, where the owner, Mr Cornell, who expects us, receives us like old friends.

July the 2nd.—It was in the spring of 1876 that the existence of gold in three or four valleys opening on Deadwood was officially recognised. Emigration flowed there immediately, and about July in that year the town counted about seven thousand inhabitants, but now it contains no more than six thousand.

Like all towns of the frontier, this one has had a boisterous infancy. The rising tide of civilisation, like that of the sea, has a foam or scum, and it is by this scum that each announces its arrival. The new comers, miners chased from the Californian placers by "Judge Lynch," Indian traffickers, or innkeepers run away from their creditors—all these adventure-loving people could not complain of finding life too monotonous here. Hardly a convoy arrived that had not exchanged a few musket shots with the Indian parties rambling over the prairie. The Sioux even penetrated constantly into the mountains, and men were found scalped near the first houses. In 1876 there were thirty-five or forty victims officially recorded, but one will never know the number of those who, having been surprised in some lonely spot, must have added many to this funereal list. They were not till the year 1879 completely guarded against the attacks of the Indians.

The presence of the common enemy in nowise hindered these restless wild spirits from the care of keeping their hand in by slight massacres between themselves on a small scale. A few duels with rifles have left a brilliant souvenir. It is at Deadwood that a premature end overtook one of the most popular and highly esteemed personages of the frontier. This gallant fellow was actually named J. B. Hicock, but better known as "Wild Bill." A hunter of Indians by profession, he undertook *by contract* the destruction of the Sioux—so much for the scalp of a man, so much for a woman's, and so much for a child's. At other times, aided by a few comrades, he fell on some kindly Indian village, and, availing himself of the moment when the men were absent, took their horses, sold them and put the money in his pocket. Like every other profession, this one also has its dead season. At these times Wild

Bill came to Deadwood, and related his deeds of arms in every bar to his sympathetic audience.

One day he entered into an inn recently opened by a Californian, named Jack MacCall. The landlord was standing behind the bar, against which Wild Bill tottered already half drunk.

"A glass o' whiskey," he demands.

"Show me your money first," replies the other.

"Money, I've none—stay, here is a squaw's scalp well worth ten dollars."

And he draws from his pocket a handful of black hair hanging to a skin, still horribly stained with blood, and throws the scalp on the counter.

"'Tis money I want," replies MacCall, coldly.

Everybody was looking at him, for they felt that some exciting incident would occur. Wild Bill, however, seemed to be in a good humour. He burst out with a loud laugh.

"True, my little Tenderfoot! Won't you give a glass of whiskey to poor Wild Bill?"

"No."

He leaned forward, caught MacCall by the hair and putting the point of his revolver to his opponent's nose,

"Then," said he, "we must use force."

MacCall looked at him a moment, then took a glass and pushed it before Wild Bill. The latter seeing him yield, let go his head, but keeping the revolver in his hand, he made a gesture of triumph towards the spectators. Then he laughed loudly in his exultation.

MacCall had stooped to take the bottle of whiskey from under the counter, and thus disappeared a moment from the scene. Suddenly three shots were heard, then a scream; Wild Bill gave a reel, and then fell lifeless. MacCall had taken a revolver from under the counter, and between the crevices of the planks had sent three balls through his body.

Wild Bill was feared, but not well liked. A jury was formed there and then; two amateur lawyers were found at the same time among the customers, and the sides were arranged without contention. One appeared to prosecute and the other defended MacCall, who meanwhile continued behind his bar quietly smoking his cigar. The jury and counsel quickly dispatched the cause between them. Half-an-hour after the murder, the president of the jury re-appeared from the back parlour, where he had retired with his colleagues to arrive at a verdict, and declared MacCall as white as snow; after this the culprit *at the bar* was respectfully invited to treat the whole company, including the court, the jury, and the bar, which he readily did most graciously, and the quantity of *gum-ticklers, eye-openers, corpse-revivers,* and other delicate beverages so highly appreciated by the Yankees, that were absorbed that day nearly cleared out the stock in trade of this generous bar-keeper.

The lawyers of the country very much admired the regularity with which the affair was conducted, and everyone believed the case closed, when in the month of March 1877, some news so strange was announced, that no one would believe it. MacCall, passing through Yankton, had met there a Federal judge, who caused him to be arrested. He had, still more unluckily for himself, fallen among a stern jury and an incorruptible sheriff, and had been hanged high offhand. The strangest part of the affair, however improbable were some of its details, was that this news turned out to be true.

These recollections are now already old. The Sioux hardly ever come prowling around the neighbourhood. Now and then, a cow-boy or a pot-valiant miner in high spirits fires off a few revolver charges in the street, and the ball hits a passer-by, but it is without malice, being solely by way of amusement. They have also lynched five or six men these last few years, and now the business is done the lynchers have discovered, with sincere regret, that they had got hold of the wrong men, the hanging having come off in the night. But after all, it is the general opinion that the good town of Deadwood is one of the quietest and best regulated that can be found within a hundred leagues of the spot. It has had, like all other American towns, merely its maladies incidental to growth, and has besides in these submitted to their ordinary trials. The first buildings were log-houses, but a vast conflagration having destroyed them all, the town has been rebuilt in plank. In the future, which probably will not be distant, brick will replace wood. These are the stages invariably passed through.

The first impression we had on coming down from our rooms this morning has been good. The town is so closed in between two hills that the whole is comprised in a single street. There are seven or eight grand hotels, whose wooden walls since nine o'clock this morning have had their habitual contingent of idlers, who are smoking their pipes with their feet well elevated. We spy out the "establishment" of a shoe-black, consisting of a stylish easy-chair placed before the little brush box. Monsieur Bouverie, whose ideas of propriety are sorely tried by the neglected state of our dress, cannot resist this inviting opportunity, and accordingly seats himself in the easy-chair, patiently waiting for the shoe-black. One of the smokers with a good-natured countenance withdraws his pipe from his mouth, spits ten paces with admirable dexterity, and then says,—

"All right, stranger! Wait a bit, the gentleman is coming."

At this moment a "gentleman," more elegant than the others, appears at the door of the saloon with a newspaper in his hand.

"Bob!" cries our new friend, "here is a *man* who wants you."

Bob comes up with his newspaper, folds it carelessly, lights his cigar, and then, first contemplating with a dreamy look the curling smoke, and next a passing dog in the street, seizes Monsieur Bouverie's foot with one hand, and, with a brush in the other, executes the work offhand for the small charge of twenty-five cents—almost gratis.

This morning we have business at the banks. There are two principal: "The First National Bank of Deadwood," and "The Merchants' National Bank." Both have been established about four years with a capital of ten thousand dollars, but it was soon necessary to double this sum, and then still to augment it. At present they have each a hundred thousand dollars of capital, and have constantly given from 35 to 40 per cent. in dividends to their shareholders in operating with the highest prudence.

These figures, which seem to us fabulous, convey a great truth. "This is not a poor man's country" is a favourite saying, and one unquestionably in accordance with fact. Without capital a man can do nothing, but the smallest capital brings in extraordinary interest to him who knows how to turn it to good account. Let us take, for example, a ranchman. He has invested five thousand dollars in the purchase of a herd, and established himself gradually in a ranch. He is not proprietor of the ground he occupies; it belongs to the government. He settles down, and one fine day he sees a batch of emigrants arriving, who begin exercising their rights, and take the best lands of his ranch in order to cultivate them. He is then obliged to decamp and go, sometimes three or four hundred miles, to choose another ranch, from which he will shortly be again driven by the rising tide of emigration. It is then for him a matter of life or death. He has only one way of getting out of the dilemma, and this is to become the owner at least of all the land he occupies that may be available for culture; but in order to carry out this operation, he must look out for a banker, who will advance him the money at three per cent. per month, in taking first a mortgage on the bought land, and next a security on the herd. These combined operations make an excellent piece of business.

But what surprises us is, that these enormous profits do not tempt competition. The Far West is astonishingly little known in New York. We had already noticed this fact when we were in that city a fortnight ago. We had the greatest difficulty in the world to get the most simple information, and we found out every day that most of that given to us in perfect good faith turned out to be entirely false. Lord Beaconsfield wrote "Sybil" to show that England was composed of two nations, the rich and the poor; there are decidedly two nations in America, and these are separated, not by their social status, but, geographically, by the Alleghanies, and every day they are becoming more estranged to one another.

The cashier of the "First National," Mr Alvin Fox, receives us with the utmost cordiality, in an office ornamented with a splendid naturalised head of the great moose of the Rocky Mountains. Upon the table a sack filled with nuggets is poured out among the books; it is the produce of a week's work in a neighbouring placer. The purchase of gold is still one of the sources of profit of the banks, and it is not the least important.

CHAPTER IV.

THE GREAT MINES OF DEADWOOD—WHAT THE ABSENCE OF POLICEMEN COSTS—CALEDONIA—A *SOIREE* AT DEADWOOD—THE JESUITS IN AMERICA.

HAVING transacted our business, we return to our hotel, loitering on the way. Deadwood makes really a very good appearance. The shops are large and well furnished, and, to judge from the groups of horses, all saddled, standing before the balconies, customers do not seem to be wanting, even at this early hour. The *saloons* also are crowded, and Monsieur Bouverie remarks to me how much all these people are like one another. They have the same beard, long and ill-combed, flannel shirts, and trousers big enough to serve as models for a new "divided skirt," or to contain a cabinet of mineralogy, for one might find in their folds specimens of mud scraped up from all the mines in the neighbourhood. All these men look tired out and prematurely old, and as if their long, lank bodies were constantly exposed to the risk of slipping out of their loose wrapping. To see them gulping, silently, with an automatic movement, their whiskey, glass after glass, one readily suspects long nights passed on the prairie under a soaking rain, or at the bottom of a damp, ill-ventilated mine, with insufficient nourishment, and, as a consequence, disordered stomachs, leading to periodic drunkenness during their sojourn in inhabited places.

The proprietor of Wentworth House, Mr Cornell, is doing his utmost to please us. His hotel has already been burnt down, and the new one has very narrowly escaped being carried away lately by the floods. He seems, however, to give himself little anxiety about these incidents—to him trifles as light as air. But, with an eye to business, he desires us especially to speak of his hotel to our friends in Paris. Our business accordingly is cut out for us.

About ten we go to the livery stable for our horses, in order to visit the mines. We are joined by Mr Dickerman, a young mining engineer, who has most courteously offered to show us about the country, where he has been living with his family the last two years.

We first take our route along the river, known as Deadwood Creek, which we crossed last night over the temporary footway. The mountains alongside, denuded of their forests, no longer retain the heavy rainfalls, consequently this little river, whose stream formerly maintained a flow at a uniform level, becomes an actual torrent after a heavy flood of rain. This is what occurred three or four weeks ago, and the sudden swelling waters, rushing on their course, overturned a whole quarter of Deadwood where we are now passing. As I look at these houses, I am again struck with admiration at the surprising ability of the American carpenters. All these constructions, raised entirely with planks and pine beams, without a nail, are so well adjusted and firmly put together, that when thrown on their side they lie absolutely intact; and I do not speak merely of the huts, but also of houses having an upper storey and a façade of a dozen yards.

We pass through three villages in succession, Gayville, Central City, and Lead City. They are collections of houses grouped around the four principal mines, Homestake, Deadwood Terra, Smet, and Highland. We go at once to the first, which is at once the farthest off and the most important.

Mr Gregg, the manager, gives us a thorough welcome. Having had our horses put up in the company's stables, he takes us into his office, to show us the plans of the mine, or rather mines, for he now manages the four great mines. Originally he was merely the manager of Homestake; but since, an arrangement having been made between the different boards of directors, he has taken the management of the others, although the companies are quite distinct from one another. Such a combination as this, by-the-bye, would have little chance of succeeding elsewhere. But in this country, in military as well as in commercial life, the staff or superintendence is extremely simple, still it is a simplicity with its advantages and disadvantages. Yesterday, at Galena, I was then astonished at seeing Mr R—— undertaking the sole superintendence of the working, the assaying, the keeping of the accounts, and the pay. Here, in a mine at full work, with an immense plant and machinery, and six hundred miners and workmen, the whole management consists of only two persons, Mr Gregg and a draughtsman, acting also as secretary.

Homestake mine, discovered in 1876 by two brothers of French origin, named Emmanuel, was sold by them for forty-five thousand dollars to some speculators, who re-sold it to some Californian capitalists for the sum of one hundred and twenty thousand dollars. These immediately formed a company, who issued a hundred thousand shares, on which less than two dollars each was called up as capital. They have expended in the preliminary installation of the works, together with their completion, more than five hundred thousand dollars; but the first returns having been devoted to the partial re-imbursement of the advances that had been made, the capital now to be remunerated does not amount to two hundred thousand dollars.

At the moment I am writing these lines, the company has distributed fifty-two monthly dividends, amounting to three hundred and forty thousand dollars. There is a good prospect of a still larger return, for three reasons:—Improvements are being constantly made in the methods of extraction, since last year the economy effected being thirty per cent. per ton of quartz crushed; the wages, the average of which is now four dollars a day, have a marked tendency to diminish, in consequence of the increase of population; finally, when the railway is opened to Deadwood, the expenses of carriage will diminish again considerably. As to the stock of quartz, there is sufficient to feed the works for twelve years to come at least.

All this information is most obligingly given us by Mr Gregg, and it is all the more interesting, because it is usually difficult to get anything of the kind from companies having a good thing on their hands. I do not quite understand why it should be so, but I notice the fact. We enquire if an annual report is communicated to the shareholders, and we are told that none is furnished. One can readily understand, however, that the shareholders, on receiving a simple telegram every month, announcing a dividend of forty cents on a share of one dollar and a-half, are well satisfied with this sort of literature, and find it more eloquent than the most glowing report in the world.

I clearly see, also, that the numerous duties of this good Mr Gregg do not leave his mind sufficiently free to give finishing touches to the prose of his reports. While we were examining the plans of his mine hung against the wall, we saw him suddenly seize a Winchester rifle—one kept ready loaded and to hand—and rush towards the window. I asked him what the cause was for this alarm.

"Well, I must tell you," he said, joining us again, "that I am a little nervous just at present. To-day we are casting our ingots and sending them to Deadwood.

Now, I know from good authority that there is a scheme afoot for seizing the waggon. I have taken my precautions ; but, you understand, until I get the receipt from the superintendent of the express, I shall not be quite at ease. I thought I heard a noise under the windows, but it was only a few ladies that had come to see the melting. If you like we will go and join them ?"

"By all means, my dear sir ; we follow you, of course."

We cross the street and enter into a little isolated house, where two men are drawing off from a furnace the liquid metal and pouring it into pyramidal moulds ; many of these ingots are already on the table, where a man is punching them with the company's mark. In a corner four lusty young fellows, armed with revolvers and rifles, are quietly waiting till the operation is over. These are the *fighting men* of the establishment. They have a more dare-devil look even than their colleague of the Spotted Tail, and I accordingly compliment Mr Gregg on their warlike appearance.

"Oh!" he replies carelessly, "at present the country is quiet enough, therefore we save something important now in this item of cost. There was a time, sir, I can tell you, when I spent seventy-five dollars a day on nothing but *fighting men !*"

"Have you been sometimes attacked ?"

"We ? never ; but the people of the express have been."

"How do you manage, then, to send your gold to New York?"

"Ah! I will tell you. There is a company formed for that object, who takes charge of it for a commission of one per cent. They have an office at Deadwood; my responsibility ceases and theirs begins so soon as the ingots get there."

"Well, have they ever been attacked?"

"Yes; about four years ago. It was in 1878. Seven cow-boys seized and drove off their conveyance that was escorted by six of their *fighting men.* There were in it one hundred thousand dollars' worth of ingots."

"How did they manage to do that?"

"They began by taking possession of the first station on the prairie on the other side of Rapid City. There were there only three drivers, who had no suspicion of anything. They pounced on these poor devils, gagged them and bound them hand and foot in the stable. Having secured them, the cow-boys then made loop-holes in the doors and window-shutters of the house. The express for transporting the gold make. use of closed vans, under lock and key, and the *fighting men* are seated on benches on the top. When they arrived in the yard of the station, suspecting nothing, they saw at once the muzzles of rifles levelled at them, and they heard a voice commanding them to surrender. Two showed signs of defending themselves, but were shot down on the spot; the others then surrendered themselves. The cow-boys, having made them safe, put them among the drivers already bound in the stable. They afterwards broke in the van, took out the ingots, and then decamped in the direction of the South. But they were encumbered, for our ingots weigh nearly one hundred pounds, and their shape renders them inconvenient for a man to carry on horseback. In short, the express had a very good chance of recovery. The alarm was given, the thieves were pursued from all sides, and in less than six months they were all taken and hanged."

"And the gold?"

"This is the most astonishing part of the affair. They found eighty thousand dollars; no more than twenty thousand were lost."

The ingots we came to see are all melted; there are seven altogether, for the dispatch to-day is of the value of one hundred and fifty thousand dollars. In the last twelve months, the value of gold extracted has reached a total of two millions three hundred thousand dollars.

Having seen the van and its escort safely off for Deadwood, we walk, accompanied by Mr Gregg, to the mouth of the shaft, which is on the top of the mountain. Here we see everything set up on a larger scale than among our friends of Uncle Sam. When we arrive at the mouth of the mine, we find a series of large plates moved by a steam engine. These bring to the surface the trucks loaded with quartz, which then, left to themselves on the inclined wooden way, follow this course and disappear one after the other in the works which are behind us half way down the hill. We get on to one of these plates, a steel wire rope unwinds on a windlass, and in a few seconds we reach the low level of working at 450 feet below the surface.

The vein of auriferous quartz of Homestake goes down into the earth almost perpendicularly. Its horizontal section represents nearly a rectangle, the longer sides of which would be double the shorter, which is from 250 to 300 feet. It is included between two beds—*walls* as they are very properly called here *—of slate. Its average richness is four dollars and a half to the ton, and they have never found it more valuable than seven dollars. In many places the return is only half a dollar. This does not represent the expense of extraction and crushing, which is about two dollars. These poor minerals, however, often cover up others much richer; they must be removed, and it costs less to pass them under the crushers than to transport them outside.

At the bottom, we keep close behind Mr Gregg, following him through a labyrinth of levels and vast chambers, and arrive at the spot where they are at present working. The direction is revealed to us by the sound of a blast of dynamite that still rings in our ears. In these mines, the air is always perfectly pure. The humidity and the abrupt passage from the hot air outside to the chilliness below are alone to be found. But the mode of working unfortunately gives rise to many accidents.

* The sides of a mineral lode have been called *walls* in Cornish mines from time immemorial. In French mines also the lower inclined wall is called *le mur*, though the upper, *le toit*; but since they are parallel to one another, this is not so reasonable.—W. C.

In this sort of mine, every part of the lode being good to take, the whole is taken, and nothing is reserved in the way of pillars to support the overhanging rock. They simply undertake a little timbering, and, here and there, in the most hollow places, they strengthen the ground with a buttress of fir poles. All these appliances are insufficient for safety. At all events, they are not desirous that one should be solicitous about the falling of the ground, which, in displacing masses of quartz, renders its extraction very easy. Mr Gregg explains to us that the timber props decay in a period varying from two to five years. When they are rotten they fall away, and if one could only succeed in establishing them on a large scale, so that the 450 feet of rock above our heads might all break away, it would be a brilliant operation, for then they would only have to shovel away the debris by open working. It is by no means desirable to be below when these falls of ground take place. About three weeks ago, a great mass of ground fell away. It was during the night and no one was touched, but two of the company's workshops above dropped into an immense pit of sixty to eighty yards in diameter, at the bottom of which we were shown their *débris*, when we were about to descend into the mine.

When we arrive at the spot where the explosion took place, we find the smoke dissipated and the miners resuming their work. By the light of our lamps we see the ground strewn with *débris*, which they are going to put into the trucks. Three or four men are sounding the vault with long poles, in order to bring down all loosened rocks. All at once, we hear a fearful crash, as if the mountain had fallen away; a cloud of dust blinds us, and half of the lights go out. I see Dickerman and Parker running as if chased by demons, and take refuge in a level. As for myself, it struck me that in running into the obscurity, there was much danger of plunging into a great gulf. Besides, the manager ought to know what was best to do under the circumstances, it being his business, therefore I took shelter with him against one of the great timber buttresses I have already alluded to. The noise continues for two or three minutes, though it seems much longer; we hear a tremendous clattering, like a cascade of rolling rocks falling together above our heads, and nearly to our feet, and a few of them pass so near us, that we feel the current of air they make. The impression produced on me is decidedly unpleasant, and all the more so, perhaps, because I am certainly not made for underground work. This absolute darkness of the mines is always for me something painful to undergo.

At last the noise ceases, the dust disappears as if at the touch of a wand, and our lamps light up the dark recesses around us. We distinguish a man taking shelter, like us, behind a timber prop.

"Well, Sam, where is your mate?" asks Mr Gregg.

"He must have run away, sir."

"All right! all right! I thought he was dead!"

The miners reappear from all sides. The fall has produced an enormous cavern, one so high that you cannot see the roof of it from where we stand. It seems quite a miracle that no one has been hit, and the men are astonished at it. I ask if accidents are frequent.

"Oh! yes," says one, "there are many arms and legs broken; but in this mine we have much good luck; there are very few killed."

"What does the company do for the injured?"

"The company! It does nothing; but all the miners subscribe a dollar a month towards the maintenance of an hospital, where the injured are cared for."

This is not the first time that I have noticed in America this supreme indifference of capital towards labour. In a new county like this, this policy is thoroughly understood on both sides; but in the Eastern States I have never found, either among the railway companies or the great manufactories, which by-the-bye are not wanting, any trace of those institutions of superannuation funds, which all our work-people make it a duty to establish in their works, and for which they often impose on themselves such heavy sacrifices. It is possible, and even probable, that they exist in America, but I have never heard of them. The position of the employed with regard to their employers seems here throughout to be strictly regulated by the law of supply and demand, without even in the management of companies the most solidly established, any account whatever being taken of length of service, nor of any of those moral considerations which with us have so much influence. From this a sceptic might perhaps conclude that democracy demands all these things, though excellent in themselves, only when capital, which in the long run should incur the expense, is in the hands of political adversaries.

Mr Gregg having ascertained that all his people are safe and sound, we go in search of Parker and Dickerman, who, on their part, went to see if it would not be necessary to clear away a mountain of quartz, in order to find us; then we remount from stage to stage, admiring the arrangements made by Mr Gregg for the great fall of ground, which should furnish him for years to come with the means of satisfying the formidable appetite of his crushing-mill, without prejudice to that remaining to be worked in following the lode deeper. When we at last arrive at the surface, it is with some apprehension that we hear this terrible man invite us to follow him to his works, for we are so bedaubed with auriferous mud from head to foot that we fear it might be considered a profitable operation, from his point of view, to pass our clothing under the crushers.

In order to get there, we follow the tramway, and this conducts us to the spot where the trucks, stopped by a projection in the rails, discharge their load over a grating formed of enormous iron bars, laid down with the object of arresting the passage of the larger stones.

These are quickly reduced to a convenient size for passing through, by two or three men wielding large sledge-hammers. We are at the upper floor of an immense wooden building, covering the two hundred heads of stamps of the company. As Mr Gregg observes to us, with pride, they are the largest works of the kind existing in the whole world. They are probably also the noisiest. These two hundred heads of stamps, ranged in two parallel lines, and back to back, make an uproar that cannot be easily conceived. We must give up the idea of asking for explanations, for hearing a human voice is out of the question. Moreover, the mechanism is so simple that it would be superfluous. We go down to the ground floor: the tables of copper, covered with amalgam, regularly receive their sheet of muddy water, which subsequently runs into the river, and gives to it the red tint we noticed on coming here. All these brave miners are doing work like the good God, as sung in the psalm *In exitu:* they level the valleys by throwing into them mountains. But their work is pernicious. In California they have transformed rivers, formerly navigable, into pestilential marshes, and here they are doing all they can to produce the same result. All these stamps are kept going by a fine Corliss horizontal engine of fifty horse power. It must not be forgotten that all this has been brought here in oxen waggons over 400 miles of prairie. The boilers are heated with wood. They have already consumed all the timber that covered from 25 to 30 square miles, and they are only just beginning.

It is noon when we have finished our visit. We shake Mr Gregg's hand most cordially, for he has really done us the honours of his mine most graciously, and we go away to satisfy our hunger at an execrable meal in the Grand Hotel of Lead City, where we eat beside fifty miners coming direct from their work. What countenances all these unfortunate people have! but then, what food they subsist on! In our arsenals, in our great manufactories, I have often been present at the workmen's meals. I state as a fact, that the poorest calker of the port of Brest, who with a pay of three francs a-day maintains a family of three or four persons, consumes more wholesome, more nourishing, and especially more palatable food than these men, the worst paid of whom gains nearly seven times as much,—nearly four dollars a-day,—and this too in a country where meat costs three-halfpence or twopence a pound, and where wheat is so abundant that it floods the markets. But then, how can a man who calculates on becoming a president or a millionaire, or at least a "prominent citizen," consent to turn his attention to cooking? If the American people, who read the Bible so much, ever have the chance, like Esau, of selling a good share of their rights for a dish of lentils, especially if they are *à la brétonne*, and he gets the receipt into the bargain, I would persuade them seriously to accept the offer. They could not fail to gain by the exchange.

The Company of Homestake have left us the care of looking after our meal, but they have generously provided for our horses, and these, having well feasted on oats, carry us off at a smart gallop in the direction of Central City, where we are going to visit de Smet's mine. This one is more recent than Homestake; it has only eighty heads of stamps, and in point of financial results they are rather less brilliant than the former. In order to reach it, we have crossed the railway which, running beside the crest of the mountain, brings the wood necessary for the boilers of the four mines. Having again descended into the valley, we see overhead a train discharging. The method of executing this is again quite characteristic of the country. The permanent way goes along the brink of an actual precipice, about a hundred yards deep, at the bottom of which the road we are following takes its course. Directly underneath are the buildings of Highland Mine. A log escaping from the trucks would fall straight on to the roof. On the other side, the valley is so narrow that a slide, however little inclined it might be, would bring its end to bear at a point half-way up the opposite side. The American engineers have had an idea of engineering which certainly would never occur to any one in France.

They have made their slide terminate just above the roof of their works. There it is interrupted by a plane formed with great beams, making a sharp angle with its axis. The logs, abandoned to themselves on the top of the hill, arrive there with a vertiginous run. Stopped abruptly, they rebound in the air at least forty or fifty feet, and, exhausting in this vertical leap all their momentum, they shower down on one another, forming a great heap at the door of the works. Now, the road passes by here, but in this country they are not particular about such a circumstance as this. At the moment we reach here, logs of fir, as big as a man's body and two yards long, come down about our ears like a shower of hail. Dickerman affirms that if the passer-by keeps close in beside the wall, accidents rarely occur, and then gives us an example. I wait for a momentary lull and then pass at full gallop: the others follow, and actually get clear off, but it is by a narrow chance.

We are going to visit, a little lower down, two more mines, and first, Smet's mine. Dickerman, who has superintended the construction of the works, makes it a point of shewing us a special arrangement, of which he is very proud.

The amalgamating tables, instead of being placed against one another, back to back, and separated by the stamps, are disposed face to face, on each side of a walk along the middle of the building. I notice, however, that this arrangement, by throwing back the horizontal shafts and the stamps against the sides, shakes the whole timber work of the building terribly, and must produce constant displacements. In spite of the evident pride Dickerman takes in this, I cannot refrain from remarking it to him.

"Oh! that is true," he admits; it is a disadvantage. But just see what economy is realised on the other hand! In the other works they are obliged to have, during the night, two *fighting men* to overlook the two rows of tables, because one man cannot see both at once; but here, a single man sees the whole at a glance. Only just look, with a good Winchester you could easily pick off anyone coming to steal the amalgam.

I must admit that this side of the question had escaped me, but it undoubtedly has its interest. It was the mode in France a few years ago, when the Republicans were not in power, to laud the economies realised by the Republican form generally, and in particular the government of free America. It is quite true that, in this country, one pays neither local rates nor *prestations*, but then they have no roads and they have no police; still they are obliged to pay for *fighting men*, which cost dear enough, if I may judge from an official estimate of the cost of returning the mineral, just handed to me by Dickerman, which I copy in all its eloquent simplicity.

Cost of the treatment of a ton of quartz. (Calculated for 120 heads of stamps.)

		D.
Crushing of the mineral		0·0372
Workshops:	Forge	0·0512
	Foundry	0·0162
	Sawmill	0·0078
	Engineer	0·0148
Roads and accessory roads' maintenance		0·0044
Wages		0·4603
Fighting-men		0·1179
	Total	0·7098

More than a seventh of the expense arising then from want of a police! In France, the army, the navy, the sergents de ville, and the 500,000 *employés* who oppress us, do not cost us so dear.

Let no one suppose that this is a fact peculiar to a locality situated on the borders of civilization. In the most populous states of the East, though things do not take the same course, the result is the same from the point of view of economy. About twenty years ago, the municipal council of New York decided on building a mayoralty house. The auditing of the accounts subsequently revealed details decidedly interesting. The furnishing undertakers had been duly informed that they would be paid no more than about 8 or 10 per cent. of the amount of their invoices, the remainder being about to be shared between the members of the council. It was carefully calculated, that if all the carpets fully paid for had been furnished and laid down, they would have filled the apartments to the ceiling; as for the rest, *ex uno disce omnes.*

It is getting late, and yet we do not want to return to the town without having seen a new mine, the Caledonia, about which people are beginning to talk a great deal. It has not yet paid a dividend, and its shares are not much over par at one dollar; but we know from good authority that for two or three months it has returned sufficient to pay all the costs and reimburse to different creditors more than 30,000 dollars. Besides, hitherto it has been a tributary to Homestake for its water, for which it paid the enormous sum of four dollars per head of stamp per week, something like £4000 a year. Now they have just learnt that its mining engineer has found the means of utilizing a considerable source found in his mine, and the supply being ample, he has given notice of the annulment of the contract. All this excites the curiosity of the good people of Deadwood to the highest degree, and they are looking forward to the first day of a sky-rocket rise, that will shoot up the shares of the Caledonia to nearly a level, probably, with those of Homestake, which are about sixteen dollars. The mysterious attitude of the board of management seems to confirm this rumour. Strangers are never admitted to see the works; for all that, we venture to send in our cards by Parker, the negotiator in difficult matters. In a few moments we see him returning with Mr Allan, the fierce-looking superintendent they had told us about. He receives us with the utmost cordiality, and shows us over his mine himself. So much for the popular opinion of a man.

The ore of the Caledonia has quite a different aspect from that we have hitherto seen. The quartz has no longer the appearance of alabaster, and the bright fracture that characterises it elsewhere. The presence of a rather large quantity of iron gives it a bluish tint, very singular, without rendering it, however, less hard, for here it is still more difficult to crush than elsewhere. The mine is worked in much the same manner as Homestake, in view of a great final ready sale. The return gives nearly the same result, 4 dollars 59 cents per ton.

After all, from what we have seen to-day of this country, two important facts come to light; the extraordinary abundance of its ores, not their richness, and especially the high perfection of the means of extraction. I have given above the cost of the work of obtaining the quantity of gold it contains from a ton of quartz; it is 0·71 under the most favourable conditions. The managers of De Smet cannot reduce it below 0·86. This is their cost of return:—

	D.
Extraction of the ore	1·29
Extraction of the gold from the quartz	0·86
Sundry	0·65
Total	2·80

Now, the average richness of the ore treated has been for the year 1882—

	D.
In May	3·80
„ June	3·75
„ July	3·46
„ August	3·79

The profit per ton was therefore about one dollar, which has permitted the company to give eight dividends of twenty thousand dollars each, equal to twenty cents per share—shares that now sell for about five dollars.

This evening we have been dining with Mr Dickerman. He has introduced us to his wife and an aunt, who, for the last two years, have been sharing his adventurous life in the Far West. These ladies relate their little troubles to us. A few days ago, having gone to pass the evening with some neighbours, they found on returning two feet of water in the house, which is, notwithstanding, on the flank of the mountain at three-quarters at least of its height. This is again the result of destroying the timber. It required no more than two hours of heavy rain to form a fine cascade that quickly discharged itself into the kitchen. Their poor little girl, a fine child of four years old, was navigating the room in her cradle. On the other hand, the water disappeared as quickly as it came, when the rain stopped; everything dried up as if by enchantment. Evidently, they had not to complain of bad drainage.

After dinner, Dickerman shows us a very interesting collection of the minerals of the country, and the list of them is very long. By successive cleavages, the specimens are rendered to the smallest size, and then by means of a grindstone, they are still reduced to a thinness much less than that of a sheet of paper. They then become quite transparent, and the microscopic examination reveals with remarkable clearness the disposition of the veins of metal. It is the most interesting object one can imagine. We have seen innumerable specimens of auriferous quartz, and the gold therein can be distinguished admirably in the form of lace work, sometimes of a tenuity one can hardly imagine to be possible. It looks like veins running beneath the epidermis.

We get back to our hotel about eleven o'clock. All the bars are blazing with light in the profound obscurity of a starless night. While I am writing these lines a terrible storm is raging and the thunder is roaring as it does in the tropics.

July 3rd.—This morning we have indulged ourselves a little till late, in order to repose ourselves from the fatiguing peregrinations of the last few days. The storm of last night has refreshed the atmosphere, and now the weather is delightful. On coming down from our rooms, we find the hotel and the town in a great commotion. To-morrow is the 4th of July, and they are preparing to fête the hundredth and seventh anniversary of the Declaration of Independence. All the farmers of thirty miles round are coming in, some on horseback and others in carts. As the newspapers say, the programme of the féte is quite alluring: first, there is to be a procession essentially popular, of course; a marching past of firemen; a triumphal car; and then a grand *Fourth of July oration*, pronounced by Judge MacLaughlin; at last, to crown the whole, the reading of the Declaration of Independence by Mrs P——. All this promises us a complete study of manners. The citizens of Deadwood appear to be quite decided on giving a lively *éclat* to the ceremony. The national flag is already waving at all the windows. Unlucky little fir-trees, cut down in the flower of their youth, rise again as if by enchantment before the doors. The table d'hôte, ready at all hours, is invaded; but the delicacies of the American *cuisine* are not likely to be more tempting here than we have found them elsewhere. At the hair-dresser's there is quite a file waiting for their turn. The stores also are doing a fine business. A crowd of cow-boys are coming there to buy white shirts which they will probably throw into the basket, if they have such a luxury, to-morrow night. We are entering one of these shops to purchase a few trifles. A young Hungarian comes up to us and offers us his services in good French; this son of Arpad was last year at the *Bon Marché* in Paris. A little further, a shipowner recognises in Monsieur Bouverie a fellow countryman. He is one of Liége, who has quitted the Belgian service, and subsequently that of the Foreign

Legion. It would be perhaps a delicate matter to ask him under what conditions he left.

The lovers of patriotic emblems are crowding round a workman who is selling a nest of eaglets. It strikes me, by-the-bye, that this bird personifies admirably the American race; they are always eating and are ever lean. Neat-looking Chinese in white vests, with sleepy countenances and glossy heads, are wandering up and down without seeming to trouble themselves much about the new law of Congress, that exiles them from America in the name of liberty. As these do not indulge themselves with a quart of whiskey daily, they seem quite satisfied with their lower wages.

After all, this crowd looks bright, and, for the first time, we notice in them an expression of gaiety. The cow-boys have not yet had time to get "in full swing"; not that it takes so very long, but they have only just begun with "a drop." We evidently excite their curiosity to a high degree, but this curiosity is not hostile; quite the contrary. A big fellow, passing on horseback, cries out to us: "Halloo, boys! Let us have a drink!" I have always heard that, in the Far West, a refusal of an invitation of this sort was an insult that invariably provoked a shot from a revolver. To give a little local colour to the scene, I should like to be able to affirm that I heard a ball whistle past my ears; but as a conscientious historiographer, I am obliged to admit that I have heard nothing of the kind, not even the air of *Yankee Doodle*, and that this great strapping fellow appeared in nowise sanguinary. Parker, however, tells us that the streets to-night will not be safe.

A little further I am accosted by a tall, simple man, having somewhat the cast of a Don Quixote, in blue spectacles and straw hat, who gravely hands me a card—Freiherr von ——, Homœopathic doctor. I shake his hand which he holds out good-naturedly, assuring him that I shall come to him if I want his pills, and go my way. I fear the poor wanderer is not doing a very thriving trade. He has probably overrated his prospects in quackery in the land of Barnum.

We return by the bank, where we have still some business to finish, and on reaching our hotel we hit against a superb lady in a bright pink robe and a big Mexican hat, which appears to be quite the *chic* at Deadwood. Under this "attractive" costume we recognise Sally Rodgers, with whom we travelled from Pierre to Deadwood. When one has passed so many creeks in company, friendship springs up. She puts on her most captivating little ways. It seems that the theatre of Deadwood is about to re-open, and everything leads her to anticipate that she will have a brilliant success. Unfortunately, she is obliged to do without a certain robe of red velvet—one that never fails to produce a most imposing effect. It had been so moistened in the journey that mushrooms were springing up between the folds on arrival. We begin now to account for the red hue of Plum Creek when the coach was lying there in distress on its side for two hours. At all events, the company has handsomely recognised its responsibility, and has promised to indemnify her for the damage.

This evening we return to dine with those good people the Dickermans. During the *soiree* we are presented to a few notables of the country, particularly to Judge MacLaughlin, who is to pronounce the famous *oration* to-morrow. He is a man already aged, grave and earnest, possessing, it seems, a considerable fortune and a high reputation. He has passed all his life on the frontier. For a long time he lived among the Mormons, where the strictness of his religious principles—being a fervent Catholic—has obliged him to pass many an anxious moment at the time when the apostles of Joe Smith did not fail to dispatch an exterminating angel at the heels of those Gentiles able to trouble him. He relates to us, with a delightful freedom, a few of his adventures in that charming country. But how is it that a man of his stamp set his foot in that *galère?* this is what I shall never be able to understand; and why, on having got clear of it, did he come here? this also is a mystery. He has had with him for a few days his son, an agreeable young man of twenty, who has just finished his studies in a Jesuits' college. We hear that he was on the point of becoming himself a Jesuit. I can hardly fancy a true Yankee taking this course. There are some, however, though not many, who do so. Besides, American society, constituted as it is, with its good qualities as well as bad ones, does not appear to me a social medium in which the celebrated company would find its place easily, in spite of the marvellous aptitude through which it has been enabled to succeed everywhere else. It has, however, many colleges, and they are constantly increasing in number; but I cannot conceive that it is able to maintain over its disciples any great influence, or that its recruiting can be carried on easily. On the other hand, the "souvenirs" left by the Père de Smet of his experiences in this country prove that among the Indians no one will be able to replace him.

There is a German Catholic Priest here, whose chapel is much frequented by the Canadian, German, and Irish miners. Since I have been in the country, it is, indeed, only among the Catholics that I have noticed any serious manifestation of religious sentiments. There is, however, at Deadwood, a Protestant chapel, but the dominical repose so rigidly observed in every country of the reformed religion has no existence whatever here. I have never seen any works or shops closed on a Sunday.

CHAPTER V.

THE FOURTH OF JULY AT DEADWOOD—A MONARCHIST DISCOURSE—THE MONARCHIST JOURNALISTS OF NEW YORK—THE JURY AND LYNCH LAW—THE MINISTER'S PRAYER—THE COW-BOY AND THE BARON—INTRODUCTION OF THE SPIT INTO THE BLACK HILLS—LITTLE GIMLET—THE ART OF BECOMING A PROPRIETOR IN DAKOTA.

July 4th.—One hundred and seven years ago to-day the thirteen English colonies in America, feeling annoyed at the policy of the English minister, Lord North, in still compelling them to pay a petty duty on tea, proclaimed their independence, which has cost them, to begin with, an eight years' war, and subsequently another of five years, in which a million men at least have perished, in order to get rid of slavery. And in return for these sacrifices the Americans have enabled themselves to become, indisputably, the most pilfered and the worst administered of all nations, whilst their neighbours of Canada, or their cousins of Australia, though they are still subjects of Her Majesty, Queen Victoria,—whom God preserve!—do not pay so dear for their tea, are not plundered by anybody, and are ruled admirably by themselves alone—facts that would lead one to infer that the Yankees, with all their shrewdness, have seized the shadow and let others enjoy the substance.

In order to celebrate this glorious anniversary, all the inhabitants of Deadwood and the neighbourhood have been thronging since six o'clock this morning in the bars or in the barbers' shops, saturating their stomachs with ardent spirits or smearing their hands with highly odoriferous pomatums and oils, for without these two preliminary operations there is no good fête in America. When we make our appearance in the street, they are snatching up the newspapers giving a programme of the ceremony. The morning edition announces that a new element is to contribute to the interest of the spectacle. The miners of the Caledonia, it seems, are in rivalry with those of the other four mines under the united management of Mr Gregg. Hitherto this pot-valiant party spirit has manifested itself simply in a few shots from revolvers, exchanged after " a drop " of whiskey, and no one has paid much attention to the diversion. But now to-day the Caledonians have set forth in the newspapers a proclamation, announcing that they challenge all the others, not to single combat, but to a simple trial of proficiency in mining work. It is the question to determine which gang of miners can break down the most mineral in a given time. The stake is sixty dollars a-head. This is an affair quite to the American taste, and bets are being booked on both sides. The first cow-boy I meet, " a little elevated," will absolutely give me the Caledonians at three to one.

The procession is not to be formed until nine o'clock, but the first *rôles* are already on the ground. First there are the *marshals.* They are gentlemen in black frock-coats on horseback, with a great sword, the hilt of which is in the form of a cross, and a chain around their neck, and they are galloping frantically up and down the street, admonishing some, and trying to arrange others in file, without producing any appreciable effect. They remind us a little of the *Cirque.* There are also firemen in red shirts; a few Indian hunters, great brawny fellows with faces by no means reassuring, their hair falling over their back, and clad in doeskin jackets and mocassins prepared by their Indian wives—for it seems they are all married to two or three squaws of different tribes, in order to multiply their relations, and are accordingly called Indian scouts or squaw-men, but they are not held in high estimation. They are the chief personages in the Indian wars; they fire the first shots, and when hostilities are once engaged, they betray alternately both parties, acting as spies on each for the account of the other; but, after all, they have more affinity with the red skins, whose mode of life they have adopted, and generally adhere to, taking care at the same time to fleece them well of their horses, their buffaloes, and even to the hair of their heads.

At last, about half-past eight, the *marshals* succeed in obtaining some appearance of order, putting themselves at the head of the procession, which begins to move. First, there is the inevitable fireman, who, in this country, no more resembles the active little soldier which one sees behind the scenes of our theatres, making love to the supernumerary actresses, than the puppet with the enormous helmet in the pantomime. In America the fireman is an institution; the smallest button of his uniform, as well as the pettiest hose-screw of his pump, is the product of the meditations of all the sagacious big-wigs of the country. All these admirable precautions, unfortunately, are invariably useless; nowhere are the people so well provided against fire, and nowhere else does it make such ravage. I have never seen a city that has not, once or twice at least, been almost totally burnt down.

Behind these comes our friend, Judge MacLaughlin, he who is to deliver the *oration.* He comes in a buggy, which he drives himself; beside him is seated the other heroine of the fête, Mrs P——, whose rôle is to read the Declaration of Independence.

After them follows the military band mentioned in the newspapers. It is a flourish that recalls that of French villages. They play different airs, which should be national, but which are difficult to distinguish, each performer being too deeply penetrated with the principles of independence that are glorified this day, not to play his own little favourite melody, without troubling himself about the notes produced by his comrades. The great drum here makes an imposing figure. The unhappy individual that bears it, a German emigrant recently arrived, moves one's heart with compassion to look at him. His poor battered felt, his long faded black coat all frayed and fringed, shining with grease and riddled with holes, his begrimed trousers and shapeless shoes, his haggard, flabby face—all this forlorn figure, from top to toe, is oozing with misery, with that dire misery of the dark alleys of Berlin, with that misery which, from the time of Aristotle to our days, has provoked those risings of peoples who, emerging from the "off-scourings of nations," as mentioned by Tacitus, have thrown themselves on the south of Europe in search of all those enjoyments refused to them by a sterile earth and a sunless sky. Here they are now flowing into America, and all the efforts of the great Chancellor will be powerless to arrest the tide of emigration. We next see passing a triumphal car containing about forty little girls in white frocks singing *Hail Columbia;* each of these represents a State or a territory. After these come a straggling crowd of good simple people belonging to different societies.

In about half an hour the head of the procession reappears. Judge MacLaughlin gallantly aids Mrs P—— to mount a stage, erected almost facing our hotel. Many persons and the band of music instal themselves there in their turn. One of the eaglets we saw selling last evening is perched on the rail. A shrivelled, old gentleman, whom they call the "President," then rises and begins to speak.

"Gentlemen," he says, "you have all, no doubt, taken notice of the programme of the day in the newspapers.

However, I think I had better read it to you. Will you, then, listen to me?

"At half-past nine, procession.

"At ten o'clock, after a prayer said by the Reverend X——, speech by Judge MacLaughlin.

"At eleven o'clock, reading of the Declaration of Independence by Mrs P——."

Mrs P——, a pale-looking little lady in a white dress and with a great hat, puts on charming little ways, agitating a roll of paper she is holding in her hand. The crowd is evidently thoroughly sympathetic.

The President continues—

"At half-past eleven, luncheon. Those who belong to Deadwood will go and take their meal at home; strangers who have friends here can go and enjoy their hospitality, if they are invited; the others will find in the hotels, and especially at the Wentworth House, a meal as abundant as delicate, provided, however, they have the means of paying for it, which they should be sure about previously on examining their pockets. If not, they would do better to keep away."

An allusion of this kind would be considered with us in the worst possible taste. Here it produces no unfavourable impression, it is simply a joke. Poverty is not, as in Europe, an habitual condition, involving a kind of degradation in the eyes of those who suffer, as well as for the public. It is here a situation that may be prolonged, but which is only transitory; the man who to-day has nothing to eat is quite convinced that, one day or other, in "prospecting," he will find a mine as magnificent as the treasure of Monte Christo, and this, perhaps, is already come to his hand. With these sentiments, an allusion to his poverty, however coarse and heartless it may be, does not hurt his feelings, for he no more takes it seriously than the young scapegraces of the Latin quarter of Paris in their "vie de bohème."

While the President is speaking, one of the marshals comes to invite us to take a place on the platform; but as our costumes are too *négligés*, and we do not intend to remain long, and, besides, fearing I shall be booked for a speech if I put my foot on it, I decline the proffered honour.

Judge MacLaughlin rises afterwards, and begins to speak. His speech, from the commencement, appeared to me so remarkable, that I have taken notes, and if I am not quite sure of the exact words, I am at least of their purport.

"My dear fellow citizens," he begins, "we are assembled to celebrate the hundred and seventh anniversary of the day on which our ancestors proclaimed their independence. On a day like this it is good to commune with one's-self, and, while returning thanks to God for the unparalleled prosperity which He has deigned to grant us, to ask ourselves what are the moral and material causes that have led to this prosperity. Some attribute it to that republican form that has been given to our government. But this is an opinion manifestly false. In ancient times, as in our days, in the Old Continent as in the New World, nations of different race have had the same experience, but very unequal success. Let us consider, in fact, what has taken place in the old Spanish colonies, which, in proclaiming their independence, have desired to adopt a constitution modelled on that of ours. Everywhere we see nothing but civil wars, oppression of the feeble by the strong, a violent suppression of all liberty, and a fatal return to barbarism. The same experience has been tested in Spain; in France at three different times, and with what signal failure I have no need to tell you.

"It is not, therefore, to the republican form that we are indebted for this prosperity of which we are so proud. What, then, is it due to? Gentlemen, I am going to tell you: we owe it, in the first place, to the Divine Providence, who has led us by the hand like the Hebrews on coming out of Egypt, in order to bring us into the land of plenty.

"But we owe it also to the circumstance, that labour among us has always been honourable, that every one was ready to sacrifice his life and his fortune to defend the life and fortune of his brethren; that, when poor, we were frugal, pure-living, and laborious, and having become rich, we have not given way to the allurements of luxury, but, in retaining all the virtues of our poverty, we have employed the acquired riches simply in the development of civilization in the immense continent that has fallen to us as an inheritance.

"There, gentlemen, these are the causes of our prosperity: it is not the Republic that has given us all these qualifications; it is all these qualifications that have rendered us capable of living under a republic. Now, those virtues of our youth, do we possess them still? It is with profound sadness that I put this question to myself; for, in truth, when one sees what is passing around us to-day, we no longer know whether it is with an affirmation that we should reply: when one sees the fortune of the nation in the hands of a few shameless speculators; when the public coffers are pilfered by the very hands entrusted with them, as we have just seen in the affair of the *Star routes;* when the Jay Goulds are in power; when the elections are no longer free, but are disposed of by the railway companies at their free will in trafficking with the public conscience, and when justice is powerless to suppress abuses of this kind; then, gentlemen, it is urgent to recognise, if the republican form is incapable of arresting such a disorganisation of the social body, that the time is not far off when we shall be obliged to demand, in another form of government, both liberty and security."

I was astounded on hearing these words: had they been pronounced at New York or Washington I should have been less astonished.

When I left Paris, a few weeks ago, the *Directeur* of one of the great Paris newspapers had asked me to procure an American correspondent for him. On my arrival in

New York I spoke to several persons of this commission, one that drew on me, during my entire sojourn at Fifth Avenue Hotel, a long file of journalists who came to offer their services for this post so highly esteemed there. They all naturally spoke of political matters. At this time, the acquittal of the accused in the *Star routes* case deeply interested public opinion.

One of the first who came to see me, said to me quite naturally :

"Oh! things cannot go on in this way much longer : the acquittals at present are nothing more than a question of money. In the country, security is still guaranteed in a certain way by the good custom the inhabitants have adopted of administering justice themselves by means of lynch law ; but this reaches hardly any other than ruffians ; with a little money the rest are quite sure of escape. If this sort of thing goes on, we shall soon be obliged to resort to monarchy."

"You are joking," I said ; "to talk about monarchy in America is almost a heresy ; if there is in the world any nation republican by tradition, by experience, and by instinct, it is surely yours."

"But, not at all, I am not jesting ; what you say is true, we are all that, but we are eminently a practical people ; we are not bamboozled with fine phrases, and be sure, the day, when it will be proved that the republic and security are become incompatible, that it will not be security we shall sacrifice ; only," he added, smiling, "if we must have a king, I do not know very well where we shall find him ; we shall be obliged to resort to the productive capabilities of foreign countries, for we have not got the home-made article."

I thought he was only in a jesting humour, and simply laughed at it; still, wishing to confirm what I suspected, I had the curiosity to lead the conversation to the same subject with another. To my great astonishment, the idea did not at all seem new to him ; he discussed it. I tried others in the same way, always journalists. Everyone of them spoke to me like people who had already well considered the question. A certain number, a few only, said openly, that at some time or other the form of government would be modified in the direction of monarchy ; others, and these seemed to me they must be right, simply regretted that the thing was little possible; a very few declared themselves absolutely opposed to the idea.

Politics are of all subjects of conversation the most agreeable to Americans. If there is an opportunity for the topic they will impose it on you, and they are always ready to listen to and discuss, with the most perfect courtesy, ideas quite opposed to their own. In this we are bound to recognise a great superiority of education over ours. It is therefore never inopportune nor disagreeable in a discussion of this kind to touch on subjects that may seem the most delicate or dangerous.

If, however, by chance, rare indeed, your adversary loses his *sang-froid*, he would immediately be called to order by those present, whatever class of society they may belong to. I well remember an incident in which I was struck by a fact of this nature.

One day, while travelling by rail, a stranger came to sit beside me, and began to relate that he was going to France with his brother-in-law, who was a deserter from the French navy. I replied, that if the said brother-in-law was not disposed to serve his country for three years at a third of the pay, he would do well to deny himself the pleasure of this little voyage.

Upon this, my man got into a rage, declared to me that his brother-in-law having become naturalized, 50,000 Americans would invade France and beat them into a jelly in a trice, if they tried to meddle with his liberty. I replied that his brother-in-law was quite free to remain in America so long as he liked, but if he came back to France, the *Commissaire d'inscription maritime* of his quarter would be pleased to have the opportunity of getting him arrested by two gendarmes, without thinking of the 50,000 Americans ; and that it would be far too easy a matter to elude the laws of his country, if a young man of eighteen had only to make a voyage to America for a month, in order to escape subsequently the military service.

I touched there as I well knew, I must admit, a particularly sensitive point. The question interests so many people yonder, especially among the German population, that it was discussed under a variety of forms, and always with much warmth. From all corners of the carriage, adversaries sprang up. The discussion lasted a full hour, but was always perfectly courteous; and strange to say—a thing that would never happen in France—in the end many of my interlocutors were of my opinion.

In these conversations on politics, which are impossible to avoid in America, I always took pleasure in leading on, by some means or other, to a discussion on the subject of the form of government, repeating the views of the journalists of New York. So long as we were in the Eastern States, and even at Chicago, it excited no astonishment, but in proportion as I advanced further into the West, it was not the same; and this was the reason I was so much surprised at Judge MacLaughlin's speech, and especially at the reception so evidently sympathetic the crowd gave to his ideas. I believe, however, that these are shared here by a very small minority, while they become more general as one advances into the East beyond the Mississippi.

And the reason is very simple. In the States of the East, a middle class is rapidly forming, composed of people who have not themselves made their fortune, but who have inherited one made by their parents, and this they will by all means enjoy in peace.

These people have no longer the energy, somewhat stern if not fierce, of their ancestors; they are not rich enough to be confident of their ability to "grease the paw" sufficiently of the first elected judge, who might take it into his head to set a ransom upon them.

Below them exist the populace, constantly fed by fresh arrivals from Europe, chiefly Irish and Germans, who sometimes become for the moment absolute masters by reason of their number, and who feel themselves constantly menaced by these evil-doers; for in the cities, bands of malefactors are constantly formed that are openly protected by the magistrates, elected by their votes, and there is no other way of dealing with these vagabonds than a summary execution by Lynch law. Now, it is not at all agreeable for a good, peaceful citizen to go away some fine night with a hundred others to besiege the prison, and take and hang at the first telegraph pole some scoundrel who, in a well-ordered country, would, years ago, have infallibly figured at the end of a rope.

This middle class will certainly, in the long run, impose its will, for, besides having the advantage of number, it contains all the living strength of the nation. This class clearly sees that, however good a thing liberty may be, security is far better, and it is quite ready to sacrifice so much of the former as may be necessary to obtain the latter in all its plenitude.

But will the people go so far as a monarchy? I think not. It is, however, a fact that some think it possible. At all events, they will surely modify the form of the Government with the object of securing more executive authority.

In the West the conditions are quite different.

It is generally imagined in Europe that it is the vast solitudes of the prairie that absorb all the emigrants which one sees, at certain periods of the year, encumbering the quays of Liverpool and Havre. I once thought so too myself, but it is an error. In the Far West I have hardly seen any of them. All the farmers, all the miners I have met, were, with three or four exceptions, Americans. The poor creatures, broken down with misery, which old Europe sends across the Atlantic, have nothing like the energy requisite for a life of the frontiers.

They nearly all stop short of the great manufacturing centres of the East, where they take precisely the places of those who are led by a love of adventure, or driven by a hatred of the restraint of civilisation, to seek more freedom in the Far West. The old farmer of Arkansas, whom I met on the way to Pierre, setting out for the Yellowstone, expressed the idea that led them forward. He told me that the country he quitted had decidedly become *too crowded.*

A population recruited with such elements has necessarily the taste for liberty, and for equality also, strained even to excess. In the matter of security, they are satisfied with that which can be guaranteed by a revolver of large calibre. The existing régime, which allows them to live absolutely as they like, delights them. To be free to lynch, from time to time, some lubber or miscreant they have the good luck to catch, is for them a refreshing diversion, and they take good care not to miss an opportunity of sharing in the enjoyment.

During my sojourn yonder, I have never taken up a newspaper without reading in it some execution of this sort.

Between two populations of a turn of mind and aspirations so different, there cannot exist much sympathy. Hitherto the West has been too thinly peopled that much notice should be taken of this feeling in a country where number imposes the law, but I fancy that the state of things as they exist will, before very long, be singularly modified. I have an idea that the first question cropping up will be that of the capital. In a federation of States, where its *rôle* is so important, the metropolis should exist nearly in the centre of the agglomeration. Washington has, for a long time, tolerably well fulfilled these conditions. At present the Californians begin to find it rather hard to be obliged to send their senators and deputies to a city from which they are separated by an eight days' journey by railway. The prizes of good places besides fall too much to the share of the old states: therefore, all the politicians of the West are not backward in declaring that some day or other it will be necessary to rebuild the White House on the right bank of the Mississippi. When this question arrives at a stage when its solution can no longer be deferred, great complication may be expected, and the separation of States, which could not be effected for the benefit of the South in taking a line from East to

West, may still be accomplished in favour of the Western States and territories by drawing a line from North to South.

All these fine speculations have taken me far away from Deadwood and the fête of the fourth of July. When Judge MacLaughlin had finished his speech, he turned round, making a gallant bow to Mrs P——, who, rising in her turn, began reading the Declaration of Independence. Unfortunately, this excellent lady, who, on getting up, revealed to us a situation generally agreed to be held interesting from their point of view—though we much need a better term that would express also the sentiments of the disinterested—this excellent lady, I say, did not seem to be much accustomed yet to speak in public. It is certainly not I who am going to find fault with her for it, nor with the worthy Mr P——, who, standing up at the foot of the platform, was looking most tenderly on his wife. But the result was, that, not having heard a word of what she said, it is impossible to state here precisely of what Mrs P—— and the inhabitants of Deadwood have declared themselves independent; at all events, the list of their liberties is long, for it took twenty minutes to read it. It might, perhaps, have been shorter and more useful to have read an enumeration of their duties.

When Mrs P—— sat down, I expected an explosion of cheers, but, to my great astonishment, there was no greeting from any one. American crowds are remarkably silent. The President merely rose at once to announce that the ceremony was going to end with a prayer, to be delivered by the Reverend X——. We then see a stout man in a black frock coat, who, in very good terms, improvises a prayer, which is listened to most reverently. One detail, however, makes us smile a little ; it is the care with which the reverend minister enumerates the various things on which he appeals for the Divine blessing. "Bless, O Lord," he exclaims, "the standing crops and those that are in the ground ; multiply the flocks and herds ; may our mines, which are being worked, continue to give dividends more and more considerable ; help us to discover new lodes ; may the rain be abundant without having any innundation . . . " and so forth. If, after this, the good God does not specially watch over the inhabitants of the Black Hills (Dakota), which, by-the-bye, must not be confounded with other Black Hills that exist elsewhere, it certainly will not be through any fault of the reverend gentleman, who evidently took scrupulous care that every i should have its dot.

During a good part of the ceremony, Monsieur Bouverie abandoned me ; perched on the balcony of Wentworth House, he has been photographing the scene, and has obtained two or three very good negatives, and when I rejoin him I find he has already made up his luggage. Satisfied that we have the requisite money in our pockets, we run down to the dining-room, where we are lucky enough to find room, notwithstanding the crowding. We devour something, take leave of Mr

Dickerman, who is come to say good-bye, and hurry to the livery stable to saddle our horses and start.

While I am just putting the bridle on *Jean-Leblanc*, a drunken cow-boy comes reeling into the stable, screaming with all his might.

"They tell me there's a cursèd French Baron here, and I want to see a cursèd French Baron."

Upon this, he stumbles against me. I seize him by the belt of his trousers and send him rolling into an empty stall, where he sits on the straw with his legs apart, holding in his hand a big revolver, which he has not the strength to lift, repeating, with persistence, the same phrase.

We set out now with the conviction of having contributed our part, in his case, to the rejoicings of the fourth of July.

We are going to visit one of Parker's properties, the Little Rapid Creek. Now, it is forty-five miles at least from Deadwood; we are therefore come to sleep with our friends of Hilly Ranch, in order to break the journey. Parker has led us over such roads that he was obliged to march afoot a good part of the way, taking the horses by the bridle. In this country one is not driven to this extremity by a trifle. We have managed to descend sloping hills where it seemed to me lizards would have maintained their equilibrium only with difficulty. For the first few miles the country, laid quite bare by the industry of Mr Gregg, is grievous to behold; but we soon arrive at the border of a forest, and then it becomes lovely again. At last, about six, we see before us the hut where we have already passed one night, but the door is closed, and it seems that every one is absent. Parker, however, succeeds in entering by a window, and returns with the old Confederate, who informs us, in a husky voice, that his family has gone to Deadwood for the fête. For his part, he is celebrating it with a bottle of whisky before him.

"Is there anything to eat?"

"No," he replies; "besides, if there was, 'tis no good —I ain't no cook. I'll make you some coffee; I am a bully-boy for coffee."

With this announcement he assumes a very droll air, nods his head with a knowing look, and winks an eye slyly. I cannot help laughing at these grimaces, in spite of the gravity of the situation revealed by his words.

"Oh! if there is no one here, all the better," says Monsieur Bouverie. "You are then going to have a dinner, and you will be able to tell me how you like it."

We are then most agreeably surprised to see him draw out of his courier-bag a fine leg of mutton, which he had the happy idea to bring from Deadwood this morning.

We walk into the house. At the end of five minutes a fire fit to roast an ox is flaming on the hearth; a cord, suspended from the mantel-piece, replaces the spit, unknown in this barbarous land; and an hour afterwards the first roast leg of mutton ever eaten on the Black Hills displays on the dish all those qualities characteristic of this excellent joint. But now, as I am writing these lines, there remains nothing but the remembrance, which is delicious, and a bone well scraped —thanks to the hungry Confederate, whom we were obliged to invite. If all Lee's soldiers had this devouring capacity, they must have ravaged the plains of the Potomac like a swarm of locusts.

July the 5th.—This morning, on coming down, I found the old Confederate again wrapped in his blankets, and lying across the door-way, as I had seen him five days ago. But the great revolver, which is generally within convenient reach on the floor, was replaced by a bottle of whisky, or, at this hour, a bottle without the whisky.

Having pushed the master of the house aside as gently as possible, we succeed in opening the door. The sun is already rather high. The cows, which have not been milked for two days, bellow so pitifully on seeing us that we proceed to relieve them of two or three quarts of delicious milk, and then we go to catch our horses that were let loose last evening in the corral. This is no easy matter. Monsieur Bouverie's buff mare is terribly wild, and she sets a bad example to the others, they keeping close to her side; they let us approach quite near, and, when we fancy we have them safe enough, they start off at a gallop through the long grass, steeped in dew, without allowing themselves to be allured by our soothing words, or to be caught by a handful of good oats that has not the semblance of chaff. We must, therefore, have recourse to force. We put ourselves in line, holding between each of us the ends of our bridles, and at length get the unruly animals into a corner, when, seeing there is no escape, they prudently surrender.

Parker at last puts himself at the head of the column, and we say good-bye to the old Confederate, this time definitely, leaving him to sleep himself sober with his empty bottle. From Hilly Ranch to Little Rapid Creek there is not even so much as a pathway. Parker points out to us a mountain peak of a particular form, which commands his property, and we make as straight as possible for this, plunging at once into the forest we have to traverse.

But however straight the way may seem, it is no easy matter to get there. We stumble every moment against dead, fallen firs, whose trunks, bristling with stumps like chevaux de frise, compel us to make long *détours*. And then, we have to make head against thickets of wild rose trees and wild raspberry canes. If the raspberries were ripe there would be some compensation; because, first, we might have some fruit, and next, we might have a good chance of coming on a bear, for these animals, frequenting the forests about here, are very fond of this delicacy. Yesterday, the Confederate, when he was not "too far gone," related to us that, three or four days ago while ploughing in a hollow, he saw a great bear coming out of the wood. He thought at first that the beast would simply cross the valley ; but the animal having stopped a minute to watch him from a distance, at length came towards him, and the old man seeing this, hastened to take out his horses, to stride one and lead the other, and scampered away for his life. Arrived at a safe distance, he saw the bear squatting beside the plough, which he had turned over on its side and was examining with much curiosity.

For our part, we have seen nothing of these interesting animals. We have started three or four spotted deer, and constantly see vast numbers of squirrels feeding on the fir cones. I understand now why the Indians live more on the prairie than on the mountains. We see much less game since we have left Rapid City. I have been deceived also in another particular. An Englishman, a great traveller, had strongly advised me before my departure not to omit taking a fishing-rod, and accordingly I furnished myself, not only with a rod, which much encumbered me, but a book full of artificial flies that cost a lot of money, and there is not, it seems, a trout in the country. This I can well account for ; the water of the Cheyenne, which they must ascend to get here, is too much charged with elements from the crushing floors of the mines for them to brave the passage.

After two or three hours of tiresome marching, we arrive at the crest of a lofty hill, where Parker makes us linger awhile to explain to us the topography of the country. From Deadwood we have been taking a line that extends a considerable way across the circle formed by the Black Hills. As all the valleys have been formed by the waters flowing from a central mountain mass towards the circumference, we have been obliged in passing near the centre to traverse all the lines diverging therefrom, and it is this that has rendered our march so fatiguing. We shall soon reach the head of a valley that leads to his property, only, before getting there, we must pass over a region of the mountain eight or ten miles wide, which a conflagration some years ago has totally devastated. We plunge at once into the midst of a labyrinth of carbonised trunks. In some places, sheltered from the wind, there are some still standing, as if kept afoot by a miracle, for I see in many instances that the boles have been burnt around, leaving only the thickness of a few inches of solid wood, the fire not having extended further upwards. On pushing one or two of these with the butt end of my whip, they fall away and bring down their neighbours like a house of cards, making, however, much more noise.

About ten o'clock, we at length arrive at the skirt of the forest at the far end. Parker calls our attention, with all the pride of a landowner, to the fine growth of the timber around us. The fact is, we have not hitherto seen such fine forests; the average diameter of the trees is certainly from 16 to 20 inches.

And Parker flatters himself he is the proprietor of all this, though he is not legally so, for the law forbids the alienation of the forests ; but, since it permits everybody to use the timber, it virtually belongs to him who has at his disposal the most economical means of access. Now Parker had bought a river course, Little Rapid Creek, the principal tributary to Rapid Creek, which we saw at Rapid City. In a few months, when the laying down of the railway begins, he will be the only one having a right to float to their works the timber of his region, consisting of eighteen or twenty thousand acres.

Emerging from the dark shade of these fine fir trees, we come on the brink of a little natural basin formed by a magnificent source, whose waters, as clear as crystal, issue from a great schist rock.

While our horses are here refreshing themselves at their ease, we are enjoying the delightful view we have before us. The little brook, escaping from the basin, flows down an admirable valley that unfolds its verdant bosom before us as far as a vast wall of rocks four or five miles beyond, and the upper layers of these, of a bluish gray, are flooded with sunbeams. At the foot of this rampart runs the Little Rapid, and this brook, to which they have given the significant name of "The Little Gimlet," empties into it its limpid waters. This valley, of a width varying from eight to nine hundred yards, is also Parker's property. It is deeply set between two walls of rocks crowned with fir trees, and the ground between is covered with natural sainfoin, so thick that our horses find it by no means easy to beat down a road through such a store of forage.

These valleys between the mountains must have been anciently nothing but a series of little ponds, the one emptying itself into the other. Then great floods having carried away the natural dams that had formed them, the waters drained off, leaving a series of little long plains, closed in between the meandering course of the brook. They are called *bars* in the country, where they are highly appreciated for rearing cattle, in the first place, because the grass there is magnificent, and next, because snow does not stand there in winter. Parker is going to put six or seven bullocks in there next autumn. In one of them he set up a saw-mill last year, which has transformed the firs of the neighbourhood into a pile of sleepers for the new railway.

The Little Gimlet deserves its name, for it makes so many turns, and these we are obliged to ford continually, the great floods, about a month ago, having carried away the planks of all the bridges. At one of these passages, Jean-Leblanc gives me a fresh example of his sagacity. The river is not very wide, but it has a bed of mud ; I take it into my head to cross by walking over one of the horizontal beams that support the flooring of the bridge, when there is one. It is a fir tree with its bark on as thick as a man's thigh. My horse, which I was leading by the bridle, began passing through the mud, but, finding himself sinking into it too deep, he leaps out at a bound upon the fir tree, and follows me along the narrow foot-way, applauded by Monsieur Bouverie, who, having witnessed the feat as well as myself, could hardly believe the evidence of his eyes.

We arrive at last at Little Rapid Creek. It is a fine river, about twenty yards wide and four or five feet deep, whose waters like crystal flow over a bed of sand that fills the interstices between large schistose rocks. It runs also from one side of the narrow valley to the other, forming thereby a series of *bars*, completely isolated from one another, for the sides of the mountain are so precipitous that they seem like actual walls, and of this we are soon only too well assured. During Parker's absence from the neighbourhood, the Little Rapid has had also its floods, and these have carried away all the planks of the bridges likewise. Not being disposed to recommence our experiences of passing rivers by swimming, we follow our guide, who tells us that a pathway has been formed along the flank of the mountain by the passing of the workmen in the spring. It is a fearful precipice, after half-an-hour's uneasiness we are thankful that our necks are safe, and we reach a group of houses, well built and surrounded with a large garden, the first we have seen in America. Upon the threshold of the first appears a nice old gentleman in spectacles, to whom Parker presents us with a good deal of *sang-froid.*

"Captain Hughes, here is Monsieur Bouverie and Monsieur de Grancey."

Captain Hughes is Parker's assistant. Just at present, he is quite alone at the house. We unsaddle our horses, turn them into the grass of the *bar*, and then take shelter just in time to escape a deluge of rain, which, having considerately waited for us thus far, continued for the rest of the day.

I employ the leisure thus forced on us in examining all the documents relating to the acquisition of Little Rapid Creek, and am interested in the art of becoming a proprietor in Dakota.

About three years ago, different miners recognised the existence of a considerable quantity of gold in the sands of the Little Rapid. They began by fulfilling the formalities necessary to acquire the property. This is what is called a *placer claim*, and is secured by a simple declaration and a payment of 2s. per acre. This having been done, they began to work. The operations went on very well, when a speculator from New York appeared, who proposed a certain sum for their claims of auriferous sands. The negotiations came to an issue, and the New York speculator then formed, in his city, a company for working the gold with a capital of 200,000 dollars. Superb machinery was bought, and thirty workmen, the least of whom cost four dollars a-day, arrived in the valley, and there constructed a road, a saw-mill, five or six houses, stables, warehouses, &c. A year passed away in this preliminary work. Engines arrived, and were set up. They had already spent £100,000, and the cash-box was empty. The salaries and wages were not paid regularly. The best workmen, seeing a ruinous failure in prospect, relinquished the precarious service. The engine, entrusted to an inexperienced engine-driver, became so seriously damaged that the repair required an important piece from Chicago, and this was the bottom of a boiler to replace what had been blown out. Then the desertion and break-up commenced. The directors, who seem to have acted well at this stage of the affair, advanced some funds on their personal responsibility, and then convened a meeting of shareholders to demand from them fresh sacrifices. These being dissatisfied, refused to comply, preferring to lose what they had already staked to continue "watering" a badly-managed affair. During this time the expenses were still running on. One fine day a waggoner disappeared with his team. About this time Parker appeared on the scene, and proposed to take up the affair on the following conditions: The company was to assign to him all its rights as proprietors, in consideration of the payment by him of the debts incurred. His proposal was accepted with enthusiasm. A special provision of the law of New York relating to companies, however, rules that the bargain will not be definitive till the end of the year 1883.

Although becoming proprietor of these claims, and of the magnificent plant, machinery, and buildings on the spot, Parker has no intention of working them, at least immediately. His chief object was to secure the ownership of the water-course; for, having ascertained that the two ranges of hills between which it runs contain a large number of lodes of quartz and of copper, he was sure that a day would come when other companies would be formed for working them, and, as in the working of auriferous quartz mines water is an absolutely indispensable factor, not only as a motive-power, but for the washing, he was certain of being able on that day to dictate his terms. A speculation of this nature, which would be strange in any other country, is sure here of success. Besides, it has already been tried in other quarters. Under similar conditions, the "Calcdonia" pays, as a water-rate, to the proprietor of a stream, 400 dollars a-week.

These Americans are certainly very extraordinary people. I have known Parker formerly at Saïgon and at Hong-Kong. He had there three or four horses in his stables, and half-a-dozen Chinese boys in white silk jackets for his personal service. He used to give us very good dinners, at which many a bottle of iced champagne was uncorked. He lived, in short, like all the rich merchants of the country.

Knowing that he has been living in these parts for more than a year, I had imagined we should find there, if not a certain luxury, at least ordinary comforts. Alas! what a deception. He sleeps in a bed without sheets, wrapped in a blanket. He eats the bacon of the country with his workmen; I should mention, however, that his is not rancid, and his engineer, the good old Hughes, does the cooking. To-day the workmen are absent enjoying the after-fete of the 4th of July; we are therefore all alone. When Monsieur Bouverie was informed of the domestic arrangements, he declared that he would himself do the cooking. Hughes, therefore, has undertaken simply to make the nasty cataplasm which they call bread in this country.

Feeling ashamed of my idleness, I have offered my services, but they have thought proper to confide to me only the rough work. Consequently I am armed with a heavy hatchet, and I have to keep up the fire, which I do at the cost of some blisters on my hands in chopping a fir tree into convenient logs.

When I came in with my load of wood I found old Hughes quite excited. He had just learnt that a mysterious composition, to which Monsieur Bouverie was giving the last touch, was that French dish, the renown of which had often reached the Black Hills, and which the epicureans of the Old World called an omelette. And it was really one with bacon, and, moreover, exquisite.

Old Hughes has tasted an omelette; he has lived seventy years, and this is the first time in his life! And the Americans pique themselves on their civilisation, forsooth! A single fact will give an example of their total ignorance of the culinary art. The Bordeaux fresh-water lobsters are unknown at Chicago, a city of 600,000 inhabitants, and these excellent crustaceans, positively swarming in the neighbouring brooks, and treated there with cold contempt, would actually boil with excitement if some Frenchman, while wandering along these brooks, would only give them a warm reception—in a saucepan!

CHAPTER VI.

LITTLE RAPID CREEK—THE BEAVERS—THE PAN—BILL—THE MARQUIS DE M—— AND THE COW-BOYS—TIGER HUNTING—FAIR VIEW—THE MARMOTS.

July the 6th.—It has rained all night, but this morning the sun is shining, and on putting our heads out of the window before leaving our bed-chambers we enjoy a pretty landscape, all fresh and tranquil, which at once consoles us for the bad night we have passed, stretched on a sack of dried leaves, and badly covered with Indian blankets of brilliant colours, so gay withal, that they would make a great show in a little room in the way of curtains, but certainly do not make a good bed. There is one advantage in these arrangements for reposing; they do not encourage laziness, and we accordingly quit them without regret, and walk into the principal house to rejoin our hosts.

We find only Captain Hughes there. It appears that Monsieur de M——'s mare has again played one of those freaks she is so fond of. Parker, on finding her absent this morning, has saddled a horse and gone on her traces in pursuit.

We console ourselves for this unlucky incident, by

swallowing a glass of coffee, and then go to take a glance at the property. We see that the former owners did not spare their money. They have done everything well. There are, to begin with, five or six wooden buildings well turned out, one of which is very large with two side wings, another filled with reserve pieces of machinery and stores, a central one serving as office and refectory, with a kitchen beside it; then, higher up, another house where we slept, containing three or four rooms, a third destined for a lodging for the workmen, and finally, lower down, stables, sheds, smithy, and carpenter's shop with all their appliances. The machinery, which we shall examine later, is on the other side of the river, along whose banks we are sauntering. We find first, the remains of a dam made by the beavers to establish there their habitation. Parker did not wish to disturb these industrious, interesting animals which abound all along the river, and have there two ponds, the work of their ingenuity. During the late extraordinary floods, a lot of dead firs, carried along the current, have totally demolished these interesting constructions, and now they are busy every night in rebuilding them. We see a tree which they are about to bring down to the ground; it is a birch, ten inches in diameter; they have made a cutting with their teeth as regular as if done by the woodman's axe; and the branches we pick up are severed as cleanly as if they had been lopped by the woodman himself. As soon as the tree is felled, and they contrive that it shall fall, as they want it, across the river, they will cut down one or two others, interlace the branches, plaster them with a mortar made of mud well beaten with their tail, and on the dam constructed in this manner, they will raise their new houses.

> " Quatre dents, ou plutôt quatre terrible scies,
> Qu'en un tranchant acier la nature a durcies,
> Et sa queue aplatie, et ses agiles doigts,
> Voilà de ses travaux les instrumens adroits."

The old habitations unfortunately have disappeared, and " leave not a wreck behind."

At the spot where we have stopped, an eddy of the current, caused by a turn in the river, has accumulated a large bank of black muddy sand.

" Now, suppose we dig here for a little gold," suggested Monsieur Bouverie.

He runs back to the house, and presently I see him returning, accompanied by old Hughes, who wishes to gives us our first lesson in *panning*.

Armed each of us with a *pan*—an iron plate a little larger than a soup-plate—we fill it with mud and sand, and then stooping down at the edge of the water, in conformity with our instructions, we give to the contents a circular movement, throwing off at each turn the gravel and muddy water. After three or four minutes of this manipulating, there remains no more than a handful of very fine sand deposited in the water, which, as soon as the agitation ceases, settles down on the edge of the plate. We then see already here and there some little shining specks appearing, and these are spangles of gold. It is the critical moment. They are so thin, that if they are not shaken very gently, they will be carried away with the water; and if not agitated sharply enough, it is impossible to get rid of the earth. Monsieur Bouverie, who is wonderfully clever, got the knack of it at once, and astonished old Hughes. Our instructor then lets us into all the secrets of the art.

"You see, when one wants to buy a placer, one must be wide-awake and distrustful. The seller always proposes *to pan* before you. But at each trial he drops into the water a small quantity of gold dust, which he holds in reserve in his nails, or even in his mouth, and in doing this dexterously, he may add a very sensible quantity to the proportion of gold as it actually exists in the ground. This is what we call *salting* the mine.*

"Well, Captain, how much gold is there in this pan?"

"Oh! You have not searched at a very good spot; there is not more than five or six sous' worth of gold to the pan. Come a little higher up and you will see."

He makes us walk a little way through the grass turning our back to the river, and then stops over a little depression in the ground.

* There is another trick of *salting* much practised. They charge a gun with some gold dust, and then fire into the spot, which is afterwards *panned* before the unsuspecting buyer.

"Do you see that great rock yonder, at the entrance of the *bar?*" he says to me, pointing out an enormous mass of schist, that blocks up half the valley.

"Certainly. What then?"

"Well, do you notice in the mountain that great gap just above it? That is where it came from. It had rolled down here into the bed of the river and changed its course. Do you see? Formerly, it passed by the spot where we are standing."

"I understand, perfectly."

"Let us dig here and you will see what a *pan* we get."

With a few strokes of his pick, he carefully turns aside the clods of turf, comes on a layer of vegetable mould and then a deposit of water-worn river pebbles, and removing this, he lays bare some black mud, exactly like that we have just seen in the river. The good man shows it to us with a triumphant look. We fill our *pan*, and after five minutes washing, we have each a streak of gold three times as much as we had before.

"Now, do you see?" he says. "In prospecting along the valley, I have sometimes found so much as two shillings worth of gold to the *pan*. Last season, Mr Parker was not here, and I allowed some workmen to work on their own account. They paid us a dollar a day, and made five or six dollars for themselves for their day's work. Ah! Here are our horses!"

On the other side of the river, we see Parker coming back, galloping as if pursued by a scalp-hunter, and making for the ford a little higher up, near the beaver-pond. He brings back the buff-mare. Fortunately, yesterday, we left the halter on her; the great knot at the end caught in a root, and she was stopped about six miles from here in a wood. Without this lucky halter, Gods knows where she would have gone! Without Parker to release her from her perilous situation, what a nice mouthful for a bear!

We hasten over a breakfast composed of bread and Chicago corned beef, and then set out again in our journey, for we have to visit the three or four mines which Parker intends reserving as his exclusive property. On going down along the river, I notice a group of firs of colossal proportions; we measured the largest at a yard above ground, and find the circumference to be eleven feet ten inches: many others are above six feet.

We are obliged to climb the flank of a mountain to a great height. I feel quite ashamed to be out of breath, and often to be reduced to hold on by my hands when I see old Hughes, with his seventy years, marching before me with ease, without appearing conscious that he has a pick and a hatchet over his shoulder. We at last arrive at a drift, cut into the side of the rock but a few feet only, the green hue of which contrasts strongly with the grey masses of schist surrounding us. It is a copper mine, which is simply taken up, the working of it being deferred. From the point where we stand, we can survey the valley, which, three or four miles lower down, is cut off abruptly by two walls of rocks of stupendous height, and so close together that they leave only a very narrow gorge for the river to pass. Ravines of this kind are here called *cañons.* On the other side of this is Rapid Creek. Old Hughes calls my attention to the vein of quartz. It cuts all the spurs of the mountain chain obliquely, and we see it very distinctly, especially where it is washed by passing streamlets.

Here the walls of schist, gradually worn away by the friction of the water, leave it jutting up in a dazzling white mass. We are led to a point a little further on, where a shaft has been sunk to determine its depth. At this spot the metal displays itself through the vein of quartz, and even impregnates a neighbouring layer of singular matter, which looks something like a *nougat de Montelimar* with a golden iridescence of superb colour. The iridescence is due to the presence of iron ore: the gold therein, mingled very irregularly, is, in some parts, very abundant.

On following the mineral vein, we at last come to the bank of the river. It is now late, and we are three or four miles from the house. Darkness comes on much sooner in this valley, where the oblique sun's rays cannot reach. The mosquitoes take advantage of it to pester us, and thereby hinder us from enjoying the fine scene of nature with the necessary tranquillity. In spite of these torments, what we see is very fine. The river, deeply seated in the ravine, rushes foaming over its rocky bed. Huge firs interlace their branches over its banks, and mark out the innumerable windings, for, in this respect, the Little Rapid is not inferior to the Little Gimlet. But its endless meanderings compel us to cross it frequently—passages that are not always free from danger, arising from the rudimentary character of the bridges and roads in this country. Generally, the wanderer is obliged to cross over a fir tree thrown across, and Parker and old Hughes accomplish this feat with a dexterity that makes us ashamed of our limbs. Gliding over these slippery trunks with my big boots, and my rifle over my shoulder, I fancied two or three times I was on the point of "taking a header" into the dark water bubbling and boiling a dozen feet beneath, but luckily I escaped falling into these rapids.

I have been edified again to-day by another example of the "free and easy" habits of certain people. On entering the house, I went straight to my room to put down my rifle, and, in a few minutes, Parker comes in, handing me a letter.

"One of our workmen has just come from Rapid City, and the postmaster has given him this letter which is arrived for you."

"But," I observed, examining the letter, "how is it that it is open?"

"Ah! I did not notice that. You are right. Let us go and ask him the meaning of it."

"What was he doing, then, at Rapid City?"

"He has been on the jury; and he has been away a whole fortnight."

We go into the kitchen. A great hulk of a lout, with

a gallows-look, is sitting beside the fire with his hat on. That he does not rise, on seeing us, need hardly be mentioned.

"Bill," says Parker, "this gentleman is Monsieur de Grancey."

"Ah!" says Bill, without stirring an inch. "What do you call 'im? I haven't heard his name."

"Monsieur de Grancy," repeats Parker.

"Delighted to see you," says Bill, with a rather patronising air.

"And I also," I replied to him, a little irritated. "Is it you who has brought this letter?"

"Yes."

"Could you explain to me how it happens to be open?"

"Ah! yes, to be sure. The bar-keeper says to me, 'You must go to-day to take it;' but I didn't want to go till the next day. Then I opened the letter to see if there was anything pressing; but it was in French, and I couldn't understand it."

And for the last fortnight this bumpkin has been sitting in judgment over his fellow-countrymen! With instances of this sort, can anyone wonder at the way in which justice is administered in this country?

July 7th.—This morning Parker comes to tell me that the amiable Bill has disappeared during the night. He had complained, it seems, to Captain Hughes that I had not treated him with sufficient consideration.

He had been feted on the 4th of July, but I do not know where. In a newspaper, *The Yellowstone Journal* of the 30th June, which he brings, we find some very interesting news of one of our friends, who has just entered on a great ranch, a few hundred miles from here in the North, on the North-western line. This is the article:

"ARREST OF COW-BOYS.

"Last evening at six o'clock a goods' train arrived at Mandan, bringing the Marquis de M—— and his friends, Sheriff Harnow and his escort, and also the desperadoes that have just been arrested, Frank O'Donnell and John Reuter, the latter known also under the name of Wanegan. A large crowd had assembled at the Station to see the prisoners, but they were immediately driven off to prison. O'Donnel is a tall, well-made man, dressed in an Indian costume of leather, fringed on the seams, and a white felt hat, such as worn by the cow-boys. He was handcuffed. Wanegan, who is much younger, had nothing on but a shirt and trousers.

"The examination of the prisoners was made by Judge Bateman at ten o'clock. The Marquis has chosen for his attorneys Sowel and Allen. The culprits are accused of having threatened to kill the Marquis and his workmen, of having destroyed his fences, and committed divers other acts that are crimes or misdemeanours.

"The two prisoners declared they were not guilty of the offences with which they were charged. They have been required to find two sureties of six thousand dollars each, and have been summoned to appear on Tuesday next. Everyone present manifested much sympathy for the Marquis.

"Wanegan and O'Donnel, not having been able to find sureties, have been remitted to prison, which is guarded with special precautions. The reporter of this journal has had an interview with the Marquis, who gives the following account of the affair.

"'O'Donnel is one of the first persons I have met at Little Missouri. I should say that his bravery and his address as a hunter had prepossessed me so much in his favour that I was disposed to do all in my power to render him a service, and this I have proved to him on many occasions. Last Friday, about eleven, I arrived at Little Missouri from Miles City, where I had been since the evening before last. Finding many letters arrived during my absence, I passed the whole of Friday, and of Saturday also, without going out, busy in writing letters for the post. In the evening I saw Mr Paddock arrive, who came to tell me that I must take precautions, for O'Donnel was saying everywhere that he was going to assassinate me. On Sunday I went to Mandan in order to procure a warrant against him. The Judge not only gave me one, but he told me also that he fully authorised me *to defend myself if I was attacked.* At four I had returned to the station of Little Missouri, from which I would not go at first as a matter of prudence.

" 'My presence there was soon known. O'Donnel, and his companions, Luffecey and Wanegan, warned by one of their spies, prepared immediately to come in search of me. Being informed, about eight, that they were approaching, I escaped into a little wood near by, where I met Mr Paddock, who, seeing we were pursued, took me into his house, where we stayed all night, and whence I was able to send a telegram to the Sheriff of Mandan claiming his protection.

" 'During the whole of Tuesday morning we saw O'Donnel watching the house. About eleven he and Luffecey approached from two different directions; but seeing we were on our guard, they went away.

" 'I sent word to Howard Eaton to go to the station and see the Sheriff, who was expected by the 12.30 train, to tell him what had taken place and inform him that our *cow-boys* had been ordered to guard the roads going out of the town, in order to stop the offenders if, as soon as he arrived, they tried to escape.

" 'Three roads meet at the station where they were. Frank Miller and I were on the first, Captain Paddock and his nephew on the second, and Dick Moore with another man on the third.

" 'When the train entered the station, O'Donnel, Wanegan, and Luffecey were on horseback on the platform, facing the line with rifle in hand. The Sheriff stepped out of the car and began reading the warrant which he bore. O'Donnel interrupted him, saying they should not take him alive. About half-an-hour later, the train set off again, and I saw the three men coming up at a galop, rifle in hand. Miller and I immediately fired on them. At the first shot, my ball broke O'Donnel's rifle and then lodged itself in his thigh. Riley Luffecey fell dead on the spot, Miller's ball having broken his left arm, then passed through his heart and lungs. O'Donnel, feeling himself wounded, tried to escape, but Dick Moore, who came to our succour and was posted on the road, brought down his horse dead under him, by a shot from his rifle, whilst Captain Paddock and his nephew laid hands on Wanegan. We then conducted our prisoners to the station, and handed them over to the Sheriff, who, having identified them, conducted them to Mandan.'

"This narrative has been confirmed by all the witnesses of the scene. Howard Eaton affirms that these three men have, for some time, been the terror of Little Missouri. They roved through the town, firing off their revolvers at random into the windows of the hotels, the banks and bars. O'Donnel has refused to give any account to our reporter. He simply declares that all the accusations made against him are false, and that the most respectable men of the country will come to bear witness in his favour. In spite of these assurances, they seem to understand that their situation is bad. All the inhabitants of Little Missouri, as well as the escort from Mandan who accompanied the Sheriff, concur in saying that the Marquis has committed only one fault, and that is in not having killed all three, for they are ruffians of the deepest dye.

"What are the real motives of this aggression? This is what we do not yet well know. It is possible that these three men merely intended, through intimidation, to procure the departure of the Marquis, whose presence, notwithstanding, contributes so largely to the development of the riches of our country. If this be their object, it will not be so readily attained, for this nobleman is going to return to his lands so soon as tranquillity is re-established. He says that the unhappy victim who has succumbed, Riley Luffecey, was the bravest and the least culpable of the gang."—*Bismarck Tribune*, 28th June.

Another newspaper of the 5th, the *Black Hills Pioneer*, happily gives us the *dénoûement* of this adventure, in the following note:—"Last Saturday, the Marquis de M——, Frank Miller, and Dick Moore appeared before Judge Bateman, charged with having occasioned the death of Riley Luffecey, at Little Missouri. A great number of witnesses were heard. The Judge acquitted the accused, declaring that they had been menaced, and had only acted in self-defence. The two men at present detained at Mandan—O'Donnel and Wanegan—will be tried at the assizes, accused of manslaughter and of having occasioned the disturbance, in the course of which Luffecey was killed."

Parker and Captain Hughes highly admired the *sang-*

froid and prudence manifested by this brave Marquis. In such a dilemma, an American in his situation, with a hundred cow-boys in his service, believing his life to be in danger, would not have failed to get at once the start of them, and, with a rope, make short work of O'Donnel and his confederates, and every one would have applauded the promptitude of their procedure. But his position as a foreigner rendered the matter more delicate. He had the tact to allow his enemies to commit themselves, and acted only after having given information to the Sheriff.

Consequently, his conduct has been approved by everybody. In spite of this I have a notion that he will be obliged to pay a considerable sum to wash his hands of the affair.

But what must we say of the situation of a country, where such doings are possible, where, in a large village of some hundreds of inhabitants and on a line of railway, three scoundrels can stalk about with impunity for two days, firing their revolvers through the windows of the houses, besieging a railway station, occupying it in force, pursuing an unfortunate stranger to the woods, without the population, who are almost entirely indebted to him for their living, appearing to notice it, and where this state of things goes on till this stranger, aided by his servitors, puts an end to it by executing justice himself, in the presence of a Sheriff, accompanied by his escort, who has not, perhaps, either the will or the power to stop the affray!

The people of the West, who for the last few years

have been trying so much to attract European capital to their side, should understand that it does not require many adventures of this sort to repel those who have a wish to go there. They should, however, throw down flowers on the paths before emigrants of the stamp of the Marquis de M——. The eldest son of the Duc de V——, having at his disposal an enormous capital, he came, about two years ago, to set up in Little Missouri an establishment on a vast footing. In order to avoid the great expense incurred by transporting living animals, he decided on sending to Chicago his beasts already killed. Every day they kill at Little Missouri two hundred and fifty bullocks, and these are cut up, packed, in refrigerating waggons, constructed *ad hoc*, and immediately dispatched by special train. One may fancy what a source of riches such an industry is, which succeeds admirably, they say, in the town where it is established.

The Marquis is not the only Frenchman who has come to seek the employment of his energy and his capital in the Far West. One has hardly any conception of the immense loss to the French nation by the dwindling away of its living strength since the establishment of the third republic.

All the young men, the issue of the old military families, have no longer any employment; for, through a phenomenon of heredity that admits very few exceptions, their aptitudes that would almost always make them excellent officers, often distinguished diplomatists, judges, or ministers, render them, on the other hand, very nearly incompetent for the sedentary occupation of business, even that of a first class bank. Nine-tenths of those who have already tried their hand at it have not succeeded, and even have often left there, unfortunately, a share of their gentlemanlike bearing. In every position that suited them, they have been beset to that degree, that they have either quitted them or are on the point of quitting them. The officers insulted, in the estimation of inspectors by the functionaries, obliged to humiliate themselves before the pettiest *sous-préfet,* retire from the service as soon as they can, and their sons rarely take their places. Twenty years ago, at the examination to enter the *École navale* there were a thousand candidates for fifty places; there are now no more than two hundred and fifty for eighty admissions, and before long they will be obliged to establish a conscription for the officers.

During this time, they have been taking school-masters to make ambassadors of them; consequently, there is a school-master's place vacant, an ambassador incompetent for his business, and a competent ambassador sauntering on the boulevards for want of occupation. Now, this is the main fault of the system; when a barrister is appointed a magistrate, the magistrate, whose place he takes, may take his at the bar. It may indeed strictly be maintained, that from the point of view of the nation generally, there is nothing lost; still, when you have, through distasteful proceedings, compelled a good officer to resign, there is, somewhere or other, a young man who might have made a very good merchant or an excellent attorney, who will be tempted to choose the career of an officer, for which he has little taste, whilst he who has just quitted the service will be neither a merchant nor an attorney. There is therefore a loss on both sides; but this is not all. This man who, in his element, was a useful servant of his country, becomes not only useless, but perverted; for the idleness of an entire, large class of rich men in a good position, can only produce, for themselves and for society, calamitous consequences.

Many young men, without clearly understanding results so complicated, are beginning to perceive these truths instinctively. For them, what is to be done in France, when the magistrature, diplomacy, politics even, are closed against them? when the army, if these things continue, will before long be so also? To remain at home with their parents and do nothing, is to resign themselves to become worthless members of society. Those who have the most blood in their veins are often those who the least resist a life so void of all interest. It is in this class that are recruited the men that have made France so conspicuous for colonizing. And in past time, these were also the men who had given her Canada and India, the loss of which, by-the-bye, is hardly compensated by the acquisition of Algeria and Cochin China. Besides, those who would now go and establish themselves in these countries, would find, in the local governments, the hostility that pursues them in France. Therefore, the number of rich young men of good position, who suffer themselves to be allured by the free and adventurous life of the *ranchmen* of the West, is rather considerable. Important sums have already been drawn from France to be employed on the other side of the Mississipi, and, if we are not deceived, the amount will, before long, be still increased.

We have spent the whole day in rambling about the neighbourhood. First, we went across the river to examine the machine for washing the sand, which is set up. It is a kind of suction-pump with a large bore; the suction-pipe, about five or six inches in diameter, sinks into the black mud, which accumulates in pockets without cohesion, in the depression between the rocks, lying in the bed of the current. The auriferous sand is thus abstracted with great force, then projected on to a wooden inclined plane, and there washed by a stream of water brought from a great distance in a kind of wooden tube called in the country a *flume*. This inclined plane is cut by a multitude of transverse furrows, where the water lodges. Some legal difficulties relative to the acquisition, which cannot be determined till the end of the year, have compelled the work to be suspended for the present.

Monsieur Bouverie has passed his morning in crushing, under the stamps, all the specimens we collected during our wandering yesterday, and he finds himself in possession of a good pinch of gold dust. During this time I took it into my head to go and verify the statement of Captain Hughes that there is no fish in the Little Rapid. I was pretty sure, however, of having seen some yesterday. I take my famous rod and make my way to the beaver pond, where I land, in about half an hour, a dish of excellent fish, but of very strange shape. I have often heard of queer fish, but I have never seen any so queer as these.

Old Hughes is quite a type that would be very extraordinary in Europe. For twenty years he commanded a schooner on Lake Michigan. In winter, when the lake was frozen, he worked as a carpenter in the building yard of his shipowner; for in this country, a man, who has been educated and has practised a liberal profession, finds it quite natural to work occasionally with his hands. In this they show a great superiority over us.

One fine day he got sick and tired of navigation, and came to try his hand at agriculture at Yankton. Then he turned his attention to mines, and, in a short time, acquired quite a reputation as mining engineer. He has, in fact, an extraordinary "scent." Latterly, in returning from a visit to his son, who lives near here, he discovered a little mine, and made him a present of it, which he immediately sold for ten thousand dollars. He is now seventy-two, and quite as active as a young man. When he learnt that I had been a sailor, he took quite a fancy to me, and every evening we had our corner by the fire, with long conversations that interested me very much. He appears to me to be quite the type of the good sort of Yankee. Yesterday, he spoke to me about Canada, where he has been very often, and which he much admires. He praised especially its good administration.

"Do you think," I asked, "that the Canadians are better governed than you Americans?"

"Ah! to be sure they are! They are not pilfered as we are, and when they have a lawsuit on hand they are not sure beforehand of losing it if they do not give money to the judge. Now, here is an instance. One day I was on the coast of Canada. One of my men had had some affair ashore and had been fighting. He was put into prison. I thought it was just the same as with us, and that I had only to give twenty dollars to the magistrate to obtain his release. Only fancy my reception! They very nearly put me into prison also."

"But the day before yesterday you all went to celebrate the anniversary of your Independence. It seems to me that you have not gained much by being independent. The Canadians, who have stuck to England, are not much to be pitied according to your account."

The good man looked at me with an air of surprise, drew five or six whiffs of smoke from his pipe, and then remained in contemplation before the fire for a long time without saying a word. Afterwards he changed the conversation.

This morning after breakfast he took me aside.

"You mentioned to me yesterday something that I have never thought about. I have been reflecting on it during the night. It is quite true that the Canadians are more favoured than we are in every way. But for all that the Declaration of Independence is a good thing. Only see, we are already too vast. It will not be very long before America can no longer remain united in a single nation. If we had remained English, do you suppose that the other powers would have tolerated the existence of a kingdom comprising all America, Australia, India, and what I don't know besides? No; we should have had constant wars so long as that would have lasted. It is for this reason that the separation has been a good thing."

Sunday, July the 8th.—Last evening, after having written down our notes, Monsieur Bouverie and I took it into our heads to go and lie in wait for game. Parker pointed out to us a spot by the river where he sees constantly the footsteps of deer and even elk, for there are still a few of those magnificent animals, as he found only yesterday a splendid pair of horns of one. As a rule, however, I have quite a horror of lying in wait, and I have good reasons for it too. While in Cochin China a few years ago all my comrades affirmed having killed one tiger at least each of them. The position of a gentleman who could not exult likewise in his prowess in hunting or in the killing of any felines bigger than a cat was becoming so painful that I felt bound to give in. I was then on a surveying party not far from Vinh-Lhong, and tigers were not wanting there: they were heard every night growling round the survey, in a jungle that extended as far as the parapets of the fort. Still, it was necessary to go to them, and that was the rub.

One morning when my advisers were assembled, I put to them this question:

"What is the greatest height a tiger is capable of springing?"

The discussion was long, but it was interesting. In the end the *om-sha*, a little old man with a white beard condensed the opinions of his colleagues, declaring to me that tigers had been seen springing over barriers three yards high. With this information I sent for the *doï* of my *matas*.

"You will go off to the jungle," I said, "and cut a number of arecas sufficient for the purpose, and make a platform, four yards high (thus giving myself an extra yard for precaution), and a ladder to mount on it. You will buy a live calf this evening and put it there, and to-morrow morning if it has been killed by the tiger you will come and inform me.

The *doï*—a Cambodian—struck his forehead three times on the ground, declaring he was "the dust of my feet," which is a form of politeness habitual in this country, a complaisance existing there, perhaps, to an excess that no one would dream of reproaching the

Americans with. Having performed this homage, he took a dozen men and went to execute my orders.

The next morning on rising I saw my *doï*, who brought me a calf's head; it was all that remained of the animal. I had it made into mock-turtle for my *déjeuner*, and in the evening, a little before sunset, I walked towards my observatory, followed by my *doï*, who was leading by a cord another calf, and by my servants, who placed on the platform quite an arsenal of rifles of divers calibre, and also a little meat-supper to minister to my patience, for I intended passing the whole night there.

When every one had retired, after having wished me good luck without end, I installed myself peaceably on the platform: they had brought me a comfortable easy-chair, and I was soon at my ease. The calf, ignorant of the painful rôle he was destined to play, seemed to be perfectly happy, nipping off the young shoots of bamboo within reach of his tether.

Darkness came on with that suddenness usual in tropical countries. I had gone so far as to ask myself whether I should not enjoy a little nap, to pass away the time till it should please the tigers to announce to me their presence, when a sharp sting in the calf of my leg attracted my attention. I stooped quickly to see what it was. By the feeble light of the stars and the moon, I saw a procession of ants scaling my leg. They were little black things. I got up and shook myself, pushed away my chair, and sat down again; in a minute, another procession was on the march, and, at the same time, my other calf was invaded. This time they were red, great red monsters, advancing in good order, with superior officers at their head, throwing out skirmishing parties right and left, reconnoitering the country in all directions, and leaving very sensible traces of their ravaging course. But this was not the only attack, for next came the advanced guard of a swarm of mosquitoes, sounding the charge ; fierce little assailants with grey-spotted wings, which alighted on my skin and as quickly departed, leaving traces of their marauding in specks of blood.

"Oh! oh!" I said to myself, "I am not going to stand my ground against such a decided superiority in number, and shall beat an orderly retreat, if I can only find my way through this infernal jungle."

Taking the first rifle that came to hand, I prepared to descend the ladder, and no sooner had I set foot on the first round than a growl, gently modulated, came from a spot near behind me. I did not see the beast, but the calf, for his part, was by no means deceived: he trembled in every limb, and nearly pulled his head off, dragging the cord. I remounted at a bound. Another low growl, this one coming from my right, replied to the first. Evidently, the tiger, whom I had invited to dinner the preceding evening, had, in his turn, gallantly invited a female friend to a little supper of cold veal, and I was on the point of interrupting this *tête à tête.*

The ants and their allies, the mosquitoes, recommenced hostilities whilst I was meditating on my situation, and meditation is certainly not under favourable conditions when one is fully occupied in repelling an attack. Three or four times, being driven to extremities, I tried to descend, but then this terrible low growling recommenced, and it expressed so clearly: "Wait, my friend, I will have him by the leg as he comes down the ladder, and then we shall have something more delicate for supper." Indignant at the mean *rôle* circumstances compelled me to play, I had no alternative than to seek safety on my platform, but there, however, I could defend myself, if not against all my enemies, at least, armed as I was, against the most formidable. "Let them come on," I said to myself, "I will give them a warm reception, and prepare for myself an oration on my return."

At six in the morning, when day appeared and my men came to look for me, my head had swollen to the size of a pumpkin, and my legs were studded with bites, which were burning like a scald. As for the calf, he appeared to have recovered from his fright, and was eating with a good appetite. I kept him a long time, but I never returned to lie in wait for a tiger, nor have I ever recommended this kind of sport, but to one person alone, and this was a learned German tourist who had been pursuing me for three days with questions on statistics.

This incident, that really occurred to me in the East,

came to my memory last evening. The post for watching indicated by Parker is a little beach of sand, at the spot where the water is turned into the *flume*. Monsieur Bouverie, who is an inveterate hunter, pointed out to me all the foot-marks imprinted on the soil, and then went to hide himself in a thicket of willows, whilst I tried to cover myself in the branches of a fir, and there we remained two hours watching a little gap in the rock, the sole path open to the game coming to the watering place. Alas! we were bound to believe that the fallow-deer and the moose-deer were no more thirsty than the beavers were hungry, for nothing came down from the wood, and the sheet of water was not rippled by the pettiest beaver. On the other hand, we were so well punctured and scarified by the mosquitoes, that, about nine o'clock, being unable to hold out any longer, I prevailed on Monsieur Bouverie to beat a retreat—a manœuvre that was not easily accomplished in this country without roads, in the dark.

When we returned from our hunt we found Parker still up. He told us that during our absence he had received a visit from Mr Cockries, the proprietor of one of the neighbouring mines with whom he is engaged in business, and who, hearing of our presence in the country, came to invite us to breakfast, that he might at the same time show us his mine.

Having plenty of time to spare before going there, it being only half-an-hour's walk, we have employed the morning in *panning* in the river. Monsieur Bouverie has decidedly missed his vocation; he should have been by all means a gold-digger. At the end of an hour's work, when we compared results, he had a little heap of gold four times as much as mine. It is a great pity our rivulets in France do not bear gold, for really *panning* is an exercise as healthful as amusing. It would be an invaluable resource for the country when one has visitors and does not know what to do with them.

Immediately facing the house, a little dell, in every respect resembling that of the Little Gimlet, by which we came, descends into our valley, and to this they have given the name of Fair-View. There are three like this, and these constitute the sole means of access to the Little Rapid. It is the little dell of Fair-View (called here a *gulch*) that we are now going up on horse-back, after having crossed the river, to get to the mine, which is quite at the end near where the streams separate. We soon arrive at a little log-house, which serves as a lodging for the proprietor of the mine, Mr Cockries. He is a fine young man of about thirty, who shakes our hands so heartily as almost to dislocate the joints, and seems quite happy in having the opportunity of showing us his lucky find. We are obliged to leave our horses at the house with a sack of maize between them to keep them employed, and, while clambering up the mountain to get to his mine, which is much higher up, he relates to us its history. It is that of a prospector on whom fortune has smiled, and who well deserves his good luck.

About two years ago, passing by this way, he remarked a cropping-out of quartz quite at the top of the mountain. It contained no gold there worth mentioning, but Mr Cockries concluded from many indications that there would be some lower down. He joined with a friend in the adventure. As it would have been too long to follow the vein by sinking a shaft down into it, he considered it would be far better to intersect the lode further down by means of a level driven in from the flank of the mountain. They worked together for seven or eight months. At the end of this time they were already seventy feet below the soil, and had not yet come up to the quartz. They would have perforated the mountain from one end to the other by continuing in the same direction without finding anything. Every thing was to begin again. The vein, not having been intersected, evidently was inclined in a contrary direction.

They then recommenced lower down, and after a year's toil, they were 130 feet below the surface. One day at last they came on a lode, but one as yet of doubtful value. The two adventurers were not discouraged. At the end of their "adit level" or drift they sunk a shaft, and in proportion as they got deeper, the lode became richer. They had at last found gold.

Capitalists came to the spot immediately. They made a bargain with one of these, and the sum paid for it represented exactly the cost of two years' working! But it should be explained that a quarter of the profits is reserved for the two partners.

At present the machines are ordered, and shortly the first consignments of materials will be on their way across the prairie. Mr Cockries remains here waiting for them. With four or five miners, he is making trials with the view of ascertaining the exact width and the bearings of the lode. At present his fortune is secure.

Having gone down the shaft, we returned to his dwelling. It is a square log-house, the sides of which are not more than four yards long. Within there is nothing but a stove, a table, and two stools. In a corner are thrown the blankets that constitute the whole of their bedding, and here these two men have been living for two years.

After an excellent *déjeuner* of preserved meats, which Mr Cockries served up for us himself with a hospitality that prompted me to ask him if he were not of Scotch origin, we went to smoke a cigar at the foot of a tree, in company with the miners, who did not eat with us on account of the insufficiency of table accessories. While we were talking with them, I caught a few words between Parker and our host, which induced me to open my ears. It was about Bill, that amiable personage whose feelings I am reproached with having so inconsiderately wounded regarding my opened letter. It seems that this choice specimen of a juryman has a brother who has just been caught stealing, and that he himself is suspected of the same offence. Consequently, it is a question of giving him notice to *skip the hills*—an order that must be obeyed, if given, under the penalty of being shot at the first opportunity. If a dozen men like Parker and Cockries are to be found in the neighbourhood, the system is admirable, and they will speedily be rid of Bill: if, on the contrary, the Bills are in the majority—and here, unfortunately, they are often in the majority—the consequences are very serious. One of the newspapers that came to hand this morning, relates that a town in the West—I forget the name—is, at this moment, in the power of a band of *desperadoes.* Having elected the mayor, they pillaged the property of the peaceable inhabitants, so far as formality of procedure is concerned, in the most strictly legal way.

We separated from our friends of Fair View about two o'clock. Parker has made us return by the upland, and we have rejoined the river on descending the third valley. The water of the brook flowing there is highly ferruginous, having a strong taste of ink, and yet the animals drink it with avidity. We pass beside an old tunnel, pierced in the flank of a little hill, the timber work of which has entirely fallen away decayed. They suppose it was made in 1852. That year there was a party of nineteen miners, who, coming from Fort Laramie, had been able to penetrate into the Black Hills, which were then little known. There is evidence that they succeeded there, and even remained some time, for remains of work have been found at different spots, which appear to belong to this date. But they must have been all massacred by the Indians, and their scalps, perhaps, are still hanging in the tent of some

Sioux warrior. The vocation of a *prospector* is still very hard, but in those times men who led such a life must have been daring even to recklessness.

We return to the house by way of the river. In one of the *bars*, Parker's little dog started two animals about the size of foxes and of nearly the same colour, which run away among the rocks, uttering shrill cries. We run after them and kill them with our revolvers, and discover that they are marmots. There are enough here to make the fortunes of all the Savoyards in Europe, judging from the innumerable holes they have made in the mountain dales. We asked Parker what they were, and he called them *mountain hogs*, which did not enlighten me much.

A little further on, a beaver files before me across the river, but before I can unhook my rifle from the saddle it has disappeared.

This evening we are busy making our preparations for departure, for to-morrow morning we leave Little Rapid Creek.

CHAPTER VII.

DEPARTURE FROM LITTLE RAPID CREEK—CASTLETON—KING SOLOMON—FRENCH *CUISINE*—A DEAD CITY—AN IRISH RANCH—CUSTER—THE WHITTLERS—THE CONQUEST OF THE BLACK HILLS—DEATH OF COLONELS CUSTER AND CROOK—SITTING BILL AND MANITOBA—THE MICA MINES—THE YELLOW STONE—THE MISFORTUNES OF A SHERIFF—THE PHILOSOPHY OF A COW-BOY.

July the 9th.—To-day we are obliged to leave Little Rapid Creek, and it is with a feeling indeed of regret that we say adieu to the people as well as the places. Parker comes with us, for we have still to see the property which is now in course of improvement in the South, and in the centre of which they are going to raise a town. Before getting there, we have to turn out of our direct way in order to visit Custer City, where we have some business to transact ; but we say good-bye to old Captain Hughes, who has truly inspired us with the warmest regard for him. Here he is at seventy-two, passing the remainder of his days far away from his family. During the fine season, he has still a few workmen and the benefit of their society, but when winter comes, the poor old man remains almost entirely alone, compelled to go out every day, whatever weather it may be, through snow or storm, to look after the bullocks. If he were a European I would pity him with all my heart, and yet I do not understand him, for the good man is rich, and by no means visibly employs the large salary he gets here. But truly, the people of this country are made of such stuff, that situations which would seem to us intolerable suit them exactly, apparently, and what we like is distasteful to them.

While we are saddling our horses, he and the workmen come to say good-bye. They all absolutely force us to accept, by way of souvenirs, little nuggets or specimens of quartz, which every good miner makes a point of carrying in his pocket. In all these demonstrations—we must speak out plainly—there is not the slightest thought of self-interest; petty gratuities are quite unknown here, and would not be accepted, as we well know from experience. If, however, they accepted such a thing as a knife, or some other trifling object of little value, this is quite as far as they would go.

We cross the beaver pond where we have *panned* so much. It seems that our operations have frightened these brave little creatures, for their work has not gone on very quickly during our sojourn. The tree is leaning very sensibly, but has not yet fallen. They have promised me not to disturb them, and if beavers have poets among them, I hope they will not forget to sing praises in my behalf.

As we have not a long stage to do to-day, we set

out rather late, about two o'clock. We march due south, and we have to cross in succession two deep valleys, Castle Creek and Tigerville, before entering into the one that is to conduct us to Custer—the city in which we are to sleep to-morrow night. The Castle Creek is a little stream parallel to the Little Rapid. The valley, wider than the one we are just leaving, is very fertile; one or two farms are established there, and constitute the town of Castleton. As we remove further from Deadwood, marching towards the south, we find the vegetation much finer. From the Little Rapid to Castleton, but especially on the side of the Little Rapid, the fir woods we have crossed are very fine. Trunks two yards round are common.

Beyond Castleton we have some trouble in crossing the *creek*, which is much muddier than we see any need for. Besides, the inhabitants have taken it into their heads to lay over the bottom planks of fir, perforated with a multitude of little incisions in the form of cups, and these boards are held fast by big stones. From time to time they take them up and turn them over, and they collect in this way a large quantity of gold dust; but the horses have much trouble in coming to a decision to put their feet on the unsteady planks. The sojourn at the Little Rapid appears to have benefited the little buff mare. She always keeps at the head of the column, and seems now to get on very happily with Monsieur Bouverie, who looks as if he were riding a horse with six feet when he is mounted, for his own almost touch the ground. He is carrying with him a basket of little fir trees, which he dips into the water at every brook, flattering himself he will find them fit for planting on his return to Belgium. In his long conversations with Captain Hughes, he has made great progress in English. As politeness is in him quite instinctive, he has devoted special attention to acquiring a thorough knowledge of the forms of politeness in use in the country. The list of them is not very long. So soon as we meet any cow-boy whatever on our road, he bawls out as loud as he can: "How do you do?" and this never fails to produce an impression.

As night is coming on, we see, in a glade, an immense wooden construction, surrounded with several houses, looming before us, one of which looks very elegant.

"What is all that?" I ask Parker.

"They are the buildings of a mine, *King Solomon.* Our friend at Deadwood, Mr Dickerman, was the manager here, but I believe it is now abandoned. But look; do you see that big house? There is a man at the window! That is where he lived."

"Halloa, boys!" cried the man in question.

"How do you do?" roared Monsieur Bouverie.

"Can I do anything for you?" I replied.

"Are you not French barons?"

"Well—what then?"

'Why: Professor Dickerman telephoned to me this

morning that two French barons would pass, perhaps, by this way. He says that I must offer you a bed here instead of letting you go to Tigerville. Besides, there is not one at Tigerville."

"Well! here is a piece of good luck," says Monsieur Bouverie.

"Could we have something to eat?"

"Ah! That is not quite so easy. I, for my part, can give you nothing, but there is a French lady here who can, perhaps, prepare you a dinner."

"Ah! ah!" exclaimed Monsieur Bouverie to me aside, giving me a sly poke in the ribs, "are we not lucky fellows of the first water? We were speculating on a problematic dinner at Tigerville, and upon a night passed in the open air, or, at best, in a stable, and here we are going to sleep snugly between sheets after a good dinner, prepared by the hands of a French lady, too! But who the deuce can she be?"

"She is the wife of one of the enginemen of the mine," explains to us the friend of this excellent fellow Dickerman. And he takes us into a magnificent stable, where we fasten our horses before mangers filled with oats and racks stuffed with hay, and having done this, we enter into the house. It is quite a little palace. When we see there on the first floor beds with their clean sheets all ready, looking as if expecting us, our first impulse is to rush to the telephone in order to thank the good-hearted Dickerman. Unfortunately a great storm is gathering over the mountain, the thunder is already beginning to roar, and the communication is interrupted.

"I assure you," says Monsieur Bouverie, "that nothing less than a conspiration of the elements was necessary to hinder us from, in the first place, testifying our gratitude. Suppose we now go and see what there is in the larder; I anticipate something quite appetizing from the hands of this French lady. Let us go and pay her a visit."

We explain what interests us to this servitor of Dickerman, who conducts us to a house, close by the machinery. We knock at the door, and this is opened to us by a clean, very fair, little woman, who makes her courtesy.

"Oh!" explains Monsieur Bouverie to me, "she has an apron."

And she has made a courtesy to us! At all events, she is not an American. The little woman looked at us with an embarrassed air.

"*Madame,*" I said in French, "you see before you two famishing fellow-countrymen, who would be very grateful if you could give them something to eat."

"*Ich verstehe nicht!*" replied the little woman.

I jabber a little German. This expedient had indeed been very useful to me during the war. Every time that a German officer pretended not to know French, I spoke German to him. He coloured immediately for his ignorance, and entreated me to speak French. Recalling these incidents, I give out to her a few phrases from Ollendorff. I mix these up with a few examples from Ahn's method, and, after all, I express myself with an ease that astonishes me. The little woman understands immediately, a circumstance that astonishes me still more. She lays the table with three covers, gives us genuine bread with some butter, and then we see her taking from some mysterious corner a few eggs, and from another, a great joint of meat, which she holds out to us in triumph, for, in this country where seven or eight hundred thousand bullocks are pasturing on the prairies, it is a *gourmandise* quite unheard of to eat beef. What she shows us is a haunch of venison. While we are eating excellent *œufs sur le plat,* waiting for the stewed venison with potatoes, the odour of which would draw all the wolves of the forests around us, if there were any, we get our pretty hostess to entertain us with her talk. She is an Alsacian, and her husband is called Enrick. He was a non-commissioned officer, and came to America at the end of the war. He was then an engineman in Dickerman's service and earned six dollars a day. Unfortunately the works have been stopped for four months, and, in this interval, he has gone to work in another mine, leaving his wife here till King Solomon resumes. Parker, gallant as usual, feels in duty bound to interfere.

"Madame," he says, "we should not think of allowing a lady to do the cooking for us. Permit me——"

"Ah! excuse me, Parker," I said, "I cannot suffer you, in my presence, to lead the wife of a fellow-countryman astray from her duties. If the Americans like women who read Longfellow, like your friends of Hilly Ranch, but who do not sweep their floors, and who leave their husbands to do the cooking, it is their business; and I hope they are happy! But here is a brave little woman who has never read Gœthe nor Schiller, I am quite sure."

"Have you ever heard of Messieurs Gœthe and Schiller, Madame?" asks Monsieur Bouverie, who has his mouth quite full, but who highly approves.

"No, Monsieur," she says; "they do not live here."

"Ah! you see! But just look at the floor: it is so clean that you might eat off it. And this *gibelotte de darin!* This is the third time you have been at it. For God's sake just let Madame Enrick do the cooking, she understands it perfectly."

And I also spoke with my mouth full, for indignation did not deprive me of appetite; nor has appetite, while being gratified, hindered me from being ever eloquent, apparently, and yet Parker, who, on his part, is eating like an ogre, has not said a word: as to Monsieur Bouverie, he is actually devouring. But I must shorten these notes, for the bed Dickerman has placed at my disposal attracts me irresistibly.

July the 10th.—We had to make rather a long stage to-day—nearly twenty-five miles. We did not, however, start very early. For, in the first place, it is no easy matter to tear one's self from the seductions of a good bed furnished with clean sheets, especially when one has been deprived of such a luxury for a week. Next, we wished to send to Dickerman the expression of our warm gratitude; but, after a few vain efforts, we found the communication still interrupted. This seems to me to be the normal state of the telephone in this country. I remember in Cochin China, when we had installed the telegraph there, the wild elephants took it into their heads to follow the posts and pull down the wires with their trunks, for the humming of which when vibrating with the wind, was a kind of music that did not seem to please them. I do not know whether bears are to be held responsible for accidents of the same kind produced here; I merely notice their frequency.

While waiting for our *déjeuner*, which our friend Madame Enrick is preparing for us, we pay a visit to King Solomon. Alas! the lucky day of dividends is not yet arrived. The mine which they intended to work regularly was, however, tolerably rich; still, facts have once more proved the truth of the axiom, the essence of which Parker is always giving in a few words: "If you will have gold, first have water," but which may be also expressed in a way less concise, but more comprehensible by this formula:

"If you have two gold mines, the one rich and far from a water course, the other poor and near one, do not hesitate to work the latter and sell the other."

The King Solomon comes under the first of these

two conditions: the only serviceable water course in the neighbourhood is two or three miles off, it seems; and there it is where the stamps would have to be set up, if the working had gone on; and then to connect it with the mine, a little railway would have been necessary. The shareholders, probably, have set their faces against this great expense as a supplementary estimate, for, unfortunately, all their capital has been already absorbed in making preparations and trials, and this is the stage at which they have now arrived.

Parker shows no ill-will towards me for the good rating I gave him yesterday. His chivalrous feeling, underlying his American habits, left him no peace of mind when pursued with the intolerable idea that a woman was going to work for him in preparing a *déjeuner;* but now, nothing but a sigh escapes him—a feeble expression of the dominion of the senses over intellect—as he surveys the venison cutlets prepared and brought in by Madame Enrick, which he soon attacks with a voracity, excited probably by a long diet of bacon and "canned meat." But the grosser part of man, however, having been once appeased, his spiritual essence quickly reassumes its authority, when he sees Madame Enrick, coffee-pot in hand, preparing to make the coffee. His conscience accordingly troubles him so much that he seems as if he were on the point of snatching it from her; but I give him such a stern look that he dare not rise from his seat. And lucky for us too; for, in the end, we get coffee, "the genuine article," instead of the muddy water stirred up and served by the Americans. When they pretend to make coffee, they throw a handful of grains, imperfectly ground, into a saucepan of cold water, make it boil and bubble over, serve their decoction, and then scald their throats. Their tea passes through the same stages, and one may fancy the result. While sipping with calm contemplation the nectar served up to us by Madame Enrick, I raise my head and perceive the family library on a shelf. According to habit I go and consult the backs of the volumes. There are three: a missal, an almanac, and a translation of "La Cuisinière bourgeoise"!! Happy Monsieur Enrick! I hope he appreciates his happiness.

It is a fact known from remote antiquity that horses never march better than in the interval just after their riders have made a good dinner: in this respect, the American horses quite resemble our own, and accordingly in quitting King Solomon we make our way at a rattling pace. Jean Leblanc, especially, rushes on at such a rate that I soon find myself alone in the sole avenue of Tigerville. The word *avenue* requires some explanation. At New York the city is divided into squares, bordered on two of their sides by an avenue, and upon the two others by a street: the streets are 80 feet wide and the avenues 160. It is a very convenient arrangement for a large city; but as every village founded in America is, in the idea of its founder, or rather in his prospectus, destined to become much more important than New York in a not distant future, he invariably takes care to divide the ground into avenues and streets, unless, which is generally the case, he stops for the present at the first avenue. But nothing looks more wretched than the effect produced, when the rising town is, for instance, composed of only ten houses. The poor plank huts or log-houses, instead of closing in together and compressing their ugly uniformity in a single group, spread it out on each side of what looks like a field encumbered with weeds, but which is actually an avenue. Before each rises a pile of empty meat tins, for just as the civilization of the Kelts is revealed to us by their dolmens, and that of the Scandinavians by their mounds and kitchen-middens, so will the antiquaries of future times immediately recognise the spots inhabited in India by the English by the piles of soda-water bottles heaped up before the cantonments, and the dwellings of the Americans by their deposits of empty meat tins. And yet, who can foretell the stores of wealth they are laying up for future generations, and whether, when the Cornish tin mines shall have been long worked out, the New Zealander, who in the remote future is destined to sit on a ruined arch of London Bridge, may not actually read an account of the exploitation of post-tertiary beds of stanniferous iron in the United States?

The aspect of Tigerville is desolate in the extreme. Founded in order to provide shelter and especially whiskey for the miners of King Solomon, this unhappy town has been struck down in the flower of its age by the interruption of the work of the mine. Its ruins are wanting in the poesy that characterises those of Palmyra or of Thebes, of the valley of Tempe, or the woods of Olympus. Its marbles are not yet *in loco.* Half-a-dozen timber public houses falling to decay, which expose to us their desolate bars, are no more frequented by men than by the bears of the neighbouring forest. What has become of all those "prominent citizens," who, on this corner of the earth, now a desert, caroused together, swindled and "revolvered" one another with so much spirit? Where are the flowers of last year? Perhaps, however, we may derive some knowledge from a living relic, for we perceive a survivor of this civilization. One of those citizens, doubtlessly "prominent," for he seems the only one of his kind, is seated before a mean little store, with his feet in the air, smoking sadly his pipe. He looks so dirty and chopfallen, that it is solely from principle and without hope of a cordial response, that Monsieur Bouverie salutes him on passing with a "How do you do?" shouted, as usual, at the top of his voice without producing any reply.

We are, moreover, soon reminded of the hard realities of the existence of the explorers. After having traversed a few patches of wooded upland, interspersed with grassy glades, we at length come to a little narrow valley, in which, as usual in this country, "zigzags" a strong rivulet. The nice dance the Little Gimlet gave us, was the mere prelude to the performance we had to go through here. In three hours we had to cross it seventeen times, and, as it is excessively muddy, the constant repetition of the operation was by no means pleasant.

About two o'clock we fall in with a good man on horseback, whom we ask if we could not have something to eat in the neighbourhood. He interrupts his work, which consists in nailing on the trees of the forest some little boards, a collection of which hangs from his saddle-bow, and on which is inscribed in red letters different sentences ; thus, on one of them we read :

"Where the deuce does one drink such good whiskey?" This is followed with the figure of a hand, and, guided by the direction of the finger, we see another board attached to another tree near by :

"Why, bless me! It is at P. Finigan's at Custer." From which we conclude we have the honour of speaking to Mr Finigan in person. He gives us in genuine brogue sundry explanations, from which we learn that a ranch, occupied by one of his countrymen, exists in the neighbourhood, and that, "sure for the honour of ould Ireland," they will give us there something to eat.

Cheered with these assurances, we resume our way : we traverse our meandering rivulet half-a-dozen times more, and we at last perceive at the bottom of a pretty valley, which opens on our right, two or three huts of wretched aspect. It is here, evidently, that resides the victim of perfidious Albion, of whom we have just heard.

When we arrive at the log-house that serves as a dwelling, we are received by a tall young woman, with cheeks as red as a boiled lobster. She tells us that her husband, Joe Clinton, is absent, but that he killed a deer last evening, and she will cook a piece for us. We turn our horses into the grass, where they feed beside the brook, and then return to the house. Parker, as usual, lavishes on our hostess all the hyperboles suggested by his gallantry so annoyingly held in check at King Solomon. As it is no longer the question of a compatriot, and the material and moral welfare of Mr Clinton being by no means my business, I take care not to meddle. I do not doubt that Mrs Clinton is for Mr Clinton a treasure of inestimable value, but this jewel is deplorably ill-set. It seems to me impossible that the poorest cabins of Connemara should not be marvels of comfort in comparison with that in which we find ourselves. In this, dire misery is oozing from every nook and corner. A pile of dirty rags, of which we get a glimpse in one corner, constitutes the conjugal bed. In this hovel no light penetrates, except through the open door, unless one or two cracks in the roof will permit a few rays to pass when not too clouded by the rising smoke. The few utensils and clothing are lying on the ground. In another corner, the trunk of a fir hollowed out serves as a cradle for an unhappy, pale-faced little creature, who with its hands resting on the edge watches our movements with its glittering eyes.

The poor woman by no means seems reconciled with her lot. She is only twenty, and was born in Galway, where her father must be a respectable farmer, for he holds a farm of eighteen pounds from some lord, whose name I forget. He regularly pays his rent with ease, and she has never heard of that panacea for suffering humanity, the renowned *Land League*, nor even of Mr Parnell. She married Joe Clinton, who had returned to the country, after having been long absent in America, where she then came with him. Life is very gloomy here; they make hardly any money, although they have a score of cows and a few horses, and then, again, there is neither church nor priest; her little girl is already six months' old, and has not yet been baptized; in short, she regrets Galway and old Ireland, and longs to return there so soon as they can save a little money. This is the first time I have heard this threnody. But then, when one does not feel his breast glowing with enthusiasm, and has not some means at hand, the life of an emigrant in this country seems to me to be one of the gloomiest of prospects. The saying of Dickerman at Deadwood is quite true: "This is not a poor man's country."

Having dealt out to our hostess the common-place civilities and trite compliments in use on such occasions, and, what is more important, having amply recompensed her for the dish of buttered eggs, or rather the elements for it, with which she furnished us, we go to indulge in a little siesta on the banks of the rippling brook under the shade of a great fir tree. We are advised to look well into the tufts of grass and weeds, for we are now in a country where the rattle-snake lurks, which, though almost unknown among the mountains in the interior, becomes common enough in proportion as one progresses southwards and approaches the prairie. A regard for truth obliges me to admit that I have seen neither the tail nor the teeth of one of these reptiles, and that the only tinkle I have heard was from the little bell around the neck of one of the cows of the Clinton estate.

At three, considering we have indulged ourselves long enough, we saddle our horses, and, after having crossed our brook for the twenty-third and last time, we part from it, but not sorrowfully, to plunge into a forest that borders the valley on the left. The aspect of the country changes completely. The valleys we traverse are wider; on our right the horizon stretches out a long way, and here and there we get a momentary peep of the distant prairie, still a prairie more hilly than the one we quitted at Rapid City. In sundry spots single fir trees have been planted seemingly for the sake of the prospect. On our left the forest is dense, though the trees are not lofty: it is overhung by immense piles of bleak rocks, for here the mountains are much more elevated than those we have hitherto seen. Harney's Peak, around the base of which we are journeying, is 7400 feet high, and Custer's Peak, which we see before us, 6930.

The south of the Black Hills, over which we are now journeying, is the least populous part, and yet it is that which has been first colonized, for the first specimens of gold that attracted the miners came from the South.

The Black Hills hitherto have been divided into three counties: Lawrence, Pennington, and Custer. The first, which is the most northerly, counts about 15,000 inhabitants; the second 4000, and the third 1250. It is the exploitation of the Homestake and of the group of mines around it that has drawn the population to the north. There is no doubt, however, that the mineral and agricultural resources of the two other counties are quite equal, if not superior, to those of the first. The prairies which extend towards the south are so decidedly favourable to the fattening of cattle, in the first place on account of their fertility, and in the next for the mildness of the climate, that the population there is fast increasing: to this region they have just added a fourth county—that of Fall River. They are already bringing sheep here, which succeed remarkably well, but their arrival has raised, and will still raise, many a storm. With us, the sheep is taken as an emblem of peace, but if the Americans like emblems, it should be taken by them rather as an emblem of discord. Wherever a flock of these valuable wool-producers have passed, the bullocks refuse to pasture, so much do they dislike their odour. When a cattle ranch is near a sheep ranch, one is compelled to yield to the other, though this is not easily brought to an issue without the aid of revolvers. The sheep, no doubt, is destined to occupy these parts, and the bullock the more humid territory of the north.

Parker, who has always some new speculation in his head, shows us two or three plains, covered with a short grass, fine and dry, well sheltered from the winds and bordered with plenty of firs for supplying fences and sheds. All this, in his opinion, constitutes the beau ideal of a sheep ranch ; and if he can only be free for a few weeks before winter, he will go into the country of the Mormons, who are the great shepherds in the presence of the Eternal, to buy a few thousand sheep and bring them here.

While we are discussing these fine projects, our horses continue advancing : we have already reached the banks of a muddy rivulet, which is French Creek, and we soon perceive, before us, the sole avenue and a few rudimentary streets constituting the town of Custer. We come to the hotel, which is pointed out to us, as usual, by groups of idlers sitting smoking before the doors, and, of course, with their feet duly elevated, resting on a pole installed *ad hoc.* The landlord, a fat fair man, pushes before us the visitors' book without saying a word, and we having inscribed our names therein, he reads them very attentively.

"I have," says he in German, "the city of Paris, which is very fine, and in which there are many pretty women, and splendid gardens, Mabille——"

And so on for ten minutes. We wait with a certain

impatience for the verb which should end the phrase and complete the sense. Has he helped to burn Paris like a communard? Has he bombarded it as a soldier of Monsieur de Moltke? Was he a sweeper in the old brigades of Monsieur Haussmann? Whilst these speculations are passing through our heads, he slowly enumerates diverse aspects of Paris; he interrupts himself a moment to take a cigar and drink a glass of lager beer, and then the verb at last comes, which turns out to be *inhabited.*

A Frenchman who says to his wife: "I for you have bought a pair of horses; they are beautiful; they step, gracefully, &c., &c.," is choked at the fourth word by the said wife throwing her arms round his neck: she infallibly knows all she wants to know. But a German will say: "I have, the horses which you seen have, which bay are, &c., &c., to-day, bought:" and the anxious Gretchen, who is listening in suspense, is obliged to wait till the end to know whether, instead of the verb *bought,* some other, not so agreeable, such as *seen* or *refused*, is to bring her disappointment in the place of joy, for—

"Ein einziges Wort kann Alles umgestalten."

At all events, we must render justice to the good German who has welcomed us in the town of Custer. He lived in Paris as a commercial traveller at some time or other, but he has no grudge against the Parisians because they had been starved and bombarded by his compatriots, which is something, and he receives us kindly enough. Unfortunately, his hotel is full, for we find here all the judges we had met at Rapid City. The Assizes are now filling the town as well. We manage, however, to get a bedroom with two beds, in a new brick house which he is building on the other side of the street.

After dinner, I go out to smoke a cigar: rows of smokers with their feet raised are already at their post, still I manage to find room on a wooden bench. Hardly am I seated there, when one of my neighbours rises, draws from his pocket a formidable bowie-knife, and comes up to me brandishing the weapon. Monsieur de M——'s adventure comes to my mind at once. Has he sworn to make me quit the country? I clap my hand on the stock of my revolver, determined to sell my skin as dearly as possible, but my suspected aggressor looks at me so good naturedly that I at once lay down my arms. He approaches nearer, and, without saying a word, gives me a gentle push, carries away a large piece of the plank on which I am sitting, and then, resuming his own seat, commences cutting it up into chips. I am immediately reassured, and all the more on looking around and finding all the rest busy at the same kind of work: this is *whittling*, and these are the *whittlers*.

Whittling is a special malady of the American brain, developed particularly in the West, where there are few men who do not manifest these symptoms. Its diagnosis consists in an irresistible desire to take in the left hand a piece of wood, and to reduce it to morsels of the size of a match by a gentle and regular movement of the right hand armed with a pocket knife, a razor, or a bowie-knife. The indulgence of this propensity sometimes facilitates, but more frequently replaces, conversation, according to temperament; but the predisposition—quite as imperious as the passion for opium among the Chinese—is no more easily explained than a taste for olives, or dominoes, or rancid bacon, or why Schiller could not get on with his work without the smell of rotten apples under his nose. It seems that at Washington formerly they used to deliver to each senator or deputy, at the commencement of their sitting, a little block of cedar and a pen-knife, furnished by the questorship for this purpose: they had found this to be the most effective remedy for preserving the arms of the chairs, which, formerly, never lasted out a session. The epidemic being on the decline in the Eastern States at present, I hear that paper-knives, provided they are replaced frequently, answer all the purpose of securing the preservation of the public furniture.

As a conscientious observer, I wished to account for the sensations, evidently voluptuous, which my neighbours, absorbed in this occupation, appeared to feel. Accordingly, I asked one of them to give me a practical lesson, that I might study the phenomenon. He was a cow-boy, getting grey, ornamented with a Babylonian beard, and armed with two formidable revolvers. Tear-ing from the bench a piece, six inches long, he offered his services most courteously. This fragment I took, and leaning one end of it against the pit of my stomach, I began, with his own bowie-knife which he lent me, cutting it into thin splinters, much more equal and regular than the matches turned out by the French *régie*. Encouraged by the kind glances which this homage rendered to the customs of the country won for me from the company, I continued to the end, and I am sorry to say I found no gratification whatever in the experiment; on the contrary, a disagreeable sensation in the lower region of the stomach, which reminded me of the horrible *mal de mer* I once had with the first cigar I smoked with the Révérends Pères Jésuites. Perhaps I ought to have remembered that the stomach being a highly sensitive organ, and ill-adapted to resist external pressure when there is nothing within, I should have taken "a drop" to ensure success. Besides, if the propensity be a well-established diagnosis of some obscure disease, it still may not be one so easily contracted without a little whiskey introduced into the system, though not like lymph under the skin, nor in the ordinary way necessarily in such a quantity as to get into the head, for, unquestionably, Americans may evince a disposition to *whittle* without first getting *whittled.*

July the 11th.—Custer City, the capital of the county of Custer, is a town of three hundred inhabitants. At this moment its star appears to be in its ascendant, but it has passed through strange vicissitudes. Like many other American towns, or cities as they are called, it has gone through its maladies of infancy. Founded in 1875, it had before the autumn of that year fifteen hundred inhabitants. In less than another six months, in consequence of events about to be related, it had no more than fourteen! Since then, till latterly, it has vegetated. But now it is again beginning to attract attention. Far-seeing people are unanimous in predicting for it the most brilliant future, and they are seriously proposing to new-comers to sell them a nice bit of land in order to build upon the Seventh Avenue at the corner of the Seventieth Street, close by the bank, and not far from the station of the Southern Railway. This fine project, of course, exists only in the exuberant imagination of *Nature's own noblemen*, who are eager to exchange a few acres of marshy ground for a certain number of substantial bank notes.

The history of Custer is associated with the oldest souvenirs of the conquest of the Black Hills. The whole mountainous region now known by this name, reputed to have been valueless, had been abandoned to the Sioux, as well as the surrounding prairies, by a treaty in due form, dating from the epoch when the construction of the Trans-continental, passing through one of their reserves, had obliged the Government to enter into negotiation with these native tribes.

The arrangement issuing from this, which the Sioux had accepted only under compulsion, had, indeed, put an end to official hostilities: but as bands of warriors acting independently of the principal chiefs, made occasional depredations on the frontier, the regular troops, on their part, in pursuing them penetrated frequently into the reserve. In the course of one of those expeditions, which took place in the spring of 1874, one of the best known officers of the Federal army, General Custer, penetrated as far as the Southern part of the Black Hills, and gave his troops a few days' repose on the banks of French Creek.

The soldiers, several of whom probably had sojourned in California and visited the placers there, were not long in recognising the existence of gold in the sands of the rivulet. They brought away specimens of it, and these soon passed from hand to hand in the garrisons of the frontier. The emotion was great. The treaty made with the Sioux having guaranteed to them the exclusive property of their reserves, no white man had a right to establish himself there, and the Government had formally engaged itself to compel its observance. This, however, did not restrain an expedition from being immediately formed at Sioux City, with the avowed object of going to work the placers.

The party, composed of twenty-eight men accompanied by one woman, arrived unmolested at the spot where now stands Custer, in the month of December. The adventurers began by constructing a little fort to protect themselves from any attack by the Indians, and then set to work in search for gold, with, it is said, much success. In the spring, even before the snows were melted, parties of emigrants arrived from all quarters to join them, and from this time the city began to rise.

The Indians, however, were not disposed to suffer the invasion of their territory without protestations, and even without rifle shots, for these roving in isolated parties frequently attacked the convoys of emigrants. When their principal chiefs, *Sitting Bull* and *Spotted Tail*,* representing the two principal tribes of the confederation of the Sioux, that of the Ogalalas and that of the Tetons, perceived that events were turning to an invasion, they laid an official complaint before the military commander, General Custer, who, thus consequently constrained to act, appeared at first disposed to render justice to their demand.

A proclamation, accordingly, reminded the inhabitants that the entry into the Indian reserve was interdicted to them, and patrols of cavalry, scouring the prairie, turned back all those they met on the way thither. Force was even employed, and, on one occasion, when the leaders of a convoy formally refused to

* "Spotted Tail," we regret to say, is no more, having been assassinated lately by one of his warriors. The matter has excited a certain interest, because American justice thought proper to intervene. His murderer was in prison at Deadwood when we were there. The crime will be passed over probably, inasmuch as, after the very remarkable oratorical tournaments, it was recognised that no law could reach an Indian who had killed another within a reserve.

The daughter of the defunct, Miss "Spotted Tail," is a celebrated beauty among the squaws. She had the honour of having been presented to His Royal Highness the Prince of Wales on his visit to America.

comply with these orders, their teams were seized and their waggons burnt. In his desire to compel the observance of the treaty, General Custer did not confine himself to these precautions. At the head of a considerable detachment, he himself returned to visit the spot where he had encamped the preceding year, and finding fifteen miners there, he gave them notice to quit the ground immediately. One may easily fancy the clamour provoked by this decision. General Custer, assailed by complaints and even threats, ended by coming to terms: for in America, as in all democratic countries, a functionary charged with the execution of an unpopular law inevitably finds himself disowned, sooner or later. It was therefore agreed that the work should be interrupted, in order to give the Government time to enter into negotiations with the Indians, and to obtain the cession of the auriferous lands, and, at the same time, it was also agreed that each special claim should have a man on the spot to preserve the provisional right to the property. The fort was put in order, the fourteen men designated retired therein, and all the others quitted the district. This result having been obtained, the troops returned to their cantonments.

The fourteen men left behind did not remain long alone. As soon as it was well ascertained that all the troops had retired to their quarters, miners poured in from every direction, more numerous than ever, and instantly resumed the work; and the new town, which had been baptized with a homage, perhaps rather ironic, with the name of Custer City, counted now, it is said, three thousand inhabitants, having its first avenue half a mile in length. Unfortunately, this prosperity had but a brief existence.

In 1876, Professor Jenney discovered the mineral lodes of Homestake, and the new city of Deadwood attracted thither all the inhabitants of the southern city. There remained then no more than one hundred and fifty or two hundred. This is the second period which began.

During this time, the unfortunate Indians continued protesting in their manner against the outrageous appropriation of their property. It must be borne in mind that the Sioux, being horsemen and hunters of buffaloes, have never inhabited these mountains in a permanent manner. They established by preference their villages along the rivers in the prairie. These villages, moreover, are eminently temporary, for they are hardly inhabited except in winter. During summer the *Red skins* abandon them, in order to follow the migrations of the herds of buffaloes. The establishment of the *Pale faces* in the mountains, therefore, troubled them less than if it had taken place elsewhere. The constant passage, however, of convoys was at first a constant source of annoyance, and in course of time drove away the buffaloes. War, notwithstanding, was not officially declared by the grand chiefs, but petty, obscure expeditions multiplied considerably, and very few emigrants arrived at their destination without having been greeted on their way with many bullets whistling by their ears. The principal chiefs disavowed the authors of these outrages, and attributed them either to warriors belonging to distant tribes, or to men living isolated beyond the political organisation of the tribes, known as *Renegade Indians.*

These chiefs had entered into negotiation with the Government, and admitted the principle of the cession of the Black Hills in exchange for grants of a different nature, some temporary, that is to say, a sum paid down and settled, and others permanent, such as the distribution of rations and blankets. The negotiations went on rather slowly, a circumstance of which the Americans could hardly complain, since they were in the actual enjoyment of all they demanded. Finally, the treaty was signed on the 1st of November 1876, and ratified by the Congress on the 28th of February 1877.

It might have been supposed that everything was settled, but it was nothing of the sort. The Indian chiefs, who had promised their concurrence in assuring the security of the routes, were unable to keep their promise. Perhaps they were not very anxious to do so. War, though carefully not declared, actually continued. Corps of volunteers were formed, who went to surprise the Indian villages, and, massacring all the inhabitants, carried off their horses and sold them publicly in the frontier towns. On the other hand, not a week passed without hearing of some farm attacked in the middle of the night by a band of red-skinned demons, who disappeared with the scalps of the inmates, leaving behind them nothing but corpses and ruins. The torments inflicted on these unhappy victims were appalling. Generally they were stretched on the ground on their back, with their hands and feet bound to four posts: then a charcoal fire was lighted on their chest, and carefully kept burning, whilst the assassins danced around.

Such a frightful state of things could not last indefinitely. In spite of the disavowals of the chiefs, the inhabitants of the frontiers held them responsible for all the atrocities committed. Moreover, the expeditions organised by these were often directed against those Indian villages living regularly under the authority of their chiefs, who, consequently, were obliged to defend them. War was, therefore, inevitable, and was not long in breaking out. It was discovered, all at once, that *Sitting Bull*, the grand chief of the Ogalalas, had called the whole Sioux confederation to arms, and that, at the head of seven thousand warriors perfectly armed, he was scouring the frontiers like wildfire, burning and massacring everything in his way, and carrying off immense booty.

General Custer and Colonel Crook set out immediately in pursuit. They had with them about a thousand men of the regular troops, to which flocked some corps of volunteers, and a few hundreds of the *Crows* warriors, the hereditary enemies of the Sioux. In this kind of warfare it is, in fact, almost impossible to come up to the enemy if there are not at hand a few Indian scouts, so rapid are the movements of the Red Skins. Each warrior of these leads with him four or five horses, which he treats at the same time with unparalleled brutality: when one is fatigued, he mounts another, and by this means accomplishes a course that seems incredible.

As soon as Sitting Bull found he was pursued in earnest, he began to retire towards the north, conducting before him an immense crowd of women and children. At last, at the beginning of autumn, he had the tact to draw into an engagement, in his rear, about a thousand men in a narrow valley at White Mountain, not far from Bismarck; then his warriors, commanding the heights, suddenly opened so murderous a fire on the whites, that in a few minutes the whole corps was massacred. Not one escaped.

It is related that Sitting Bull had brought to him, after the combat, the bodies of Custer and Crook; then opening their breasts with his knife, he tore out the heart and ate it before all his people.

After such a check, the pursuit was interrupted, as might well be supposed, for the other corps were not in force, and it was necessary to await fresh troops. Sitting Bull availed himself of this intermission to put the frontier of Canada between him and his enemies. In short, in this campaign, from beginning to end, the old chief proved by his manœuvres that he would have made an excellent general of cavalry.

Being well received by the Canadians, who had no reason not to consider him as a belligerent, since the Americans treated with him as between one power and another, he sojourned for some time in the plains of Manitoba.* But the populations, that had at first congratulated themselves on the distant removal of a dangerous neighbour, soon recognised that they had not gained so very much, for, in spite of the surveillance exercised on both sides of the frontier, it was constantly traversed by little bands of warriors, who, having nothing more to lose, and being entirely free from all authority of their chiefs, overran the country in every direction, ravaging it with fire and sword. Then was seen the rather strange spectacle of delegates coming from the Federal Government to propose to Sitting Bull to return to his old reserve, promising him at the same time to overlook the past, and to guarantee to him all the advantages of the treaty concluded before the recent hostilities. After a little hesitation, Sitting Bull accepted these proposals, and came to establish himself at Standing Rock in Dakota, not far from Pierre, with a group of about seven thousand of his subjects. The rest, numbering about thirty thousand, distributed themselves throughout the reserve, and there they keep within bounds, but a few ungovernable

* This Canadian province, situated to the north of Dakota, is principally inhabited by a mixed race, in which French blood participates. They proclaimed their independence a few years ago, fighting under the old national white flag of France—the last time this standard has figured in war.

marauders hardly ever showing themselves beyond. Their old chief still assembles them from time to time to receive distributions of food and clothing which are made to them by the American agent, with whom, it is said, he is on very good terms. A house has been built for him. At first he always inhabited the outside, choosing the leeward side for his couch, but he has, at length, acquired the habit of living in-doors. It is said that he even takes to agriculture. He goes occasionally to visit the authorities of the territory, and lives in peace with his neighbours.

We have begun this morning by visiting the sights of Custer. This has not taken us very long. The public buildings consist, in the first place, of the inevitable court-house, then of a timber theatre, raised in the bright days of 1876, which has never since been opened, and, finally, of the hotel, which our host is in the course of building.

On awaking this morning, we noticed, with some surprise, that the one-storey wooden house, in which we passed the night, was surrounded with brick walls, which already rose nearly to the height of our windows. We asked for an explanation of this strange arrangement, and our host, directing our attention to the back of the house where there is no wall, explained to us at once.

"As soon as the brick building is finished, I shall slide out behind the wooden house on to the ground yonder, which I have bought likewise."

In fact, there is already laid down a series of beams to serve as slides. He asserts that the operation will not cost fifty dollars: the furniture even is not removed from the rooms.

We are actually besieged by a number of pushing men of business, who will, by hook or crook, form companies for the working of certain mica mines. I confess that, my acquaintance with mica being so very meagre, I had to obtain information. I thought that mica was hardly used except for making transparent candle-screens and other like nick-nacks that form the stock-in-trade of articles at thirteen sous. It appears, on the contrary, that mica serves a variety of purposes which I little suspected. In America they make with it doors for stoves, that one may see through it when fuel is wanted; the fragments of mica, ground fine and mixed with petroleum, form the best lubrication known for the axles of vehicles. Having obtained this information, I next ask under what form this precious mineral is found, and they reply by proposing to take us to see the principal mine belonging to a Creek Indian of mixed breed, called Dempsey, who just happens to be interested in some affairs of Parker's.

An agreeable inhabitant of Custer, Mr Wheeler, most courteously set aside his business to offer us his services in showing us about the country where he has been living a long time.

Mr Wheeler is one of the founders of Custer. He was one of the expelled already mentioned, and after this expulsion joined some free bands that waged war for many years against the Indians, to whom, by-the-bye, he candidly does justice. This man, who is still young, entertained us throughout on our way with his adventures, which are very interesting.

We arrive, chatting all the time, at the mine, which is only two or three miles from Custer. The mica is found in the form of slabs, some thicker and some broader than others, embedded in the schistose rocks, kinds of coarse granite, being distributed therein very irregularly, as is usual with accidental minerals, such as talc, chlorite, &c., in crystalline rocks.

The work is not systematic; they dig into the rock anywhere, leaving chance to decide its utility or not. Whenever they see a little mica cropping out at the surface, they bore a hole, and, charging it with dynamite, blow out a block, and by this primitive process of mining they manage to get very handsome profits, which, perhaps, after all is the main point. Mr Dempsey, a lean, plain, little man, whose black eyes and tawny skin reveal his origin, works himself with three or four labourers. When the blocks come to the top of the pit, they are immediately fashioned into shape by two workmen; the first, with a knife, cleaves the slabs into a uniform thickness, which is about equal to that of a stout sheet of letter paper, and another cuts them into squares to give them a regular form. Leaves of the largest size are about ten or twelve inches by five, and are sold for ten dollars per pound, but the smaller fetch considerably less. The refuse, which will be very valuable when the railway is made, and which, naturally, is very abundant, is not sent away at present, for it would not bear the cost of transport, which is, of course, exceedingly heavy. From here to Chicago the carriage is, by express, twelve sous the pound, and by *freight*, that is to say, by bullock waggon, to the nearest station, which is Sydney, five or six sous.

On returning, Mr Wheeler made us gallop across the three or four fine valleys which meet at Custer. They are all fenced in, for the grass, which is fine and admirably adapted for the pasture of sheep, already gives some value of importance to this land.

We again find at table the whole tribe of judges and counsel whom we met at Rapid City. On seeing the flourishing aspect of these gentlemen, who are about fifteen or twenty in number, I thought to myself that the basocians decidedly thrive in America, and I wondered whether the best part of the earnings realized by the ragged miners and cow-boys, constituting the rest of the guests, did not pass into the pockets of these gentry of the long robe, as well as those of the barkeepers.

After dinner we go to see the proprietor of the livery stable where we have put up our horses. He is an elderly Englishman called Kemish, who produces a most favourable impression on us at first sight. We have retained such a disagreeable souvenir of our journey in a mail coach that we wished to ascertain if there were not some means of hiring a vehicle to conduct us to Sydney, the nearest station of the Union Pacific. It is a journey of about 250 miles to make across the prairie. To my great astonishment, Kemish accepted the proposal directly. This man, evidently in comfortable circumstances and married, finds it quite natural to quit his business and his home for a fortnight at least, to undertake a journey that may be accompanied with some danger, certainly with some hardship, and clearly more for the love of adventure than profit, for he asks us no more than eighty dollars. In France, a driver would demand considerably more for such a job. Parker has found here two neighbours from Cassade, who are going home : he will go with them, taking away our horses : we shall see him again to-morrow evening.

Having made our arrangements so far, we pass the rest of the day in going to the shops in order to buy provisions, for we desire to avoid by all means such poor cheer as we had on coming. We are informed that there is plenty of game along the route ; they have killed there even these last few days a few buffaloes. The prospect of so many barons of beef, with which they will furnish us, does not render it superfluous to provide ourselves with something already "run down," and we accordingly purchase a few cans of corned-beef and some French preserved vegetables, having luckily spied out these in a corner of some store.

A friend of Mr Wheeler's, a Mr A——, takes us into a pretty house, which he has just built, in order to show us a splendid collection of minerals gathered in the Black Hills, and especially in the Yellowstone. This wonderful region, which was discovered only a few years ago, presents mineralogical phenomena so extraordinary, and sites so curious, that the American congress passed a law declaring it a national park and prohibiting colonization therein. It is a little district, lying in the heart of the Rocky Mountains, assuming the form nearly of a square, with sides sixty miles in length. In the centre of this is a lake, twenty-two miles long by fifteen wide, surrounded with mountains covered constantly with snow.

But it is the phenomena of a volcanic character produced there that render this country so particularly remarkable. The water of many of the rivers traversing the district is actually boiling, and these rivers are derived from sources similar to the geysers of Iceland. One of these jets of water is fifteen feet in diameter, and one hundred and fifty feet in height. Rivulets of glacial water are often running at a few yards from others where the temperature is nearly 212° Fahrenheit. An amusing trapper has related to us that, one day having hooked a fine trout, he turned merely on his heel, and, without taking it off the bait, plunged it into a stream of hot water, from which he drew it in a few moments cooked to a turn. The story, perhaps, is not true, but then there is nothing at all impossible in it.*

* There is nothing improbable in this, the temperature being 100° *centigrade.* Many greater feats have been accomplished at the Strokkr,

Mr A—— is one of the fourteen men who remained in the fort. If the thirteen others resembled him, I can well understand why the Indians refrained from attacking them; for this little man, thick-set and broad-backed, with a cool look but ardent eyes, seemed to me one by no means disposed to yield his greyish crispy crop of hair on the scalp of his head readily. He is at present in the enjoyment of a nice fortune, which is daily accumulating, also from the revenues of three or four mines discovered by himself, in which he retains a share. He might live luxuriously anywhere, but he has always lived in the Far West, and cannot make up his mind to quit it.

At all events, he will make a journey to Paris in order to visit an enchanting spot, of which so many

in Iceland; the temperature there, however, appears to be as much as 109° *centigrade.* M. Leclercq, in his "Terre de Glace," mentions having met two Irishmen at the Strokkr, who determined to cook their dinner there as Commodore Forbes had done in the first place in 1859.

"They began by piling up, at the brink of the orifice, the usual number of clods of turf; then one of them took out of his trunk a flannel shirt, enwrapped in the body of the shirt a quarter of mutton, and in each sleeve a plover. The Strokkr swallowed its ordinary dose of turf, one clod after another, and then the extraordinary supplement. At the end of half an hour, just as we were speculating with anxiety whether the glutton was not actually dining instead of us, we saw the shirt hurled high in the air with the clods of turf: it fell on the brink of the well; but the moment had not yet arrived to taste the mutton, for so long as the eruption lasted it was impossible to approach the spot where the geyser had thrown it; it was necessary to take advantage of an interval between two explosions to regain possession of the shirt and its contents. The mutton, cooked as in England, furnished us with an excellent substantial dish; as for the birds, there was nothing left but the skin and bones; all colour had fled from the shirt, but the fabric remained uninjured."—W. C.

travellers have spoken to him with rapture—the *Jardin Mabille!* A word that involuntarily escapes us, reveals to him that houses five stories high are now rising on these grounds where Pomaré reigned. He supports the blow without a word; but a nervous trembling of his lips, an abrupt movement given to the rising puffs of smoke, and the dreamy fixed look of his eye into space, unveil the depth of his disappointment. The demolition of the Mabille has evidently produced an impression that the destruction of the Tuileries and the Hotel de Ville by the Communards would be quite incapable of doing.

Before going to bed I wish to pass an evening with the respectable company of whittlers, who last evening initiated me into their amusement. They are there before the hotel eagerly pursuing their work: the bench no longer exists, but it will be replaced to-morrow. The hotel proprietor tells me that it has never lasted more than three or four days; but he should try one of ebony, I will be bound to say it would last a whole month. This evening "Nature's noblemen" are talking together with animation. I hear constantly "I guess" and "You bet," and when this repetition invariably passes through the nose instead of the lips, one may fancy how disagreeable it is to the ear of a European.

One reads aloud out of a newspaper some adventure that has occurred in the neighbourhood. It appears that two men presented themselves, a few days ago, in a bank of a small town, the name of which I could not distinguish, requesting the cashier to change for them a cheque. While this one was opening his cash drawer for the gold, one of the men shot him in the back with his revolver, and killed him on the spot: then the murderer, aided by his comrade, opens the drawers and takes all the gold and bank-notes they find therein. Having accomplished all this in a few moments, they remount their horses standing at the door, and instantly disappear at a gallop.

This affair took place, of course, in open day. There was a great commotion among the "citizens," a certain number of whom mount on horseback in their turn, pursue the criminals, rousing to action all they meet on the way. In short, the following morning about six hundred men surround a little wood in which the murderers had taken refuge, and near it their horses were found worn out with fatigue.

They form a cordon of armed men all around the wood, and then they penetrate therein. Almost immediately they hear five or six reports: one of the murderers has killed three men with three shots from his revolver, and then has killed himself; the other throws up his pistol in the air without firing and cries out that he surrenders himself.

And here the story becomes very curious. Hardly had this man, named Ryan, I believe, been arrested, than they put a rope around his neck and lead him on to a bridge in the neighbourhood. They make fast one end of the rope to the post and prepare to launch him into eternity; but then, just at this moment, the Sheriff intervenes: he makes a speech to the crowd, in which he appeals to their better sentiments, reminds them of his services, observes how hard it will be for him after a pursuit so cleverly conducted to be deprived of his fees to which he is so justly entitled; first for the capture, and next for the hanging.

"But he won't be hanged at all if we let him go," cries a voice.

The Sheriff looks indignant.

"What! He won't be hanged! But everyone well knows that the jury of the good City of N—— convicts with a vengeance! Haven't they hanged Pat Rafferty? haven't they hanged Mick Murphy too?"

The crowd are evidently embarrassed; they do not wish to disappoint their good Sheriff, still, they have no confidence. At this moment Ryan asks leave to speak, and as he is so obviously interested in the question, they readily accord him this favour.

After a few words devoted to explaining that he is less guilty than they seem to think, he would not, he remarked, have the bad taste to insist on this vital point at the present moment, but he would venture to mention that he has had nothing to eat since yesterday, that he is now very hungry, and that as the discussion threatens to be rather long, he should be very glad to have something to eat.

A few men mount their horses immediately, ride off, and quickly return with some bread and cheese, which they find in a house not far away. They then loosen the rope a little around the neck of the prisoner, who is sitting on the bridge with his legs dangling over the stream, and now begins eating with a good appetite.

During this time, the good Sheriff resumes his argument, and finally proposes to decide the question by vote.

" Let all those who are for my conducting away the prisoner raise their hand."

Then they proceeded to take the votes of those who are for hanging then and there. The first count is declared doubtful ; they proceed to a second voting, and the result is equally doubtful. All this occupies some time, and the crowd in the end has sensibly diminished. Then a very sagacious idea comes into the Sheriff's head.

"You are all on the right bank!" he cries. "Well and good! Now, all those who are for an immediate hanging, cross the river!"

A loud burst of ironic laughter greets this proposal. The sight of Ryan calmly breakfasting, reminds many that they also are hungry, and others desire by all means to reach home before night-fall, fearing otherwise a scene with their wives. In short, about a score only of the most determined can make up their minds to wet their feet in order to gratify their desire to see Ryan hanged. But this time the proof of the popular will is conclusive. The Sheriff accordingly requests a few friends to come effectively to his aid, and, in the end, carries off his prisoner amid the cheering of the majority.

But the story does not end here. The poor Sheriff after all was destined to be deprived of his emoluments so well earned. About four days afterwards, the gaoler of the prison where Ryan is confined hears a loud knocking at the door about eleven at night. He opens the door, and a score of men with their faces blackened with charcoal rush in. He who appears to be the leader of these, says:

"The other day the Sheriff made game of us! We are going now to hang Ryan ourselves, and no mistake about it; hand him over to us."

The gaoler makes a show of resistance for the sake of form, and then suffers the criminal to be taken away, who is hurried on towards a great tree, and there hung in workmanlike manner. They then, by way of a supplementary precaution, send two or three rifle balls through his body, waking up the inhabitants, and, having finished their work, the band disperses.

This narrative highly delights the audience, who often interrupt with exclamations flattering to the inhabitants of N——, such as, "Very smart," "Know their business," &c. Then the conversation continuing, it leads on to a lynching that took place here some time ago. They had hanged three men at a great fir-tree which they point out to me. Afterwards they found out that one at least was quite innocent. "But then, no one knew it," they added; "he had no friend!"

"In this country," I said, "it is a good thing to have friends."

"You bet it is," says one.

"Well," says another, "I guess a friend is a good thing in this country, but a good pair of big revolvers is a deuced better one." It is my instructor in the art of whittling who pronounces these words, putting his bowie-knife into its sheath, as he throws away the remnant of the block which he has worked down to a mere chip. Everyone is applauding, and I go to bed meditating over this apophthegm: a big revolver and self-reliance! in other words: "Put your trust in God, but keep your powder dry." And then others say, "Might makes right." Will not these two maxims, which are really one and the same, be the final argument of our sociology? "There will always be a government of force," says Emerson, "where men are selfish." The fact is, when we have no longer any power, there will not be wanting others ready to show that we never were in the right.

CHAPTER VIII.

DEPARTURE FROM CUSTER — MR AND MRS KEMISH — "WAR-HORSE" AND "RED-CLOUD"—A SHEEP RANCH—ACCIDENTS—THE HOT SPRINGS—AN INDIAN PRINCESS—THE ART OF SCALPING—CASCADE—HOW A VILLAGE IS FOUNDED.

July the 12th.—This morning we quitted our hard beds and the house successively, which will soon emerge from its envelope of brick, like a snail from its shell, with the consolation that we have given trouble to nobody. For in America hotel servants do not over-load with attentions a parting guest, with the hope of a gratuity, as they do elsewhere, unless having been much neglected previously. A sudden blast of wind of extraordinary violence, but which lasts only a few minutes, has alone undertaken to call us betime, and when we, at length, arrive at the livery stable, we find the horses already put in our vehicle. We examine our equipage, and the result of this inspection is highly satisfactory. It is a kind of pleasure van suspended on springs. Our luggage and provisions are stowed away in the bottom, leaving sufficient room for our legs and our guns. The horses are two brave little animals, about 14½ hands high, having the appearance of half-blood Normans, and as if they were quite capable of undertaking full of spirit the formidable trot in store for them. Mrs Kemish is already up, and is surveying the preparations for departure. She is an elderly Englishwoman, with a clear, fresh complexion, having the look of a respectable housekeeper of a good house. I ask her why she has left England, and she gives me, without hesitation, a reply that seems to be without rhyme or reason—

"Because they make too much of the nobility there!"

As the moment is not propitious for discussions, I abstain from asking this worthy matron for an explanation. Monsieur Bouverie and I take our seat facing the horses, while Kemish installs himself on an enormous sack of oats, and we part at a smart trot.

The route glittering with the slanting beams of the rising sun is really lovely; we turn our backs to the prairie in following the valley we took yesterday to the mica mine. The carriage rolls along softly over a fine elastic grass. It seems as if we are in a fine old English park. The tall pine trees distributed singly along the valley, and the hills right and left clad with verdant woods, complete the illusion. We startle a fine buck in the wood before us. He stops a moment, then we see him running at full speed, leaping a brook in his way, and at last, before we have time to send a ball after him, disappears in the thickets on the other side. Monsieur Bouverie, as usual, is quite in a rapture with the prospect of sport so soon as anything comes within view, and now he hopes we shall at last have a chance.

A dark cloud, however, begins looming in our horizon. We are not yet four miles from Custer when, immediately after a sharp jolt, I hear a low grating metallic sound that seems to me of bad augury, and all the more so because I notice that the vehicle careens much on that side. I call Kemish's attention to it, who ascertains that the main plate of one of our springs is just broken. It is decided, however, not to stop for such a trifle. A stout piece of fir placed between the two branches of the spring, keeps it together, but deprives us of the elasticity, and we continue our way.

We certainly have not yet finished with the accidents we are doomed to encounter. A quarter of an hour afterwards comes a fresh hindrance. One of the irons that holds the pole to the body of the carriage breaks clean off. Kemish replaces it by a *woolding* with cord, the make of which leads me to suspect he has been an old seaman. He informs me indeed, that he has commanded a coaster in the Channel, which he used to load with potatoes from Saint Brienne. But while he is relating to me his maritime adventures, the second iron breaks in its turn. This time, for the honour of the French navy, I make it a point of operating myself, and I execute a Portuguese bind, which earns for me the esteem of honest Kemish, and we then start again. I begin, however, to get rather uneasy, and the optimist Monsieur Bouverie thinks the accidents come very often.

But as two or three hours pass away without any fresh casualty, we feel reassured. Besides, we are so well installed that it would ill become us to complain. Kemish has provided two buffalo hides, upon which we take our ease. These "buffalo-robes," as they are called here, are, it seems, the trophies he has brought away in his combats against the Indians. They are dressed by their wives, who make the most of the thick curly hair. The inside is ornamented with designs, representing the exploits of the warrior for whom the skin is destined. The one Kemish has taken must have been from a very terrible man. He is depicted riding a great blue horse, brandishing a long spear, from which are hanging a dozen bleeding scalps, the old proprietors of which, represented by little baboons dressed like the "pale faces," are ranged in a row before him.

While crossing a little plain, Kemish relates to us a terrible scene that was witnessed on this spot. It was the year of the great war, in the month of August. The Indians of Sitting Bull's tribe had already retired in the direction of the north, and it was thought there were no more in this neighbourhood. Four men one day came here from Custer in order to cut hay. The next day a fifth was to come for them with a waggon. When the latter arrived, he perceived three dead bodies lying on the ground. Without setting his foot on the soil, he turned the bridle and returned at a gallop to Custer to obtain reinforcement. About a score of men, among whom was Kemish, hurried to the spot. They came to the conclusion that the Indians, whose camp they find in the neighbourhood, must have seen the men coming without suspicion of danger. They had apparently hid themselves, and the moment their victims set to work they fired on them. Three were killed at the first discharge; the fourth was able to run away some distance, but was soon caught, and struck with a blow from the stock of the rifle so violently that, though a government arm, it was broken. One detail would be very droll, if the subject were not so horrible. The Indians had, of course, scalped all the unfortunate victims. But then, instead of taking off, according to the rules, a fine scalp from the crown of the head, which would have furnished them with four trophies only, they had artistically carved out from each head seven or eight round patches of hairy skin, in order to make more of them for themselves. Where next will this propensity for counterfeiting be found lurking? And Rousseau, forsooth, believed in the honesty of savages!

The details of this tragedy came later. There was then, further south, a chief called "Red Cloud." He had not only refused to join Sitting Bull at the beginning of hostilities, but had hindered a certain number of his men from going to him, and had come with these to encamp under the protection of the troops of Fort Robinson. When the first successes of Sitting Bull were heard of, great enthusiasm was manifested among these men, and a subordinate chief, named "War Horse," put himself at the head of twenty-three warriors, two of whom were his sons. He quitted secretly the neighbourhood of the fort, calculating on traversing the Black Hills without attracting attention, and then on joining, in the North, the Sioux army. They were at the second or third stage when they unexpectedly fell in with Custer's haymakers. War Horse could not resist the desire to reap the scalps presented to him so very temptingly; but after the deed, foreseeing that the passage of the Black Hills would become dangerous, he decided on renouncing the project and on returning to the fort. His sons and the majority of their companions continued their route. Several reappeared subsequently in the country.

War Horse returning to the cantonment after so short an absence, was able to explain it by a plausible pretext. When, however, they heard of the massacre, from Custer, the suspicions of the commander fell immediately on him. They sent a sergeant of the Indian police to arrest him. When the latter presented himself at the door of the wigwam, War Horse was squatting near the fire, smoking; on seeing him he got up, cleft the skin of the tent with a single stroke of his knife with the rapidity of lightning, and bounded beyond. But, at the same moment, the sergeant sent a ball through his back, and he fell dead on the spot.

We arrive at a sheep ranch, the owner of which is a friend of Kemish. Three years ago, this man, having gained five hundred dollars by working in the mines, prudently employed the money in buying sheep instead of prospecting. He has already three thousand of these animals, and every year his flocks increase enormously, for here where there is no market for meat they never kill any. The entire profit proceeds from the wool, of which each sheep yields about five or six pounds, and this sells for about tenpence per pound. This speculation is quite as profitable as that in bullocks, and requires considerably less capital and fewer employes. But then it is more uncertain, because the sheep are much more liable than bullocks to very destructive maladies.

The country we are now traversing is not so attractive. Vegetation is here sparse and stunted. We are now following the course of a little river, whose waters, singularly transparent, are irradiated in the sun-beams with opaline tints. It is very highly ferruginous. We are to stop at several mineral springs, the *Hot Springs*, which were already known, it is said, in the time of the Indians, and highly esteemed for the cure of rheumatic affections, the plague of this country. A company is now in course of formation for the acquisition of the establishment already installed there, and to give to it a great development.

It is already one o'clock, and our horses continue their course with a spirit quite refreshing to behold. Kemish declares that we are on the point of arriving. But the series of accidents is not yet exhausted. On passing the river the hind wheels sink deep into the sand, but the horses, already come to the opposite bank, throw themselves vigorously into the collar. Consequently, they go on with the fore part of the carriage and Kemish, who, another Hippolytus, has his hands entangled in the reins and is drawn on for some paces. As for ourselves, we are thrown forwards head over heels among all the objects that filled the bottom of the carriage.

A heap of valises, cans of preserved meat, rifles and buffalo-robes, have fallen on my body. While I am making strenuous efforts to wriggle out of this obstruction, and am feeling my limbs to ascertain that none of them are broken, I perceive Monsieur Bouverie, who, luckier than I, has been pitched, without much damage, on the top of a big rock in the middle of the stream. There he is contemplating the disaster with the imperturbability of Simon Stylites perched on his pillar in the wilderness.

"Well," he says, perceiving me in the midst of the *débris* of our baggage, "we have in this a sample of the hard lot to come."

"The hard lot, indeed! You are chaffing."

"But I mean what I say; and, since the accident was to happen, is it not very lucky that it should happen just here when we are quite near some houses? If this had taken place in the middle of the prairie, two or three days hence, we should have been in a nice pickle."

"That is perfectly true, but I had not regarded that contingency," I said, "but would you be so obliging as to raise the carriage a little, that I may have the gratification of withdrawing my leg that is jammed in under it."

"Oh! I beg your pardon."

And leaping from his islet into the stream, the most consoling and buoyant of travelling companions helps me out of my painful predicament.

During this time, Kemish had succeeded in securing his horses. His coolness did not abandon him an instant, and he seems to take like a philosopher his part of the disaster to his vehicle. Fortunately, his occupation has created for him acquaintances and friends everywhere. He remembers that at the Hot Springs there is a man who has a waggon, which, perhaps, would exactly suit us. It is agreed that while we are breakfasting he is to see about the business.

We sit down comfortably at the foot of a willow; then, after having taken a refreshing bath in the sandy water of the rivulet, we begin a breakfast, unquestionably a much better one than what we had at the hotel of Custer, and for this we are indebted to a can of good corned beef, and another of sardines of Douarnenez, which, familiar enough in France, we little thought of enjoying in Dakota.

As the heat is now very great, we stretch ourselves on the buffalo skins, and indulge in a little repose, a light dozing meditation, in which we seem to be floating between two worlds, belonging wholly to neither, and we indulge in this delightful state for an hour or two, when a rattle, like that of old iron, fully wakes us up to the prose of every-day life. It is Kemish, who comes up with the famous waggon. If this one breaks down we shall be unfortunate indeed. We load it at once with all our *impedimenta*, and start afresh.

In half an hour afterwards we at last arrive at Hot Springs. We take out our horses under the shade of a great tree, after having passed without stopping before "the establishment," which consists of a kind of chalet, of tolerably-good appearance. The sources are in the bottom of a little valley on the right. There are three of them, slightly sulphurous, and of a temperature which should be about 85° Fahr., but which we cannot determine exactly, having broken our thermometer in our recent disaster.

Beside the source is the veritable establishment, for the one we have mentioned is but a rival set up last year. This one is of quite primitive simplicity. A log-house is divided into three compartments: the first serves as a kitchen, the second as a sleeping-room for the gentlemen, and the third is set apart for the ladies. Three or four unhappy creatures, suffering from the ills that flesh is heir to in the form of rheumatism, are hobbling over the rocks around. Another, crippled in every joint, is being carried to the baths by one of his companions, who is not so hopelessly paralyzed. A little further, on a winding pathway, we see a woman approaching. She is a poor, little old lady, with blue spectacles, and is leading a horse at the end of a tether, which she desires to fasten to a stake beside ours. A French or an English lady would, in such circumstances, be attired in a manner becoming the situation, but this one is encumbered with a *robe à traîne!* We at once offer our services, and she half opens her mouth, which is quite unnecessary, for it is solely through the nose that she expresses her thanks, accompanied with an amiable look. She explains to us that she has come from Deadwood, with seven or eight other ladies, to take the waters. They encamp under a tent, which she points out to us at the top of the valley. Their husbands, after having seen them comfortably installed, have returned to their affairs, and now they are here all alone, doing their cooking and grooming their horses. I ask her if she is not afraid of replacing the rheumatism, which the waters are to remove, by other maladies which she can hardly fail to catch through camping a whole month in a damp valley. The idea of such a contingency does not appear to have entered her head: she smiles affably, wishes us adieu, and goes her way. It would be interesting to see the "rubbing down," particularly if the grooming is performed in the *robe à traîne.*

It is decided that to-day we obey a summons and go into society. Kemish, who went sauntering about the neighbourhood of the chalet, comes to tell us that a lady, who is staying there, having heard that we were friends of Mr Parker, whose movements and doings have been for some time past recorded in the newspapers, invites us to come and see her. We immediately make ourselves as presentable as possible, which consists in buttoning up our short coats instead of having them open, and hurry off to pay our respects to this amiable lady, who, it appears, is called Buttler and lives at Deadwood, where her husband is in business.

We find her in a room furnished with more simplicity than a wigwam. She points out to us two logs of fir, and on these we take our seats. Then she begins relating her adventures.

A German, a *soi-disant* doctor, who built this chalet and lodged his patients here, has just assigned it to the company now forming for turning the waters to account. He had not mentioned a word about the transaction, when, three days ago, Mrs Buttler, who was the sole remaining guest, saw some waggons arrive, and presently preparations made for removing the furniture. The doctor then explained to her the situation, and quickly left, leaving her absolutely alone in the house without any furniture.

"Luckily," adds the poor woman, "a gentleman, who happened to pass this way, remains with me till my husband arrives. I suffer so much that I can hardly walk."

In a corner of the kitchen we perceive the *gentleman*, who, armed with a formidable bowie knife, is peeling potatoes. He is a cow-boy of sinister look, decorated with two revolvers. Methinks, if I were to meet him in the dusk at the corner of a wood, I should fire on him at once by way of precaution to make sure. As for Mrs Buttler, she is delighted with this godsend. But then she seems to be quite inured to adventures, for she tells us that the party she came with to the Black Hills had been obliged to fight on the way. One *lady* who was among the number, whom she has long known, for she was her washerwoman at Yankton, had been scalped; but the operation, it seems, was performed by a skilful hand, for the poor woman has recovered from it; she is obliged, however, to wear a wig and has headache very often, a result by no means extraordinary.

It appears, however, there are not a few instances of people having survived the operation. In order to accomplish it, the Indians at first make a circular incision in the skin around the top of the head, then, grasping the hair, they tear off skin and hair together. Kemish, whom I suspect to have practised himself, though he affirms that he has been merely a witness, assures me that it comes off quite easily. On this point, however, the scalper and the victim would naturally not be of the same opinion.

We take leave of Mrs Buttler, assuring her that we deeply feel for her in her unfortunate position, and we prepare to proceed on our way.

The southern side of the Black Hills presents a certain peculiarity. When, in the geological era of the past, the strata were erupted and thrown up, it seems that the waters, descending from the central watershed, encountered lower down an encircling plateau, through which they made narrow breaches, though few and distant from one another. It is by one of these breaches, where all the valleys of the neighbourhood commence diverging towards the plains, that we leave the high land to descend through one of them into the region of the prairies.

From the summit of a plateau where we soon arrive, we clearly distinguish this singular configuration. On the other side of a little plain, spread out below our feet, we see a mountain whose concavity gives to the spot the appearance of an antique amphitheatre of colossal proportion. We are now passing out of this by a simple ravine, through which we already have a glimpse of the prairie, glowing with the rosy oblique rays of the setting sun.

On descending from this plateau by a fearful road, our attention is arrested by a strange spectacle. A group of large trees overhang a rock, from which a spring issues, watering a little meadow. Built against this rock stands a hut, at the door of which is leaning a tall woman of tawny complexion. Her hair, as black as jet and interlaced in two large plaits, falls on each side of her face. She is clad in a sort of skirt of red stuff, very short, showing her legs of fine outline, her feet being covered with embroidered mocassins. Beside her is a tame antelope. Kemish tells us that she is an

Indian princess, and lives there with her husband, who is of a mixed race. It appears that she is strongly suspected of witchcraft by the Red Skins, who come sometimes from a great distance, and in great numbers, in order to consult her.

It is dark night when we arrive at the breach in question. We have much trouble to get through it, for, being so narrow, the river occupies nearly the whole width. But, having once got over this difficult part, we find the solid even ground of the prairie, and our brave horses set off at a trot as if the thirty-three miles which they have already done since the morning were to count for nothing. Happily, Parker, who has arrived already some hours by a shorter way, comes out to meet us: we then cross the river and find ourselves at the door of his house, where I am now writing these lines while waiting for dinner.

July the 13*th.*—I remember having passed some very bad nights in my life, but few have left more disagreeable remembrances than my first night at Cascade. There is still only one house there provided with a roof, and this is a little log-house, about five yards long, in which eight of us were packed, lying on a kind of wooden camp-bed, in a suffocating atmosphere insufferably hot. To add to the misery of our habitation, a swarm of mosquitoes began buzzing in the middle of the night around our ears. Some one then proposed to set up a *smudge.* As I did not exactly know what a *smudge* was, I allowed them to proceed without saying a word. It turned out to be a heap of half-burnt charcoal, which they put in the recess of a window or a door on the side the wind blows. When the mosquitoes begin to find out they can no longer breathe, they prudently take their departure. Unfortunately, when this moment arrives, and even a little sooner, the room is filled with smoke to that degree that every one is seized with coughing, accompanied with a running of water from the eyes, and is eventually driven to follow the example of the mosquitoes and go outside likewise. I have seen this method employed in Madagascar and on the coast of Africa, but with no satisfactory result.

Nights like these have the decided advantage of making one an early riser, and we avail ourselves of our supplementary hours to indulge, at day-break, in a bath, in the cool stream of the river running at our feet. There is a truly enchanting cascade here, which gives its name to the place. We find now that the water, which is strongly mineralised, has a temperature of 85° F. Notwithstanding its high temperature and its nauseous taste, it is highly appreciated by bullocks and horses. It seems to be equally so by leeches, though these animals, much to my annoyance, are determined to make the first advances with the view of securing an intimate footing with new comers, two of them going so far even as to cling to my legs.

Parker is so anxious to show us his property that he gives us hardly time to dress ourselves. We mount our horses and he leads us up along the river—which, we are informed, is called the Hot-Brook—as far as the point where it flows into the plain by the breach of the Belt mountain. We admire on our way the extraordinary fertility of the soil. The muddy banks of the rivulet are covered with a kind of herbage that attracts our attention. They are actual fields of hemp growing spontaneously. So soon as the ground is turned up, it begins to get covered with yellow sun-flowers, with a black eye, the seeds of which attract a multitude of birds of all sorts—prairie hens, turtle-doves, and thrushes. A few acres have been planted in the spring with wheat, and the close-set, crowded ears will soon be ripe.

Mounted as we are on the top of a little eminence, we have a commanding view of the features of the country around. We find ourselves in the centre of a plain, almost circular, of about six thousand acres, formed in a bend of the Cheyenne, which leaves the Belt mountain at about five or six miles on our right, to join it again at about the same distance on our left. The herds pasturing on this plain are therefore in a natural enclosure, barred in on the south by the river, whose steep shores on this side permit nowhere an approach to the water, and on the north by the abrupt slopes of the Belt. Their only watering-place is the Hot-Brook, which, running along the base of the mountain, empties itself into the Cheyenne, with its left bank running along a little plateau that inclines gently towards the river, forming there the only ford that exists within many leagues around.

Parker came to this spot last year, in order to look out for a prairie, where, in the spring, he might establish a cattle ranch; the natural fitness of the locality at once struck him forcibly. The plain, opening towards the south and west, remaining warm even during the coldest months of winter; snow never stands there; the animals, shut in this natural enclosure, have not, as it were, any need of surveillance. And then the impossibility of their going to drink anywhere, except along the Hot-Brook, determines that it is sufficient to acquire the two banks of this little river to become the virtual possessor of the whole plain.

Having well ascertained these facts, he associated himself with two or three friends; for, in this country, it is neither profitable nor prudent to undertake a large speculation all alone. Then they began to carry out their plan. A band of land a few yards wide, on each bank of the rivulet, was bought of the Government, as well as the little plot commanding the ford, for it had been decided that at this spot they should found a city. Advances were made to a company to enable them to establish a daily line of coaches from Sydney to Deadwood, passing by here. They obtained from the Government a post-office. All these arrangements are to come into operation in the course of a few days. The company is building a great warehouse, in which will be established a store, and then an hotel will also be opened in a few weeks.

But Parker did not stop here with all these brilliant

prospects. Having made a rapid sketch of the spot, he set off for Chicago, and presented himself at the offices of the Great Railway Company, these having the concession of the lines that are to unite the Black Hills with the existing ones. He has actually gone so far as to prove to them—and his conclusions are fully borne out by the facts—that, instead of going from Sydney to Deadwood, continuing all the time in the prairie, they would have every advantage in taking their line across the Cheyenne at this very spot, in order to penetrate into the mountains by way of the breach, where we now are, inasmuch as, here immediately begins a long valley, which they can follow, without any special engineering work, as far as the centre of the mountain range. The engineers are at length convinced of this, and the line will be made to this spot in eighteen months.

Parker gives us all these details while he is making us galop over the plain in every direction, for, to please him, we must see everything. The Americans in speculating have a kind of blind, habitual enthusiasm which becomes contagious, and, in the long run, one no longer has a very clear conscience with regard to what is actually a fact, or what is merely in the inchoate stage of a project. I recall to memory the gentleman in the journey from Chicago to Pierre, who proposed to me that I should buy a street in a city that had no existence whatever. Parker, with the most sanguine assurance, shows to us a plain covered with grass, saying, " Here will be the station ; here will be the hotel ; there a bank, and yonder a church!" till we at last see all these things very distinctly, and come to consider the vendor of streets—that seemed very like castles in the air—as quite a rational man of business.

If the country, reserved for so high a destiny, is of exceptional fertility, it is, on the other hand, not a fine country. The heat is unbearable; the average temperature must be very high, for we see that the vegetation is quite different from what we have hitherto met with on our way. We see plants that are only ordinarily found in tropical lands. At the base of the rocks masses of dwarf cactus display their fine red flowers and prickly leaves. I fancy that this exceptional temperature is due partly to the aspect and partly to the vicinity of the hot-water river.

This water has medicinal properties so pronounced and disagreeable, that in order the new inhabitants may not thereby be frightened away, Parker has had brought here, from several miles distance, a copious stream of ordinary water, trying at the same to make everybody believe that its habitual use is attended with no inconvenience. He shows me, with some pride, eight or ten tents that are being set up on the little hill facing us. They are the tents of some emigrants who are come to examine the land, and who now announce that they shall return in a few weeks with their families.

Just as I am writing these lines, the indefatigable Monsieur Bouverie is gone to photograph a little lake, rather curious, it seems, which is on the mountain. I remain behind, because, this morning, as I was leading my horse by the bridle to make him pass a difficult path, he fell on me with all his weight, and squeezed my chest so tightly against a tree that I could hardly breathe. I am still suffering in my respiration, and must therefore nurse myself a little, for it is decided with Kemish that we begin this evening our return journey across the prairie. We shall have, I fear, a rough time of it. They say it is a course of forty-eight, or fifty miles to reach one of the stations of the line of stage-coaches, and after having passed the Cheyenne, there is not a drop of potable water to be had. We enter into what is called the "Alkali Desert," where the soil is so strongly impregnated with saline matter that the water is unfit for drinking; horses, cattle, and game, however, take it freely, whether they like it or not.

Parker's two partners, Mr Quigley and Mr Melville, have most courteously remained in the house to keep me company. We have just had an exciting moment. Mr Quigley cried out that he had seen the skin of a serpent glistening between our portmanteaux heaped up in the corner. We then set to work in removing them as cautiously as possible, and soon found one, and scotched it at once: it was about three or four feet long, but of a quite inoffensive kind. But there is a fearful quantity of rattle-snakes. Mr Melville killed a large one yesterday, and a horse was bitten in the lip five or six days ago; its head has swollen fearfully, though the animal is not dead. The danger of the bite is very much exaggerated generally.

On our way to Sydney we were told that a little girl of eight had been bitten yesterday afternoon at four o'clock. They forced down her throat two-thirds of a bottle of whisky, and the child is now unquestionably recovering from the alarming attack, and at this hour, no doubt, likewise from those effects of the remedy decidedly more widely known.

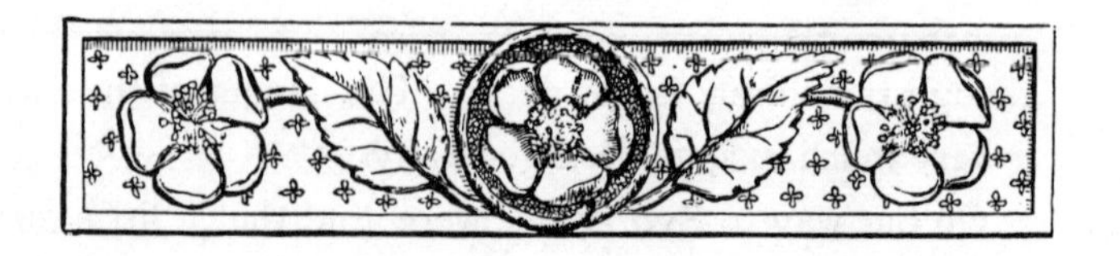

CHAPTER IX.

THE RETURN JOURNEY—THE ALKALI DESERT—THE INDIANS—THE PRAIRIE DOGS—THE ANTELOPES—A SAND STORM—WILLOW CREEK—THE RIVER PLATTE—JACK SLADE AND JULES BURGH—SYDNEY—THE UNION PACIFIC—OMAHA—CHICAGO.

Saturday, the 14th of July.—The day before yesterday, at four o'clock in the afternoon, we quitted Cascade and passed out of the great heat of the last few days. One of Parker's great merits is the tact he has in choosing his business colleagues. Captain Hughes has already left the most favourable impression on us, and, since we have been in the Black Hills, we have met very few people to be compared with Mr Quigley and Mr Melville. The former is an English Canadian, about thirty or thirty-five, whose business is with cattle. The latter is an American, and much younger. He evidently belongs to a good family, and has received a very good education. He has just been passing six or eight months all alone in that horrid log-house, which he has built with his own hands. It is this gentleman who has done the cooking for us. Where is the young Frenchman who would consent, for any amount of gold, to lead such an existence?* But how is it that a mode of education that gives results so admirable for the men, gives at the same time such deplorable ones for the women? This is a question I should indeed like to study if I remained much longer in America.

We separate from this worthy fellow Parker at last, and truly not without heaviness of heart. Monsieur Bouverie, who did not know him before coming here, is quite struck with this type of the puritan of old—one so straightforward, so profoundly religious, having always quotations from the Bible on his lips; a decided ascetic, and yet at the same time having his mind so freely open for the material things of the age. In France, where ardently religious men have generally a repugnance for business affairs, such a type could hardly be found.

These gentlemen saddle their horses to accompany us a little way on our road. We say good-bye for ever to Jean-Leblanc and the buff mare, and these good creatures are going to enjoy, in feeding on the grass of the future streets of Cascade, a repose that they have well earned; and for our part, we are now on our homeward journey.

The passage of the ford of the Cheyenne is performed without hindrance, the water being neither deep nor the current rapid. Here it is where the railway

* This admission by a Frenchman reveals the reason why his countrymen are not formed to become colonists; clearly they cannot readily accommodate themselves to new surroundings.—W. C.

bridge is to be. Parker shows us, a little way off, some coal measures cropping out, which we can distinguish very clearly on the flank of a hill, and these he contemplates working as soon as the construction of the railway begins. We next cross a marshy plain. All at once Monsieur Bouverie cries out that he sees a rattlesnake retreating in a tuft of grass. We surround the spot, and he turns out a rather big reptile, which is not a crotalus, though a very dangerous viper, it seems, known as the *spotted adder.*

On this side, the demarcation between the mountain and the prairie is much less distinct than in the north, or rather, some outlying hills of the mountain chain, detached and covered with a luxuriant vegetation, diversify the usual uniform character of the prairie it has elsewhere. We follow the wheel tracks, now half-effaced, left by the passage of some old convoy of emigrants. Mr Melville says that this will lead us to a station of the stage-coach line, called Big-Cotton-Wood, but as we are still something like over fifty miles from it, we intend to halt about eight or nine, and resume our route to-morrow.

At last, having arrived at the top of a terrible hill, which Kemish's horses carry triumphantly, we separate with a hearty shake of the hand from our three friends. We watch them a few moments as they gallop off in the direction of the Cheyenne, whose waters are glittering on the horizon, and we continue our route towards the south.

We are informed that buffaloes have been seen about here the last few days, and we are, therefore, on the alert. We have not the good luck to fall in with even one of them, but then, on the other hand, there is no end of game: its abundance is almost incredible. Whole coveys of prairie hens rise under the horses' legs; but as the young birds do not yet fly well, the cock and hen generally hop on to a clod of earth, and there, without any alarm at our presence, flap their wings and call their young together. With an eye to our dinner, which is a better excuse than the object of pigeon matches, we are barbarous enough to kill a few of these tame birds close to the muzzle of our revolvers and rifles. They resemble hen pheasants very much in plumage, though they are not so large. But then, quantities of them arrive in Paris now every winter. We are not fortunate in meeting with any wild turkeys, though they are said to be plentiful, but we see many great hares, that do not seem to be very wild, yet, for all that, we do not succeed in bagging any; this, however, is not so very astonishing, considering how difficult it is to hit a hare with a bullet. They call them here jack-rabbits. In winter they are quite white, and they have not yet wholly put on their summer fur.*

* These facts, familiar as they are now, were scarcely noticed till Darwin and Wallace cited and explained many instances of *protective colours* that conduced to the survival of the fittest in the struggle for existence. As the subject is so very interesting to others as well as naturalists, I venture to quote one of my notes on the subject from my edition, "Over Siberian Snows," of M. Meignan's travels, recently published.

About seven o'clock, a great wolf stops before us a moment, and then sets off at a gallop. Monsieur Bouverie jumps out of the vehicle, and runs some dis-

"'Many Siberian animals that are white during winter, resume, in the summer, furs of a colour which we habitually see here. The ermine is a changeable fur, and becomes yellow during the warm season. A summer ermine is almost worthless in the eyes of a connoisseur.'—*The Author.*

"These, no doubt, are instances of the *protective colours* observed by Darwin and Mr Wallace.

"'A common Indian and Sumatran butterfly (*Kallima*) disappears like magic when it settles in a bush; for it hides its head and antennæ between its closed wings, and these in form, *colour*, and veining, *cannot be distinguished from a withered leaf* together with the footstalk.'—*Wallace.*

"'With animals of all kinds, whenever colour has been modified *for some special purpose*, this has been, as far as we can judge, either *for protection* or as an attraction between the sexes.'—*Darwin*, *Descent of Man.*

"The white furs of the animals, liable to become the prey of others amid the snow, are obviously a protection from observation; and likewise in summer, some other colour presenting a diminished contrast with surrounding nature, would have the same effect.

"Perhaps this adaptation of colour to surroundings may extend also to certain animals, which would otherwise become extinct if they did not enjoy the facilities it conferred in the capture of their prey when they are placed at a great disadvantage. The Polar bear, for instance, requires no protection from its enemies, but favourable conditions, probably, for approaching its prey unobserved. It seems reasonable to conclude that animals of either class favoured with a colour that enables them either to escape from their pursuers, or, on the other hand, to approach their prey, have, in the struggle for life, the best chance of a prolonged existence, and consequently of leaving the most numerous offspring to perpetuate the race. Though colour is one of the most varying features of animals, it is, whether changing or permanent, beginning to be recognised no longer as capricious or accidental, as we have hitherto usually regarded it, but as the consequence of the survival of the most highly favoured in an endowment conducive to the preservation of the species, a discovery on which the continued observations of naturalists are ever throwing fresh light."—W. C.

tance to get a chance of bringing him down with a ball, but old Kemish, who was following the beast with his eye, suddenly cries out:

"For God's sake, call him back! Call him back directly! He must not fire for the world."

I hail Monsieur Bouverie, who returns in a rather bad humour.

"But what is the matter?" I ask Kemish.

"Why! Don't you see? Look in the direction of the wolf, where he went to fire, and you see some smoke and then three tents; they are Indians, and there are thirty of them at least. They have come out of their reserve, and certainly not for anything good."

"Bah! They are after the buffaloes that people are talking about."

"It may be so: still, if, on returning to the village, they bring back, besides the buffalo skins, a pair of horses and two or three scalps, they will be all the more welcomed. Now, it happens that, in a few weeks, the grand ceremony of the initiation of the warriors takes place. It is the time when they are most to be feared: let us get on our way as fast as possible."

"What is he saying?" asks my friend.

"Do you remember the story of Chactas and Atala related by Chateaubriand?"

"Certainly, and found it tiresome enough, too, formerly."

"And I also; but then, if Monsieur de Chateaubriand has not a little exaggerated, which, by-the-bye, is not at all unlikely, we are going to have some adventures quite similar to what he describes. Kemish maintains that the people under those three tents, which you see yonder, are going to pursue us. To-morrow morning, my dear sir, your fair curly locks will decorate the spear of a grand chief, unless some maid, like 'la Vierge des dernières amours,' allured by your personal advantages, release you from the stake of torture, and conduct you to her habitation, addressing you in a speech beginning thus: 'Oh! young, pale-faced stranger . . .' In such a case, you would become the son-in-law of some great chief, and you would ever rove the prairie with a sun tattooed on the pit of your stomach, and a moon on your back. And if, in the end, you should get tired of this sort of life, you would have, at all events, the resource of coming with your little family to show yourself in Paris, at the Jardin d'Acclimatation or the Folies-Bergère."

"Pshaw! do you suppose I should not try by all means, before arriving there, to lodge some of these cartridges in the venerable person of the said father-in-law?" says Monsieur Bouverie, showing me the reserve of ammunition in his Winchester.

We still keep on our way at a good speed. Kemish does not whip his horses, and never makes use of the long switch which replaces the whip in these barbarous regions; but his tongue is going on all the time as fast as the wheels, and it produces the best effect, for we are going at a rattling pace. Night is coming on and threatens to be very dark, and a little rain even is falling. I do not understand at all how Kemish manages to find his way. He has no compass, and not a star is visible. Besides, he declares to us that he has been this way only once before, and that was five years ago. These men certainly have some special instinct.

Twice we were obliged to cross shallow streams, so very muddy that the wheels, sunk in the ooze, could not be drawn out by the horses. We were then obliged to discharge the vehicle, carry the luggage on our backs, and put our shoulders to the wheels to get them out of the silt. At last, about two in the morning, it was not quite so dark, and we could then distinguish on our right a little hollow spot covered with a few pine trees. Kemish then told us he was going to stop here awhile to feed and rest the horses that had been running since four in the afternoon. His horses are really wonderful animals; they went on quietly feeding on their ration of three quarts of oats each, as if they had only just come off a run of five or six miles.

Kemish has not been, I think, very seriously frightened. Besides, if we were to have been attacked, it strikes me that the scalping would have been all over by this time. He tells me, however, that he is going to watch for fear of accidents. As for myself, I am going to follow the example of my friend, who is already snoring on our buffalo-robes.

I am waked in about half-an-hour by a frightful noise. A Breton of the country round Tréguier who heard such a hurly-burly about the cemetery of his parish, would swear that it was a chant of the condemned in purgatory, who had come up by a special favour to enjoy a cool night on earth. We hear at first some sharp, surly snarling, coming from five or six different points, followed by a silence, and then something like an outburst of deep sobbing. It is terrible. I have an idea that the Indians are on our heels, and I leap out of the vehicle with my rifle cocked; but Kemish, who is walking up and down, laughs at me satirically.

"Oh!" he says, "you don't know what that is. It is the coyotes.* Everything goes on well. They are the famous watch-dogs; don't be uneasy. When one hears them howling like that around one, it is certain there are no Indians in the neighbourhood."

"But are you not afraid they will take a fancy to our horses?"

"There is no fear of that; they are too cowardly; they attack nothing bigger than a rabbit or a prairie dog."

The night is so cold that I shiver in every limb. Seeing Kemish in a humour for talking, I walk up and down with him to get, at the same time, a little warmth by exercise. The good man relates to me, with a pride he glories in, all the tricks he formerly played on the coast-guard of the English shore when he commanded a

* The gray American wolf. It is precisely like the wolves in France. They maintain here that it is descended from the Spanish dogs that have become wild. But this I hardly believe.

schooner in the Channel, which did, it seems, more business in smuggling than anything else. To hear him, he led them a nice dance. It is highly probable, however, that poor Kemish had to succumb in this unequal war, and that his retirement into the Far West was not altogether irrelevant to its consequences. But then, he does not complain of his lot; he has for a long time conducted convoys of oxen-waggons, and it was during these long journeys that he sometimes traded with the Indians, and sometimes also exchanged many rifle shots with them.

And for all that he seems to judge them much less severely than the Americans do in general. According to his account, many of the ill deeds with which they are reproached are the doings of the white men who live among the tribes with Indian women. These are what are called *squaw-men*, and are mostly scoundrels of the deepest dye.

He was present once at the grand fêtes, which take place every year about the month of August. In these assemblages there are often as many as three thousand tents pitched together. It is at this epoch, among the Sioux, that the young men undergo the ordeal by which they are admitted as warriors, enabling them to enjoy the right of a separate habitation and to take part in the deliberations of the tribe. These trials, over which their priests, called by the Americans *medicine-men*, preside, are preceded by many days of rigorous fasting. Then the candidates, entirely naked and covered with emblematic paintings, are assembled in a great tent erected for the ceremony. The priest takes a knife and makes incisions through the thickness of the muscles of their chest and the calves of their legs, and inserts sticks therein with their ends protruding at each open ing of the wound: a rope, having one extremity fastened to the top of the tent, is then passed under the ends of the sticks transpiercing the pectoral muscles, and the victims are hoisted up and there remain suspended; then other ropes are passed around the sticks protruding from the calves of the legs, and these are loaded with buffalo heads, added one by one at long intervals, till the tension is overcome by a rupture and the man falls. He is afterwards dragged outside and abandoned without any care, his wounds being left to suppurate till the sticks fall out of the decomposed tissue, for they must never be withdrawn from the flesh. These horrible wounds leave naturally enormous scars, and as they are reputed to be very honourable, the Indians are consequently very proud of them.*

These singular probations, which I have heard spoken of many times, are less practised now than formerly. They produce a very sensible effect on the imagination, exalting it to the highest degree, and, through the assemblages of the people to which they give rise, gently facilitate the organisation of expeditions of war. The

* This fête has again been celebrated this year, and has terminated as usual by a banquet, in which they have devoured some hundreds of dogs.

Indian agents, accordingly, do all in their power to discourage these customs, but precisely for the same reason the chiefs encourage them. It appears that during these tortures, which often last five or six hours, not a murmur of complaint escapes the lips of these unfortunate sufferers. And yet it is not at all a rare occurrence for a few to die from the effects. After all, I am convinced that, of all races of mankind, the Caucasian race is the best for resisting maladies, but the worst for resisting wounds. Our nervous system is so far developed that suffering is much more keenly felt by us than by the inferior races. The negroes, the Chinese, or the Indians endure without shrinking tortures which the most hardened among us could not bear for a moment. I remember having seen an instance of this which has struck me very forcibly.

It was a few years ago in Cochin-China. One of the southern provinces was overrun by a band of pirates, who committed atrocities. One of my friends, an inspector of native affairs, succeeded one night in surprising the band at the moment they had just buried alive an unfortunate young girl, whose father would not send them a sum of money which they demanded from him. The leader in this affair escaped, but one of his lieutenants was taken. Having been brought up for examination, he was interrogated, but he would say nothing. At last they read to him a proclamation from the Governor promising one thousand piastres to whomsoever should cause the chief agent to be arrested.

But being still unable to get him to divulge anything, he was sent to prison.

During the night he requested to speak to the inspector.

"Is it quite true," he asked him, when he was alone in his presence, "that you will give me a thousand piastres if I put you in the way of taking the Quan?"

"Yes; to be sure I will."

"Very well, then; to-morrow bring me up before the tribunal. Interrogate me again, then order me to be flogged. After a little while, I will tell you the name of the village where the Quan retires after each of the expeditions, and where you can take him as soon as you like. After that, you must send me to Poulo-Condor (the convict prison) for three months; then I shall have my liberty, and you will give me the thousand dollars."

"Quite so: but I do not understand at all why you hold so much to having a flogging?"

"As to that, it is very simple. If they see me having a good, sound bastinado, they will consider it natural enough that, being unable to stand it any longer, I should tell the truth. But if I do it merely for the money, I am quite sure of getting a stab with a knife so soon as they find me in the country."

The next day everything was carried out as it had been arranged. The man began by refusing to speak. He was then stretched upon the ground, face downwards, and four brawny fellows, armed with rattans, emulated one another in laying on with all their might on the bare back of the prostrate sufferer, which at the twentieth lash was a complete wound. The inspector thought he was going to speak, but the old scamp merely raised his head from time to time and gave a sly wink, as much as to say—"Go on again; it is not enough yet." "At last," the inspector told me, "his back presented the appearance of a bleeding carcase gnawed by wolves. One could not look at it without shuddering." He did not speak till after the two-hundredth blow.

Who, then, is the European, who having quite made up his mind to speak, and, consequently, being sustained by no other force than that derived from the sentiment of duty and honour, having, moreover, the power to stop by one word such excruciating torment, that would have borne it for five minutes? *

* There is evidently some foundation for this opinion, that the inferior races have a far greater capacity for bearing physical suffering than the more highly developed, and I quote with pleasure, in support thereof, some passages relating to the *fellah* from my translation—"Five Months in Egypt"—of M. Gabriel Charmes's work, "Cinq Mois au Caire."

"This habit of dissimulation, this impassibility in suffering, are become the essential parts of the character of the fellah. Must we believe, according to Darwin's theory, that in consequence of their being transmitted hereditarily, they have arrived at constituting a kind of special faculty in the race? What is certain is, that the Egyptian peasant considers himself dishonoured if he pays any tax whatever on the first demand; his wife, his children, his neighbours, would scorn him as a coward shrinking from pain. When the collector arrives in his village, the fellah swears by all the gods that he does not possess a piastre, and receives with courage as many lashes of the courbache on the soles of his feet as he can bear, without being quite lacerated. If he succeeds

While we are chatting with Kemish, the sky is clearing up in the east. The first beams of the sun glancing over the prairie enable us to see well around us. We are in the midst of a sandy plain, covered very sparsely with vegetation. Behind us, on the horizon, we perceive the range of the Black Hills, the last spur of which stretches its serrated outline towards the south against the grey-blue sky, still spangled with a few stars. Along this are depicted here and there lofty rocks resembling the towers of strong castles in ruins. Our pair of horses, resting on the brink of a pond, are

in slipping off by these means from the least part of what he owes, or of what is unjustly claimed from him, he does not regret his scars. It must not be supposed that he feels the least humiliation in submitting to a punishment which Europeans find disgraceful; the shame would be, as I have said, in shirking it by paying. 'The strokes given by a master are an honour,' says an Arab proverb; another proverb of the same origin is still more explicit, 'The strokes of a friend,' it says, 'have the sweetness of currants.'

"Among the legends the most popular of Egypt, figures the story, no doubt apocryphal, but in nowise improbable, of a fellah, from whom the tax-gatherer claimed the sum of ten francs. During a month he was conducted every day to the same spot, where he bore, without complaining, fifty lashes of the courbache. It was in vain that they claimed from him, at the moment when his sufferings seemed the most acute, the payment of his debt. He invariably replied that he had not got the ten francs that were demanded. Convinced at last by this cruel experience of the truth of his declaration, the tax-collector decided to let him go; but to signify to him his discharge, he administered to him with his own hand a smart blow on the cheek. This unexpected smack jerked out of his mouth a piece of ten francs, which he had kept there in reserve a whole month, in case he could no longer support his martyrdom. One may doubt the truth of this anecdote, but Bourrienne relates one of the same kind, the *dénouement* of which, instead of being comic, is a sanguinary tragedy. Sidy-Mohamed-el-Coraïm, Sheriff of Alexandria, had plunging their noses every moment into the muddy water; they snort loudly, and then, lifting their heads, look around dolefully, as much as to say, "How bad it is!" I go and taste it, and find they are quite right. An unsavoury acrid brackishness almost chokes one at once; we are just in the midst of the Alkali Desert. On the crest of a little hill yonder, about 200 yards off, two coyotes are watching us. Now and then they lift their heads, and break out in that strange giggling noise which is so disquieting to hear in the dead of night. I take a shot at them with my rifle, scattering the sand

been imprisoned by order of Bonaparte, charged with treason. The following judgment had been given against him:—

"'Having proofs of the treason of Sidy-Mohamed-el-Coraïm, whom he had loaded with benefits, the general-in-chief orders Sidy-Mohamed-el-Coraim to pay a contribution of 300,000 francs. In default by him to pay the said contribution five days after the publication of the present order, he will have his head cut off.'

"'Coraïm,' says Bourrienne, 'was to go from Aboukir to Cairo, in order, in accordance with his demand, to justify himself of what he was accused. Arrived at Cairo, they demanded from him again the hundred thousand crowns for his justification. He constantly refused to give them. I caused him to be informed one day by Venture, our interpreter, that if he would preserve his life it was necessary to pay what was required from him for shutting our eyes on his treason; that I assured him the general was decided to make an example. He was a very fine man, whose position interested me. "You are rich," I said to him, through Venture, "make this sacrifice." He sneered and replied, "If I am to die this moment, nothing can save me from it; if I am not to die, why give them?" He was executed at Cairo, September 6th, 1798, at twelve o'clock, and his head was paraded through the streets of the city."

These facts are strongly suggestive that animals, and especially the lower animals, by no means suffer so much as is generally supposed when experimented upon in the interest of science for the benefit of humanity. —W. C.

around their ears. They scamper away with a strange pace, half-ambling, half-galloping, with their heads down and their bushy tails tucked in behind.

The report of my rifle has wakened Monsieur Bouverie, who stretches himself voluptuously on his buffalo skin. He has had only a short doze. The horses are put in, and seem quite as fresh as the evening before. At nine o'clock, we at last cross the road from Deadwood to Sydney, and, a few minutes afterwards, we arrive at the station of Big-Cotton-Wood. Since four yesterday afternoon we have done about fifty-six miles, but we are still 137 miles from Sydney.

We stop at the station no longer than is necessary to give our horses some well-water, which is not quite so bad as that of the surface, and then we encamp a little further off, on a plain, where some luxuriant grass will furnish them with a feed they have well earned. The heat is so great that we are obliged to take refuge under the waggon. We still notice an abundance of game. This morning we saw two or three herds of antelopes grazing on the hills. While we were stopping we saw two more, which advanced towards us, gazing at us attentively. Kemish asserts that, provided you remain perfectly still, you may sometimes induce them to come within reach. Unluckily these are very shy, and having approached within 200 or 300 yards, they stop a moment, and then scamper away at full gallop. They are pretty animals with their grey coats, and are about the size of a buck; their horns are without branches, like those of the roe-deer — at least they appear so to us.

About three, we arrive at the old encampment of "Red Cloud." The old chief, who led the dissentient Sioux, is now dead and his men are dispersed.* The fort that was constructed, for watching them quite as much as for protecting them from the animosity of their compatriots, is still standing, and is now occupied by a company of Federal troops. We stop at the station, where we find again the true American woman —the "genuine article." She is stretched out on a rocking-chair in the shade, clad in a dressing-gown in rags, whilst her husband, another tatterdemallion, sets about cooking a prairie hen for our dinner. Monsieur Bouverie, who spies out a herd of cows and bullocks in the neighbourhood, begs her for a cup of milk. She gives him at once a tin of condensed milk that comes from Chicago. It is not so much trouble as to go out and milk the cow. Wives are the only luxury of the Americans, but they are decidedly a very costly one.

Having had two hours' rest, we start again. We enter now on sandy ground, which, extending, it seems, as far as Sydney, will make the route much heavier for the poor horses. With this drawback, we are approaching a line of hills we have had constantly on the horizon, and we are doomed to undergo a tiresome ascent of a very long hill to reach a plateau where there are a few

* These Sioux, of the tribe Ogalalla, are distinguished from the rest by the name of "Ugly Faces."

fir-trees. Some pretty grey turtle-doves, with a white ring around the neck, rise around us, and we bring down a few for our dinner. At last, as night is coming on, Kemish halts in a plain void of water, but where there is some good pasture for our horses. We then begin making a great fire to warm ourselves, for the air feels very cold, and we prepare to pass the night under the shelter of the waggon. The weather, fortunately, is beautiful.

Sunday, July the 15th.—After the rough day we had yesterday we slept so soundly that we found it difficult to rouse ourselves thoroughly in order to help Kemish to catch his horses. One of them particularly, his favourite, "Pier," gave us a smart run for half-an-hour. His master has a manner of addressing him that is quite pleasant to hear. When he says: "Ho! Pier," he gives to this "ho!" such a tender accent that it goes straight to the animal's heart. And again, this morning, thanks to the soothing tone of his voice, he was able to come up to him; but then, the moment he had him safe in his grasp, he gave him a good drubbing, swearing all the time like a trooper. This is the kind of greeting generally accorded to wilful horses when caught, but it does not facilitate the work when the time comes for catching them again.

We resume our route at sunrise, and, an hour afterwards, we come up to the "Running Water," a little river of fresh, soft water. Our poor horses appreciate it so much that we have great trouble to get them out of it. On the banks a cattle ranch is established, and the bullocks, in groups of a score or so, quite cover the plain. There must be two or three thousand. Seven or eight cow-boys, who have just finished their breakfast, are assembled before a tent, in which they sleep when it is not their turn to watch, that is three nights out of four generally. They have thirty or forty horses for their service. We see them saddling the ones they mount, and then they gallop off, each followed by five or six spare horses, one having a pack-saddle loaded with provisions. What admirable cavalry might be made of these strapping fellows, provided one out of four were hanged to teach the others how to behave. There is one of them that I follow with my eyes for a long time. He enters into a little corral where a few cows are enclosed. He opens the gate without dismounting, picks out, among all these bewildered animals, the one he has precisely in view, brings it out with the lash of his stock-whip, drives back the others that have escaped, and then hurls his lasso at a stubborn calf that persists in running away, turning it head over heels: all this is done without a single false movement, and with an ease and grace admirable to behold.

We continued marching all day long, halting merely a couple of hours about noon. The heat is still distressing to bear. The antelopes show themselves from time to time, but give us no chance by coming within range. We traverse an immense village of prairie dogs.

Hundreds of them are crouching at the entrance of their burrows. We fire at five or six which are evidently hit, for we see spots of blood and hair, but it is impossible to take them, for they always manage, it seems, to crawl into their holes before dying. Monsieur Bouverie, however, manages to kill an owl which is not much bigger than a thrush. These birds make their nests in the burrows of the prairie dogs, which often contain also rattlesnakes. One does not know exactly what common interest unites such strange associates.

About three o'clock a storm comes on. At the same moment we see suddenly appear on the crest of the hill before us, an immense herd reaching far away out of sight and coming down straight on us in a compact body. They are the great bullocks of Texas with enormous horns. At their head are marching a few old yoke oxen that serve to lead the others. When they have a river to pass,.a cow-boy tethers one to his saddle and, dragging him into the water, the others then follow.

At this moment they are excited by the electric state of the atmosphere and the claps of thunder. The young ones leap about in all directions, trying to escape and terrify the others. Forty or fifty cow-boys, each followed by five or six reserved horses, are galloping wildly along the flanks of the column, trying to keep them in order. We hear their formidable stock-whips resounding like pistol-shots, mingled with the desperate bellowings of the herd. The scene, lighted up by the yellow glow of a stormy sky, forms a most striking spectacle. We talk a few moments with the ranchman. He is a fine young fellow, mounted on a splendid animal, with a grey felt hat set off with a goffered leathern band in the place of a ribbon. He carries two revolvers and a bowie-knife, all mounted in silver. He informs us that having the commission to furnish rations of meat that the Government gives to the Indians, he is conducting five thousand head of Texas cattle to deliver them to the agents charged with their distribution. He has been on his way during two months. How many of these bullocks will be eaten by the Sioux? This is a question that would be very curious to solve, and yet, when determined, would certainly not be very edifying. These distributions of meat are, it seems, a rather extraordinary spectacle. They give to each community a number of bullocks in proportion to the number of their members. The warriors on horseback attend at the gate of the corral, and, as soon as an animal is delivered to them, they drive it off at full speed, running after it and killing it with their arrows. Each executes in his own way the business of the shambles.

A little further on, we meet a convoy of oxen-waggons belonging to Kemish, which are being conducted by his two sons. They are two fine, tall young fellows, well built, but are far from having the polished and respectful manners of their father, who has decidedly won our warm attachment. They seemed to be quite surprised at meeting him. He will get home again before them, for they take a fortnight to accomplish what we are doing in four or five days, if our horses keep on at the same lively pace.

I have prevailed over Kemish to relax the bridles of the poor beasts. Our French bridles are already instruments of torture, carried in this direction sufficiently towards perfection; but in this order of ideas, as well as in many others, the Americans leave us far behind them. Their bearing rein consists of a simple leathern strap, which, fixed to the saddle, passes through a ring between the two ears of the horse, and there dividing in two, is brought down on each cheek and fastened to the ends of the snaffle. By compressing the nose of the poor animal, its head is therefore kept under, in a position towards the horizontal, without any possibility of giving it freedom of movement. A veterinary surgeon told me that, independent of the torture inflicted on the horses by such a detestable arrangement, there is to be attributed to this cause a large share of those very frequent cases of sun-stroke, followed by death, that happen on the streets of New York and Chicago, notwithstanding the little parasols they put over their heads during the intense heat.

About three o'clock we fall in with a flock of three thousand sheep, driven by two men on horseback, who tell us which direction to take to reach Red-Willow station, where we intend passing the night. For the last hour or two we have been beset by a sandstorm, which renders the march painfully persecuting. We traverse actual marine alluvium of a fine sand like that covering the beach of Trouville. The wind sweeping it up in thick clouds, it penetrates everywhere. Sometimes, when at its worst, our poor horses stop and put their heads between their legs, making efforts to breathe. In the end, however, we get without accident to the station.

Red-Willow has the ambition, perhaps, to become a city some day. At all events, some daring speculator has built there an hotel. It is a construction in rough planks, but, to our great surprise, capable, we understand, of supplying us with a bed, and, moreover, in the way of eating, with beef and mutton. The beef must have been cut off from some poor, lame brute that could march no further with the herd we saw this morning, and the sheep probably died of rot, for, in the Far West, though butcher's meat is sold, it is not fit to eat. At all events, we are no longer so very nice about it, and we manage to make a dinner off it—if not a very good one, one copious, at least. In this country, which should be the land of abundance, because it feeds so many others, one is reduced to remember the days when he had a good dinner. I have often heard the farmers and ranchmen say, in trying to fix a date, "That day I had a *square meal.*" What singular people!

This evening, while we are smoking a cigar before the house, we are watching a few cow-boys assembled bcfore the door of the bar, amusing themselves in throwing the lasso. I promise two dollars to the one who shall first catch his adversary at a distance of twenty paces. They place themselves in position, and, in the end, I keep my two dollars.

They excuse themselves, saying they are accustomed to throw it on horseback, then that their hempen cord is not heavy enough; but these are lame excuses. The truth is, they are very clumsy. Desiring to take to another kind of pastime, they begin wrestling. A strapping young fellow of twenty throws all the rest, one after the other. These men are very well made, but their muscular system is not much developed, due, I believe, to their bad nourishment. They have neither legs nor arms. A Breton shipmate would bring them down like a house of cards. I notice one thing that we should certainly not see in our colonies. One of these cow-boys is a negro; for all that he plays and wrestles with the others on a footing of perfect equality. It is very curious that a sentiment so rooted should have disappeared so quickly in a country where, only twenty-five years ago, a negro was admitted neither into a theatre nor an omnibus in New York.*

* As an event within the experience of the living generation, this remarkable change is to this extent curious, no doubt, but if we realise how the phenomenon, of which there are so many instances in all history, has been brought about, that is through a complete change of national sentiment and public opinion, we find it perfectly natural, and cease to be astonished. Have not, indeed, all the great and enduring changes recorded in the annals of every people been due more to these causes than

Monday, the 16*th July.*—The sand storm has been raging all night, and, on awaking this morning, we find the sheet and the floor covered with a layer of sand that has penetrated through the crevices of the partition. The wind, however, went down at sun-rise. On the hill opposite to us the sheep are beginning to march, preceded by two goats. When they go on a

to the will and action of despots and heroes, who have been so largely indebted to these surrounding circumstances for what they have achieved, and who consequently would lose much of their *éclat* if hero-worship had not been in the ascendant so many ages? Nero, for instance, with all his energy and power, could not arrest the spread of Christianity, the general sentiment of the Christian community being too deeply rooted to be eradicated; and later, it would have triumphed just as surely eventually without the encouragement of Constantine. And, on the other hand, Luther, if he had lived a century earlier, could not have effected the Reformation, for the time was not propitious, and he would have been too strenuously opposed instead of having been aided by the popular opinion and sentiment. The most extraordinary changes affecting the interests of mankind have been brought about, in the first instance, by a complete change in public opinion, and the present attitude of the American people towards the negroes, in comparison with what it was previous to the war, becomes insignificant beside many similar transformations recorded in history. Without going back to ancient times it would be difficult even to fully realise the diverse states of society produced, for example, by the general belief in the Millennium; by the duties entailed by the Crusades; by the "Black Death," when sentiments of humanity, even between members of the same family, had fled; and notably, the decline in the belief in witchcraft, during the prevalence of which every one, the most enlightened even, considered it quite proper and just that old women, perfectly harmless, but suspected of sorcery and of riding on a broomstick through the air, should be burnt alive at the stake. What was then reasonable is now preposterous.

So soon, therefore, as we realise the irresistible force of public opinion, we no longer wonder at such momentous revolutions in human affairs. Common sense evidently, as well as sentiment and opinion, changes, for journey it is always necessary, it seems, to take this precaution, otherwise they can never get them along. The flock has changed its proprietor during the night. An inhabitant of Custer, who has been here during two days, has become, after long haggling, the fortunate possessor, at the price of three dollars per head, the lambs being included in the bargain. They had cost one

"l'opinion," justly says Pascal, "dispose de tout : elle fait la beauté, la justice, et le bonheur, qui est le tout du monde." And, moreover, conscience, which appears to be merely one phase of opinion—one with reference to morals—is equally subject to modification. Without seeking support from the arguments of evolution, who can doubt the influence from the facts referred to by Lord Macaulay in his essay on Machiavelli? "Every age and every nation," says Macaulay, "has characteristic vices, which prevail almost universally, which scarcely any person scruples to avow, and which even rigid moralists but faintly censure. Succeeding generations change the fashion of their morals with the fashion of their hats and their coaches; take some other kind of wickedness under their patronage, and wonder at the depravity of their ancestors." If conscience does not change so frequently or in the same proportion, it is due principally to its resting on moral philosophy, a real science, and to the influence of a church adverse to change. But when the renowned knights of the 14th century, who had hitherto piqued themselves on their scrupulous honour, returned from the war in Spain between Peter the Cruel and Henry of Trastamare, and became "routiers," pillaging without compunction country houses, their consciences must have fundamentally changed in a brief space of time. Such a change, and that also in France, of the attitude of the people towards the nobles and the clergy after the "dernier beau jour de l'ancienne monarchie," at the commencement of the Revolution, were infinitely greater and more sudden than the recent transmutation of sentiment in the United States.

"La vaine Opinion règne sur tous les âges :
Son temple est dans les airs, porté sur les nuages.
Elle fuit et revient ; elle place un mortel,
Hier sur un bûcher, demain sur un autel." —W. C.

dollar to the man who has brought them from New Mexico, but then he has been two months on the way, and must have left a good number on the road, especially young ones, which would have been devoured by the coyotes. All the lambs that are born in the course of these journeys are immediately killed with the ball of a revolver, for they could not follow, and the dam would not abandon them alive. In similar cases with calves, it is necessary to attach the cow for a day or two to an old bullock. It is rather curious to notice, too, that these animals, living almost in a wild state, have resumed the habits their ancestors must have had before becoming domesticated. All the calves are born in the spring within a few weeks of each other.

We start again on our way, after a good repast, in company with the travellers by the mail-coach going to the north. We have still sixty-two miles to accomplish. Kemish calculated on arriving this evening, but the sands, partly moving, which we pass over, make the road so heavy, that he begins to fear we shall not do it, because his horses are getting rather fatigued. He maintains that if we had been able to continue in his little spring vehicle we had at the commencement, we should have gained twenty-four hours. For my part, I think it is very smart work to do about 250 miles over the prairie in five days with the same horses, feeding on twenty-two gallons of oats only, besides the grass cropped on the way.

The country is becoming less interesting. Water is

scarce, the ground is sandy, and, to crown all, the stand-storm begins to rage again : we, therefore, make little progress. Notwithstanding the heat, we again try to hit a few antelopes, but with no better result than before. We meet on our way two or three waggons, drawn by five pair of splendid mules. I measure one pair, and find their height 15¾ hands. They come, it seems, from Ohio, and are quite equal to our finest mules of Poitou. It is, however, the dearest animal in this country, a fine mule being worth 300 dollars.

About nine o'clock, we see from the top of a hill a large river running before us from west to east. It is the Platte, and has always been an impediment to explorers. Not deep enough to float the smallest boat, running over a bed of moving sand which renders the fords fearfully dangerous, it has often arrested the progress of emigrants for weeks together, whose unlucky star led them on to cross it. Later, the South Platte, the one we see, has served, it is true, as a barrier for many years to the Indians, who rarely ventured to traverse it, for fear, in case of a precipitate retreat, of being driven to bay on its banks. Finally, six years ago, the colonisation of the Black Hills attracting on this side an enormous traffic, a company undertook the enterprise of throwing a toll-bridge across, though they had much trouble in carrying it out. In 1877 a first bridge, when almost finished, was burnt by the Sioux. They then built at the opening of another bridge a little block-house, which still exists, and under this protection the work was resumed. They allege that the cost of construction was reimbursed during the first eighteen months it was open. This does not astonish me, considering the rate of the tolls: a person afoot pays fifty cents; a rider and his horse, one dollar; a carriage and pair, two dollars; a waggon and oxen, seventeen dollars.

While we are going over it on foot, we have time to examine it, for it is 1530 yards long. It is entirely of wood, and really a fine work, one that does honour to the American carpenters. On the other side, is the toll-keeper's house and a few others, where we have the chance of buying some bread. We are decidedly returning within the pale of civilization.

At last, after one or two halts, we arrive about seven at the last stage before Sydney, from which we are only fourteen miles. Our horses seem seriously fatigued. They have brought us along so gallantly, that we willingly consent to pass the night here, although the spot seems very unattractive. A stable, half in ruins, still stands up at the brink of a pond, with a great pile of empty meat cans blocking up the door-way. The horses, let loose in the corral, are gazing at us over the bars of the paling. The care-taker, a tall young fellow of twenty-five, politely invites us to enter into the little hovel that serves him for a lodging. The whole furniture consists of a bed that fills two-thirds of the only room, a stove, a table, and two or three stools. Herein we see two young girls, the one about fifteen and the other six months, whom I take for two sisters, but I am mistaken. The first is the wife of the care-taker, and the second his daughter. The poor people are in a state of wretchedness to make the heart bleed. The poor mother has almost no more milk. In this country, where a cow costs only ten dollars to buy and nothing to keep, they have not even one. Not a hen, not a garden. I ask the man why he does not cultivate a few vegetables.

"Ah!" says he, with a cunning look, "if the company sends me elsewhere, I should have been working for others."

"How long have you been here?"

"Since two years."

"And how much do you earn?"

"Forty dollars a month; and then the company brings me free, the bacon, the potatoes, and the flour which we buy at Sydney."

"Do you eat nothing but bacon and potatoes?"

"Certainly; nothing else," he replies, quite astonished at the question.

If French peasants were living in a cottage with the same advantages, how quickly all this would change in aspect! The poor little wife is clad in a *peignoir pompadour!* I remember having seen many more like it, exhibited in the windows of the "Grands magasins du Louvre;" but this one has neither been washed nor mended, and through the rents we can well see that she has underneath but a very poor sort of a chemise. We share with them our dinner; then, while smoking, I listen to the husband, who is relating some little stories of the neighbourhood to Kemish. One of them appears to me so extraordinary, that I get him to repeat it with all its details. I have since taken the trouble to verify them, and find them to be perfectly true.

These are the facts:—

Not far from here there is a group of five or six houses, called *Virginia-Dale.* It was formerly a station of the stage-coach line running from Denver in California. It had been established by an inspector of the company, named Jack Slade, a well-known desperado, who under different circumstances had killed with his own hand no fewer than fifteen men. Moreover, he was strongly suspected of having been one of a band of respectable people of his stamp, who, disguised as Indians, pillaged in a few months all the farms of the neighbourhood.

This gallant fellow honoured with a very particular hatred a rich farmer of the neighbourhood named Jules Burgh, with whom in 1861 he had a quarrel followed by a scuffle, in which he did not get the upper hand, and for this he often declared he would be avenged.

Many years afterwards a certain Antoine Dunnel, his intimate friend, who had a farm on the banks of the Platte, found means of enticing there Jules Burgh, and then with the help of a few employes of the company, having seized his person, he sent word to Jack Slade, who was living at about thirty leagues from there, that he had him safe in his keeping and at the disposal of the latter. When Slade heard that his enemy was at last in his power, he hired a vehicle, and, travelling night and day, arrived at Dunnel's farm on the morning of the second day. Jules Burgh was bound to a post in the corral, and so tightly, that he could move neither hand nor foot. Slade, on recognising him, began loading him with abuse; then, in the presence of seven men who looked on without interfering, he discharged his revolver at the unhappy victim twenty-three times, taking good care not to kill him, and stopping every now and then to swallow a glass of brandy. At every shot he warned the unhappy victim where he was going to fire.

This diabolic scene lasted some hours. At last the assassin, exasperated at the courage that his victim manifested, put the muzzle of the revolver into his mouth and blew out his brains at the twenty-fourth shot.

The next thing he did was to cut off the ears of the corpse and carefully salt them. From this time he always carried them about with him in his pocket, and used to show them frequently in public, and boast of his exploit whenever he visited the public-houses of Denver. Sometimes, when he had no money to drink, he threw them on the counter, offering them in pledge —a proposal that was always accepted.

After having long edified the honourable population of Denver, he emigrated into Montana, and signalised his arrival by fresh exploits of the same kind. In all these cases justice never interfered; but one fine day, at Virginia City, a few inhabitants constituted themselves a vigilance committee, seized his person, and hanged him on the spot.

His wife, warned of his unlucky mishap, arrived on horseback just as he was giving up the ghost. She was holding a revolver in her hand, and said that, knowing her husband was a lost man, she had come to blow out his brains with her own hand in order to save him from the gallows. A nice set these, in all conscience, for quiet neighbours!

Tuesday, the 17th of July.—Must I tell the truth? On going to bed last night, Monsieur Bouverie exclaimed, "After all, I shall not be sorry to-morrow night to stretch myself between the sheets of a Pullman car after having had something like a dinner."

I was quite of the same mind, and it must be admitted that the outward circumstances contributed not a little to develop these sentiments. Last night, when our host showed us our apartment, which consisted of an empty stall of the stable, in which a handful or two of hay insufficiently covered the traces of the horses, our predecessors, we could not mistake it for a bed of roses; for all that, however, we slept quite as soundly as if it had been one.

In the morning we start at an early hour for Sydney, from which place we are now only thirteen miles. The horses seem to know we are drawing near, for they are trotting briskly, and about nine o'clock old Kemish points out to us with his whip the line of railway and the town of Sydney, where we soon at last arrive.

Sydney, one of the stations of the famous Union Pacific Railroad, the first railway laid down across the American continent, is a little town of about fifteen hundred inhabitants. The "Pacific Coast Guide," from which I take this information, informs me besides that the name it bears is that of an old chairman of the company, and it is the capital of the county of Cheyenne, forming part of the territory of Nebraska. It seems to me that the worthy author of this little work was quite right in stopping there, for I do not see that he could have added anything more. The houses are of wood, of course, and the Lockwood Hotel, that opens to us its hospitable doors, is anything but inviting. But if these details were insisted on, the same qualification should be applied to all the American towns, and this would be becoming fastidious.

We begin, besides, by having a series of disagreeable surprises. First, in opening our trunks, we discover that during the sandstorm the fine dust has penetrated everywhere. The locks will not act, and we are obliged to force them. Our rifles and revolvers are so choked with it that we can neither clear them nor discharge them. Our hair is transformed into a sort of matted felt, through which we cannot pass a comb. If the sand were only auriferous we should have something in compensation, but unluckily there is no hope of paying our hotel bills out of it.

At last, with the services of the hairdresser of Sydney, a gentleman supremely elegant, we succeed in acquiring a more becoming appearance. All our equipment, saddles, boots, guns, &c., are stowed into an immense case furnished to us by the landlord, and at two o'clock we take our places in the train arriving from San Francisco, which will conduct us by way of Omaha to Chicago. Old Kemish accompanies us to the cars, and we give him a final shake of the hand with a feeling of the warmest attachment. He speaks to us again of his project that he has long cherished. He would like to come to France to buy there a pair of Percheron stallions.

" If I were lucky enough to find some one who would advance me the money, my fortune would be made," he says.

The train carries us off at full speed across the Prairie. We soon cross again the Platte, with its yellow waters rushing on between groups of little islets and along sandbanks partly submerged. We are now following its left bank, and at every moment we see immense herds of cattle crossing our way and journeying towards the north.

This is the line by which the four-year-old beasts are sent to Chicago every winter, a little before the cold sets in. The stations are already furnished with complete contrivances to receive and send on the cattle, for all these operations are carried on at the risk of the company.

As we are advancing towards the east, we see the country changing in aspect from hour to hour. Agriculture, now represented by immense fields of corn, is fast gaining foot by foot over the desert, and throwing back before it the shepherds with their flocks and herds, if this term, so eminently poetic, may be applied to the cow-boys in red shirts we see galloping in the horizon, who, seen through the windows of a comfortable Pullman car, appear to us certainly more congenial than when obliged to live among them. When we come to Kearny, a pretty little town with real houses of brick, this change is very striking. And then, at every depôt, we find monumental stations, often lighted with electricity, and in the streets tram-cars in lively movement. At last, about eight in the morning, when we enter the city of Omaha, we seem to be entering into an actual metropolis.

This city of Omaha, which has taken the name of a tribe of Indians, whom the Père de Smet evangelised about the year 1846, is the point of departure of the Union Pacific line. In 1863, at the time the concession of the railway was voted by the Congress, it was a little town of three thousand inhabitants, most of whom lived by trading with the Indians, and who only communicated with the rest of the world by the Missouri, on whose banks their houses were built. The nearest railway then was no nearer than 150 miles. It was necessary to bring the first locomotive across the prairie from Des Moines in Iowa. Within a range of 500 miles there was not a tree to furnish a sleeper: they all came from Michigan and New York, and cost two dollars and a half each sleeper.

The following figures show the rapidity with which the work was carried out. On the 1st of January 1866 there were 40 miles completed; on the 1st of January 1867, 265; on the 1st of January 1868, 550; at last, on the 10th of May, this work, one of the most colossal ever undertaken hitherto, was completed by the junction, at Promontory Point in Utah, with the line that the other company, the Central Pacific, were, on their side, laying down in the desert, taking California as the terminus. The last 534 miles were laid down in fifteen months.

During this time Omaha was becoming a great city. The poor, little straggling village of 1846 had disappeared to make room for the immense sheds and workshops of the railway, around which a population of several hundred thousands soon grouped themselves. In 1871, it was connected with its rival, Council Bluffs, opposite to it, on the other side of the Missouri, by means of a magnificent iron bridge, nearly a thousand yards long, and this now admits of the carriages setting down the travellers on the east shore, where there are the heads of four or five lines connecting this point with Chicago.

Morose moralists have often reproached young democracies with having completely neglected that worship of ancestry so prominent, for example, in the Chinese Empire, which, while reminding man that he is merely the link here below uniting the past to the future, invites him to transmit to his children the good principles he himself has received from his fathers. We have been enabled to satisfy ourselves that the people of Omaha, for their part, have determined to escape this censure; for a little pamphlet we have bought at the station is specially devoted to the early history of the city of Omaha. We have unluckily mislaid this interesting work. Its author, whose name, as well as we can remember, is Phileas J. M. T. Babcock, or something like it, has collected with pious care its ancient traditions bearing on its origin. They consist, unluckily, of three assassinations. Such at least is the term employed by the author, who remarks, not without evident pride, that the city of Rome had only one at its foundation, that of Remus by Romulus.

Here are the facts: In 1852, a jeweller, named Rhines, living in Michigan, decided on emigrating to California. On the road they naturally often spoke of the Indians. Rhines declared that he was not afraid of them, and that he would kill the first who showed himself.

The caravan, after having traversed the Missouri, encamped in the open prairie on the bank of a rivulet, at the spot where now rises the city. The next morning, as they were preparing to resume their journey, they saw two or three young Indian women crossing the rivulet and coming towards them. They belonged to a party of Pawnees, encamped at a short distance, and came, in the most friendly way, to offer some fresh meat to the "Pale Faces." The companions of Rhines then reminded him of his resolution in a jeering manner. This scoundrel took immediately his rifle and blew out the brains of one of the young squaws.

An hour afterwards, the Pawnee warriors made their appearance. They were in force, and demanded that Rhines should be delivered up to them, which was accordingly done. They stripped him: they then bound him firmly to the wheel of his waggon, and there, in the presence of his companions, too much intimidated to defend him, the squaws, armed with their husbands' bowie-knives, commenced skinning him alive, as they would a dead antelope. The operation, carried out by experienced hands, lasted, it appears, a long time, and the wretched Rhines died only a few minutes after it had been completed. Had the situation been transposed, I hardly know what the Americans would have done.

After this, the other two assassinations cited by Mr Phileas J. M. T. Babcock appear to me mere "padding." He must have been very much in earnest in the desire to eclipse Rome to give them this designation. I copied in my note-book the paragraphs relating thereto, and reproduce them here.

"To old Mr Todd redounds the honour of having been the first inveterate drunkard of the city of Omaha, who killed himself by sheer drinking. It was he who built the first house. It was situated where now rises St Nicholas, and was devoted by its proprietor to the business of grocery in general, and especially whisky. He was himself the first customer of his establishment, and soon died of an attack of *delirium tremens*. . . .

" Almost at the same as Mr Todd, Dr M—— arrived. His first patient was an Indian child, that quickly died." These are the three historical assassinations.

I am reading this interesting work while the Chicago, Milwaukee, and St Paul Railway is conducting us to the Grand Pacific Hotel, which we had quitted less than a month previously for the Far West. A fortnight later, we were again in Paris. The last days of our journey reminds us of a disappointment. On passing through New York we were unable, through want of time, to assist at the representation of an equestrian pantomime, which seems to have been a great attraction. It was entitled " The Stage-Coach of Deadwood." There was a stirring scene of an attack on the mail by the Sioux and a determined defence by the travellers; then, just as they were on the point of succumbing, a band of heroic cow-boys arrive at a gallop, and hack the Sioux into mince-meat, leaving nothing but their scalps to be carried in triumph in the highly sensational *dénoûment*.

This is the show at present exhibiting in London, May 1887.

CHAPTER X.

SOMETHING MORE OF THE BLACK HILLS.

June the 10th, 1884.—Before leaving my readers, who have been pleased thus far to follow me in my peregrinations through the Black Hills, I should like to say a few more words regarding what has passed there in the interval of less than ten months since our return.

The Black Hills form but a very small part of the Far West; but the advance in material prosperity that has taken place there has equally prevailed elsewhere and throughout, and when we compare it with the absence of progress in France in the same lapse of time, which we cannot ignore, we see how intimately these co-existing states of things are linked together.

On our departure from America, the Marquis de M—— had just come off with all the honours of war in the adventure I have herein related. A few days subsequently the Marquise bravely came to join her husband, and the pair made their triumphal entry into their good city of Little Missouri, whose name, at the close of a deliberation of the Municipal Council, was changed for that of the Marquise. All the "prominent citizens" gave an enthusiastic reception to the young couple in the same station where, a fortnight before, my friend had been chased like a wild beast. It was not the Romans only that old Ovid addressed—

> "Donec eris felix, multus numerabis amicos.
> Tempora si fuerint nubila, solus eris!"

And my instructor of whittling, the Cow-boy of Custer, was quite right in saying that a revolver of large calibre was the surest friend one could have.

At this concert one voice was wanting—it was O'Donnell's. But they had not long to wait for it. He remained in prison just long enough to get cured of his wounds. As soon as he was well and at liberty, his first visit was to the Marquise. When he showed himself, the Marquise was alone at the house.

"I come to shake hands," he said, "that all may be forgotten! I have been wrong. I did not know that I was dealing with a gentleman! Besides, those for whom I acted behaved badly. In future, your ladyship will have no better friend than me."

Everything is forgiven. O'Donnell has reconstituted his party by substituting members of the *élite* for those who suffered from the shots of the Marquis. He undertakes by contract all the elections of the neighbourhood. One moment they hoped he would get himself nominated a senator or a deputy, which would have had the advantage of ridding the locality of his presence; unluckily, he seems to have abandoned this project.

The President of the United States, Mr Arthur, having last autumn taken it into his head to visit, with a few grand personages, the Yellow-stone, a band of seventy cow-boys was immediately formed for the purpose of carrying him off and setting a ransom upon his person. The enterprise, through some accident, was not carried out. O'Donnell was credited with having originated this brilliant project, but everything now tends to show that it emanated from some other brain.

Relieved from these harassing cares, the Marquis has been able to give a fresh impulse to his affairs. He now kills from 200 to 250 bullocks a-day, and every morning sends one of his refrigerant waggons loaded with meat to New York, a distance of about 1860 miles, and every bullock there delivered returns him a net profit, they say, of five dollars! *

It will not be very long, of course, before a large traffic in the meat is carried on across the Atlantic; for when a pound of beef that costs tenpence at Havre may be bought in New York for fourpence, this inequality cannot continue indefinitely. It will be objected to, no doubt, that the imported meat, whatever the means employed, will never be equal to that of the country. It is possible, still by no means sure; but, as a Norman farmer once said to me, "bad goods always bring down the price of the good."

The stamps of Homestake crush at present two thousand five hundred tons of quartz a-day, which per-

* He has also lately sent to New York two waggons of salmon preserved in ice.

mits of a distribution of still more satisfactory dividends. The Marquis de M——, who may soon change his name for that of Carabas, is going to lay down a railway that will connect Little Missouri with Deadwood. Last spring, thanks to three or four relays arranged beforehand, he made the journey in fifty-one hours, stopping seven hours only. He had been surprised in a snowstorm, during which he was obliged to march constantly around his horse to avoid being frozen. In the north of Dakota, the cold this winter has been down to 40° Centigrade,* whilst in the south, at Cascade notably, there was hardly any frost. At Deadwood, my friend was welcomed with much enthusiasm by all our friends there, who offered him a banquet at Wentworth House, whose proprietor, Mr Cornell, is now designated in the newspapers as *Colonel* Cornell, a sign that he is getting on swimmingly.

At Little Rapid Creek also they have been going ahead like the rest. The crushers of Fair View and of Minnesota are almost finished, and will soon begin working. A line of railway coming from Sydney and passing by Cascade and Little Rapid will soon join at Deadwood the Marquis's line.

But a dark cloud casts its shadow over this picture. The good town of Galena no longer exists! Everyone knows the story of the two Kilkenny cats that fought

* If this cold could be indicated on Fahrenheit's thermometer it would be 104° below freezing point, or 72° below zero, but this unscientific scale is not adapted for cold countries; it is misleading.

in a saw-pit so ferociously that, when the battle was over, only the tail of each was left. That of the Colonel and the New Yorkers has some resemblance to this desperate fight. We have not, unluckily, the details of this great subterranean battle which, a short time after our departure, stained the mine with blood. How many *fighting men*, I wonder, were killed on each side in this momentous combat? In the end, however, the long robe vanquished the sword. The Colonel has retired under his tent, and his enemies have quitted the country; the mine is abandoned, and the lawyers are at work scraping up all the dollars that have been got out of it. I leave it to them to do it conscientiously.

At Cascade everything has been moving at a quicker pace. A few days after our departure, an assemblage of cow-boys of the neighbourhood proclaimed Cascade the capital of the new county of Fall River. A store and a post office have been established. The stage coach from Sydney, changing its old route, has been provided there with a station, with a bar and hotel annexed; and a crowd of emigrants have just been contending for the lots, of twenty-five feet of frontage by one hundred deep, that had been marked out along the course of three avenues. The Avenue of Grancey runs along the river! the name having been adopted by the *prominent citizens* attracted thither by the splendid view it commands. The doctors "the most highly qualified," strongly recommend this water, of which I have so disagreeable a souvenir. An analysis made at Chicago has proved that it contains a prodigious quantity of sulphate of magnesia, better known as Epsom salts. A moralist, perhaps, would attribute to the beneficent action of these salts that extraordinary suavity of disposition that characterises the inhabitants of Cascade. But not a single assassination has yet been perpetrated in their city, not even that of an Indian child by a quack! Evidently, in the opinion of the historian, Mr Phileas J. M. T. Babcock, its early annals bearing on its foundation are much less brilliant than those of Rome or Omaha.

The church and the school, the first in project, and the second already built, are a little behindhand in the Avenue de M——. I remember having shot a coyote on the spot last June. They intend establishing there the workshops required for the construction of the great bridge over the Cheyenne by the Railway Company.

I have mentioned somewhere in this book that the Sioux formerly wore a ring in their nose and shaved their heads, reserving only a scalp-lock; but I have done them a wrong, which I now gladly redress. These barbarous customs have never prevailed among them. They have scalped and still scalp their enemies when an opportunity presents itself; but when it is a question of an inverse operation, that is to say, when it is their turn to be scalped, they leave to the operator the care of tracing himself on their head with the point of his knife the circumference of the trophy to which the fortune of war gives him a right to claim, without having the indiscretion of imposing on him a particular form that might not perhaps be to his taste. There is obviously in this a delicacy that would be appreciated by all persons who pique themselves on good manners.

I have received also some reports relating to the Sioux established in the reserve we traversed last year.

The Indian agent for Dakota gives some news of "Sitting Bull," the hero of the war of 1876. This venerable warrior is quite well, and takes a decided liking to agriculture. His instructor, the agent, who has seen him digging up potatoes surrounded by his family, is much pleased with him. Those Sioux who were his old subjects, and who are now established in the neighbourhood, give him also much satisfaction. There are other tribes, however, that occasion him some trouble. Not far off are the "Gros-Ventres," who are really very annoying. And still further, the Tetons, who do not leave him a moment's repose. The strong oppress the weak, and these run away after having been beaten, and then he is obliged to run after them.

Some of these reports are very interesting. There is a certain Mr Llewellyn, who is clearly quite an observant philosopher. He has been appointed an agent among the Apaches Mescaleros, and describes the laws and customs of the Indians confided to his care. He is bent on leading them gently towards civilisation, and, with this object, on suppressing the customs that appear to him incompatible with it. They have, it seems, the deplorable habit of burning the old women suspected of witchcraft. One had undergone this infliction a short time after his arrival. But, since the month of May, he has kept such a sharp look out that they have not been able to continue the horrible practice.

The Mescaleros, it seems, like all the other Indians, however, always cut off the bottoms of their breeches before wearing them, which he had distributed to them on the part of the Government: consequently they are now—being incorrigible—obliged to go without.

In the moral order of things progress is equally sensible. The forms of fine language are no longer strange to them. Formerly, when an Indian spoke of his wife to one of his compatriots, he designated her, "the squaw of such a one." But now, they say, "Mrs Captain Sam!" When everybody is a colonel, they will, evidently, have nothing more to learn from the "Pale Faces."

But Mr Llewellyn, like a wise man, considers it necessary to preserve those customs that have a salutary influence on the social state. This is what he actually says of the Apaches:

"It is a fixed law with them that the mother-in-law and son-in-law never visit each other after marriage, if it can possibly be avoided. I am not prepared to say whether this is a step in the direction of civilisation or not."

I have read also with much interest the report of a head of a school founded at Hampton, with the object of giving a complete education to a certain number of

Indians of both sexes, who are afterwards sent among their respective tribes. The teachers, who are young ladies, are highly satisfied with their pupils, who are taught a variety of things, especially those concerning girls—sewing, ironing, and cooking. To this I cannot give an unqualified approval, for I fear if the instructor is an American, her work can only be pernicious. I know nothing of Indian cooking but that described by Fenimore Cooper; and the humps of bison smothered, on which he fed his heroes, Hawkeye and the Major, made my mouth water when I was a boy. If a half of what he says is true, it is the teachers of Hampton who should take lessons from their pupils.

There is also something very curious to notice in this report. It is that these people have taken it into their heads to send there a few "warriors," and these, followed by their squaws and their papooses (children), have duly arrived there. The experiment, they say, has very well succeeded. The warrior has soon lost the habit of beating his wife every night—a reform in a direction evidently acceptable to the latter. But, on the other hand, if she has contracted the habit of perpetually indulging in a rocking-chair, the move in this direction might not be so acceptable to the husband who is not prepared to forego a helpmate for a purely ornamental wife.

These experiments have been often attempted, and the difficulty is not in giving instruction to a savage, but to know what to do with him when he is instructed.

The manager of Hampton affirms that in this also success has crowned his efforts. Many young men have already been sent back among their tribes, and they are gaining very good wages as waggoners or cow-boys. If it is possible to turn the Indians to good account—and for my part I believe it is possible—it is evidently by these vocations that they should be initiated into civilised life.

I should be sorry to end my narrative without replying to twenty-seven ladies who are very desirous of knowing what has become of Jean-Leblanc and the buff mare. I have only just received news of them which is excellent. In consideration of his good services, I had strongly recommended that Jean-Leblanc should not be confided to any cow-boy. He is consequently in the personal service of Parker, and is as round as an apple. The buff mare, reserved for the pure joys of maternity, shows in her novel state as much discretion and wisdom as the young ladies, Parker's compatriots, who, after having well flirted and danced in all the capitals of the two hemispheres for three or four seasons, end equally, when they have chosen a husband, in becoming tender mothers and, in their case, exemplary wives and helpmates, provided they do not resort immediately to the rocking-chair.